S0-EAW-976

"QUOTATIONS"
from
English Canadian
Literature

"QUOTATIONS"
from
English Canadian
Literature

by
David Strickland

MODERN CANADIAN LIBRARY
TORONTO

Copyright 1973 ☉ PAGURIAN PRESS LIMITED
A Christopher Ondaatje publication. All rights reserved.
No part of this book may be reproduced in any form
without the permission of the publishers.

Printed and bound in Canada
ISBN 0-919364-23-3

To Evelyn, whose faith in this book, in myself and in Canadiana has been undying.

INTRODUCTION

The main purpose of this book is to reveal the Canadian soul. And since the soul of any people is inevitably hidden between the pages of its literature, it is there that we have searched and found the Canadian.

For too long now we have asked ourselves who we are and if we really do have an identity. For too long we have considered ourselves as English-Canadians or French-Canadians or New-Canadians. To be simply a Canadian without a prefix was never accepted. Too often the questions arose: What is a Canadian? Who is he? What does he think? Does he have any original opinions, feelings, or thoughts?

To find the answers to those questions I have gone to our national literature and discovered that the Canadian identity does exist and that we really have an individuality of our own. The Canadian originality can be seen in any one of the hundreds of topics in this book.

The origin of this collection of literary Canadiana goes back nearly seven years, when, as a student of Canadian Literature at Laval University, I began collecting Canadian thoughts for my own personal studies.

The number of thoughts in both English and French grew into the thousands. When the number passed beyond the ten thousand mark, it was suggested to me that many other Canadians would also be interested.

I have attempted to include all types of Canadian writers: poets, novelists, essayists, dramatists, and critics. All have something of value to say. In subject matter I have also tried to cover all fields. Almost every topic imaginable from Ability and Youth, to Life and Death is included. Some of these quotes may not be too flattering to the Canadian ego but they do present the reality of our society and its individuality.

I would call attention to the structure of the book. It has been arranged by topic so that the reader can easily find a quote on any subject by merely following the alphabetical order of the book. Everyone, from the curious individual to speech-writers, students, lecturers and politicans, can find a saying on his favourite or required topic.

I wish to thank all those who have been most helpful and encouraging while preparing this book. For the most part, these are the librarians with whom I have worked. Without them, the source material for this book would never have been available.

ABSENCE

Absence of the absolute results in emptiness.

Louis Dudek, *Things in Space*, 1965

Your absence has not taught me how to be alone, it merely has shown that when together we cast a single shadow upon the wall.

Doug Fetherling,
Your absence has not taught me, 1971

Absence picks up what presence has begun.

Robert Finch, *Absence*, 1961

ABILITY

I think a man carries his own ammunition with him. You can do anything that is worth doing if you try hard enough.

Nina Moore Jamieson,
The Hickory Stick, 1921

ACADIA

Happy Acadia, though around thy shore
Is heard the stormy wind's terrific roar;
Still Summer comes, and decorates thy land
Of fruits and flowers from her luxuriant hand.

Oliver Goldsmith, *The Rising Village*, 1825

They were not people of learning or experience, these Acadians. They were simple folk whose horizons were their own farms' acres.

Joseph Lister Rutledge,
This Stubborn Breed, 1956

ACCEPTANCE

To simple lives there is a secret known
Of being accepted as a person for
No other reason that oneself alone.

Herb Barrett, *A Way of Life*, 1964

We curb impatience, and disdain
To entertain this horde
Who blow themselves to bits.

Vina Bruce Chilton, *Outer Space*, 1968

Taking things philosophically is easy if they don't concern you.

Robert C. Edwards, *Calgary Eye Opener*, 1915

If we don't act the way we should too bad for you. We're here for good.

Phyllis Gotlieb, *Ordinary Moving*, 1970

What must come would come; no use trying to fight: no use worrying. Too bad if anything happened; but if it did, it could not be helped.

Frederick Philip Grove, *Fruits of the Earth*, 1933

I am sceptical that the universe has any purpose; it seems to me it just is.

D.G. Jones,
A Letter on Poetry and Belief, 1958

Since I no longer expect anything from mankind, except madness, meanness, and mendacity; egotism, cowardice, and self-delusion, I have stopped being a misanthrope.

Irving Layton,
Some Observations and Aphorisms, 1968

When we have served apprentice of the seas,
All Eldorados and old loves forgot,
We come contented to a garden plot,
Happy to watch the sun climb over trees
To warm an old dog scratching for his fleas.

Roger Peterly,
In a Garden Near Pomerol, 1952

They don't ask about the mysteries but like Job accept.

Christina Petrowsky, *Eskimos*, 1968

I do not care, because
I see with bitter calm,
Life made me what I was,
Life makes me what I am.

Robert W. Service, *The Coco-Fiend*, 1921

I am as my Creator made me, and since He is satisfied, I am.

Minnie Smith, *Is It Just?*

What are we whole or beautiful or good for but to be absolutely broken?

Phyllis Webb, *The Sea is Also a Garden*, 1963

To give up bitterness, resentment, was to bury oneself, somehow; to stop being proud, maybe to stop living a little.

Frances Shelley Wees,
M'Lord, I Am Not Guilty, 1954

And I must be content with little things
I find; for I have striven
Too hard it seems.
Ann Wilson, *Little Things*, 1939

ACHIEVEMENT

It is not under the immediate stress of a great emotion that a great work is produced; most often it is the result of the long, silent cogitation, when the mind sits in autumnal luxury thinking to itself.
Bliss Carman, *The Kinship of Nature*, 1904

Very great achievements are brought about by passion and emotion rather than by practice, training, knowledge.
Frederick Philip Grove,
A Search for America, 1927

To have done this is to have lived, though fame
Remember us with no familiar name.
Archibald Lampman, *The Largest Life*, 1899

It is always well to have a thing accomplished before one talks about it.
Isabel Ecclestone MacKay, *The Second Lie*

Who tills the soil, who builds a bridge, who plants a tree, who gives to the land his sweat and sperm, who fights for a cause of freedom, is our true inheritor,...
Edward Meade, *Remember Me*, 1946

Good taste, throughout, the victory has won,
And all that money can do has been done.
George Murray,
speech on opening of Her Majesty's Theatre (Montreal), 1898

ACTION

The principle of life is movement, and stagnation is death. So that if a thing has no play, you may be sure it has no life.
Bliss Carman,
The Kinship of Nature, 1904

Think then and plan; no more of this indecision; let action take the place of hesitation.
Frances Griffiths, *Final Assignment*, 1956

The word betrays the act;
The act alone is pure.
The rest is literature.
Irving Layton, *Silence*, 1962

By walking I found out where I was going.
Irving Layton, *There were no signs*, 1963

It rather occurs to me that it's the commonplace people who do things.
Stephen B. Leacock, *The Soul Call*, 1923

Your little narrow-chested men may plan and organize, but when there is something to be done, something real, then it's the man of size and weight that steps to the front every time.
Stephen Leacock,
Sunshine Sketches, 1912

Run. Take your dreams and run.
Take no heed of loved ones
Hear the distant calling...
Mary Jane Lee, *Supplication*, 1951

The white roads are chequered with moving oblongs of black. All Canada is on the march.
J.F.B. Livesay, *Canada's Hundred Days*

Learning has ended, now in action lives full meaning.
P.J. Thomas, *The Pear-Pickers*, 1947

ACTING

When actors begin to think, it is time for a change. They are not fitted for it.
Stephen Leacock,
The Decline of the Drama

The actor makes the word more-than-alive. This is television's famous sense of immediacy, and not to be scorned.
George Robertson, *Drama on the Air*, 1959

ADAPTABILITY

Not to be nourished by the sunshine of the hour is to begin to wilt and fail.
Bliss Carman, *The Friendship of Art*, 1904

The wise man yields himself to the moment; he is glad of the relish in toil, glad of the serenity in rest.
Bliss Carman, *The Kinship of Nature*, 1904

You adjust, yes: that is, you harden, dry up, withdraw, become indifferent to mankind, pump all your vitality and interest back into yourself, simply in order not to wither away or go mad.
Silas N. Gooch, *A Season in Limbo*, 1962

ADMIRATION

In much of our admiration for the great sights there is a great deal of sham.
Frederick Philip Grove,
A Search for America, 1927

When one admires where one loves, then in the ebb and flow of passion the heart is safe, for admiration holds when the sense is cold.
Gilbert Parker,
The Seats of the Mighty, 1896

ADOLESCENT

There is a touch of the fascist in most adolescents; they admire the strong man who stands no nonsense; they have no objection to seeing the weak trampled underfoot; mercy in its more subtle forms is outside their understanding and has no meaning for them.
Robertson Davies, *Tempest-Tost*, 1951

ADULT

Now you know that grown-ups are just very tall children.
Janet Bonellie,
Why Are The People Staring? 1968

Adults are children who have failed to find a substitute for the charm they lost.
Irving Layton,
Some Observations and Aphorisms, 1968

Adults are children merely with a larger vocabulary.
Irving Layton,
A Red Carpet in the Sun, 1959

When you reach man's estate in course of time,
With sturdy physique and strong
Will your character, too, be staunch and true,
Sustaining your journey along?
Ronald Tuckwell, *The Greater Game*, 1938

ADVENTURE

But when the lure of mystery is flown,
Will then Adventure toll its own sad dirge?
Lilian Leveridge, *Beckoning Worlds*, 1948

Having adventures comes natural to some people, . . . You just have a gift for them or you haven't.
L.M. Montgomery, *Anne of Avonlea*

ADVERTISING

Stardom is not achieved without a good deal of promotional engineering.
Louis Dudek,
The Writing of the Decade, 1969

Only the advertisements preach the lie direct,
This trumpery of the word, garbage of dreams.
L.W. Ellis, *Daily Newspaper*, 1964

Advertisers crave respectability, and have no desire to appear in publications which obviously lack it.
Robert Fulford, *The Male Mags*, 1958

ADVICE

A man shows lack of nerve when he asks for advice and still more when he takes the advice that is given.
Peter McArthur,
To Be Taken with Salt, 1903

Advice is sought to confirm a position already taken.
William Osler,
In Cushing's "Life of Osler", 1926

AGE

You take advantage of your age, measuring it, in your convenient way, by years alone.
W.H. Blake, *Brown Waters*

I've reached an age where I can't use my youth as an excuse for my ignorance any more.
Janet Bonellie,
Why Are The People Staring? 1967

I feel age like an icicle down my back.
Dyson Carter, *Night of Flame*, 1943

More lovely grows the earth as we grow old,
More tenderness is in the dawning spring,
More bronze upon the blackbird's burnished wing;
And richer is the autumn cloth-of-gold.
Helena Coleman,
More Lovely Grows the Earth, 1938

We're all fools till we get so old that what little sense we get does us no good.
Merrill Denison, *Balm*

One can always tell when one is getting old and serious by the way that holidays seem to interfere with one's work.
Robert C. Edwards, *Calgary Eye Opener*, 1913

Most people who are old enough to know better often wish they were young enough not to.
Robert C. Edwards, *Calgary Eye Opener*, 1912

We pass as time, into the nothingness
From which we came.
As nebulous as starry galaxies is life,
And no less distant to our minds.
Lorne Hicks, *Reflection VI*, 1968

No winter brings us, with its firelight,
The dreams of young adventure, gay and bold.
The fires are out upon our hearth tonight,
And we grow old.
Norah Holland, *Though We Are Old*, 1924

Our madcap youth is over,
Gone its unclouded skies,
And you and I, O Lover,
Grow old and staid and wise;
Norah Holland, *A Song of Age*, 1924

Sometimes very young children can look at the old, and a look passes between them, conspiratorial, sly and knowing. It's because neither are human to the middling ones, ...
Margaret Laurence, *The Stone Angel*, 1964

We've lost some of our hair, some of our teeth. We're disintegrating slowly. When we stop breathing the process will quicken up. That's all.
Leslie McFarlane, *A Matter of Principle*, 1936

Where can we drive to but away from fear and hellbent into age?
Peter Miller, *Motor Show at the Ex*, 1959

He is one of those people who look older than they are when they're young and younger than they are when they're old.
Alice Munro, *Postcard*, 1968

The charm of age
My dear, is not to stage
A desperate rebellion
Against what must be
But to be.
C. J. Newman,
"Instructing the Old on Growing Old", 1967

From old men to children is but a step, ...
Robert Service, *Ballads of a Bohemian, 1921*

Can nothing compensate for fading charms,
Not even knowledge, intellect nor power?
Samuel James Watson, *Ravlan*, 1876

Fifteen was a nondescript year, not marked by any change in status.
Ernesto Cuevas,
Lock the Doors, Lock the Windows

Those that we envied at twenty we pity at thirty.
Suzanne Marny, *The Unhappy House*, 1909

O midnight feast and famished dawn!
O gay, hard life, with hope alive!
O golden youth, forever gone,
How sweet you seem at thirty-five!
Robert Service, *At Thirty-Five*, 1912

No man need blush at forty for the follies of one-and-twenty, unless indeed, he still perseveres in them.
Thomas D'Arcy McGee, *a speech*, 1865

When a man is over fifty he has to expect to slow down a bit, but he doesn't want to have to remember it every waking hour of the day.
Howard O'Hagan,
Trees Are Lonely Company, 1958

AIRPLANES

The Air Age faces mankind with a sharp choice — the choice between Winged Peace or Winged Death.
W. A. Bishop, *Winged Peace*

ALCOHOL

Certainly brandy makes a woman talk like an angel.
Frances Brooke,
The History of Emily Montague, 1769

Whiskey drowns some troubles and floats a lot more.
Robert C. Edwards, *Calgary Eye Opener*, 1915

Nothing ever tasted any better than a cold beer on a beautiful afternoon with nothing to look forward to but more of the same.
Hugh Hood,
"Recollections of the Works Department", 1962

Worst thing you can ever do is laugh at a man
who needs a drink, 'cause that's what makes him
go out and get it.
Bill Howell, *A Year Ago Today*, 1970

In any position of responsibility a man has got to drink. No really big deal can be put through without it.
Stephen B. Leacock,
Arcadian Adventures of the Idle Rich, 1914

He is...like many other geniuses, a greater friend to the bottle, than the bottle is to him, ...
William Lyon Mackenzie,
Sketches of Canada and the United States, 1833

Temperance is after all in great degree a fad, like that of the health addicts who idolize buttermilk, ...
W. H. Magee,
"Stephen Leacock, Local Colourist", 1969

AMBITION

It is a fine thing to have a country to be made, and it is fine to be a man and have a part in the making of it.
Ralph Connor, *The Foreigner*

A man who walks the heights must walk alone.
Robertson Davies, *A Jig for the Gypsy*, 1954

Human motives are very mixed and...men seldom strive,...purely for the love of God and of Holy Church.
Francis W. Grey,
The Curé of St Philippe, 1899

If the desire to get somewhere is strong enough in a person, his whole being, conscious and unconscious, is always at work, looking for, and devising, means to get to the goal.
Frederick Philip Grove,
A Search for America, 1927

Once, long ago, they marched.
Eager, in the idealism of youth,
Unknowing, but unafraid.
Joyce Hailey, *Hollow Steps*, 1967

What thing is it that grows within a man such as he — a seed of ardor, that is nurtured in the memory of pain, that grows until it dominates the soul?
W. Roger Harding, *Sukanen*, 1956

The female kind of ambition which concentrates on being rather than doing.
Hugh MacLennan, *Each Man's Son*, 1951

The greater part of us spend the half of their time, running about expressly for the purpose of getting rich; yet, by some strange fatality, misfortune has fallen heaviest upon those who were most active.
Thomas McCulloch,
The Stepsure Letters, 1821

Although ambitions are well worth having, they are not cheaply won, but exact their dues of work and self-denial, anxiety and discouragement.
L. M. Montgomery,
Anne of Green Gables, 1908

Most of us who are in a hurry to attain some wished for end, are apt to take the first way to it that presents itself, without much consideration as to where it may lead us.
J. J. Procter,
The Philosopher in the Clearing, 1897

Nothing's impossible to determined men,...
Thomas H. Raddall, *A Harp in the Willows*

To fame and empire hence my course I bend,
And every step I take shall thither tend.
Robert Rogers, *Ponteach*, 1766

We live in a day of small things. We fail in respect to the bigger things, because we are not producing them.
Lord Tweedsmuir, *Return to Masterpieces*

We're all on the mountain, you know. Trying to clamber up to the peak. Or crashing on the summit. Or sliding down, down to the bottom.
Norman Williams, *The Mountain*, 1956

AMERICA

America has a great advantage over Europe in this respect, that it has a record of its birth, while the origin of the other has to be sought for in the region of fable.
T. C. Haliburton, *The Old Judge*, 1849

13

The sorrows and disasters of Europe always brought fortune to America.
Stephen Leacock, *All Right, Mr. Roosevelt*

There is a good deal of pseudo-informed and miserably envious anti-Americanism here, . . .
Millar Maclure, *English Notes*, 1959

North America is a large island to the west of the continent of Cape Breton.
Ray Smith, *Cape Breton*, 1967

AMERICANS

No matter what happens to dismay Americans, they always have their Westerns, and that is enough.
Robert Fulford,
A Myth in Every Livingroom, 1958

These Americans raise their children like chickens — Any which way.
David Kherdian,
My Mother and the Americans, 1967

Americans talked too much and the British made the mistake of underrating them.
Hugh MacLennan, *Two Solitudes*, 1945

The Americans believe they answered all first questions in 1776; since then they've just been hammering out the practical details.
Ray Smith, *Cape Breton*, 1967

ANGER

The tigers of wrath are wiser than the horses of instruction.
Dennis Duffy,
The Too-Well-Tempered Critic, 1968

ANGUISH

I doubt I know what anguish talks about. Even love is a straight deception of little merit or meaning: no heat of hell against the soul, . . .
David Knight, *Absence of Pain*, 1958

But to have possessed a unique anguish has been some solace through the years.
Malcolm Lowry,
The Days Like Smitten Cymbals

ANTIQUES

For love of vintage old,
Like old Khayyam, he hath his credit sold.
Florence C. Estabrooks,
From Out The Darker Shadows, 1938

APATHY

Indifference may not wreck the man's life at any one turn, but it will destroy him with a kind of dry-rot in the long run.
Bliss Carman, *The Friendship of Art*, 1904

The world takes no account of us because we have never adequately taken account of the world.
Louis Dudek,
Thoughts on World Literature, 1962

it is not unfortunately
quite enough to be innocent
it is not enough merely
not to offend —
John Newlove, *Ride Off Any Horizon*, 1969

Surely no violence
could bestir our lassitude,
surely no horror
nor energy loosened in hysteria
could break through this still dream
to reach our drowsy souls.
Jane Smart, *Bourgeois Afternoon*, 1938

I hear nothing. I see nothing.
Shelia Watson, *The Double Hook*, 1969

APARTMENT

The apartment house; the greatest enemy of childhood ever contrived.
Stephen Leacock, *Women's Level*

APPEARANCE

I hope she's deeper
than the gaze implies.
Dave Bromige, *The Model Lover*, 1962

Rough and ready, honest and free;
Though the hand may be black, it's the hand of a man,
And the dirt's only outside,
deny it who can!
Frederick A. Dixon,
The Maire of St. Brieux, 1875

There is so often a wonderful contrast between the ease of the man's appearance and the uneasiness that shows in his talk . . .
M. Allerdale Grainger,
Woodsmen of the West, 1908

We are all so anxious that people should not think us different.
Margaret Laurence, *The Rain Child*, 1962

Nothing in the world, short of actual dishonour, can cause a man of sensibility keener suffering than the knowledge that he has made a fool of himself.
William McLennan and J. N. McIlwraith, *"The Span O' Life",* 1899

APPRECIATION

Joy and elation and betterment reside in appreciation, not in passion.
Bliss Carman, *The Kinship of Nature,* 1904

ARCHITECTURE

We build very ugly houses in Canada, very ill laid out, and very incommodious; but this is our misfortune not our fault, for there are no people on the face of the earth more willing to learn, and if by any chance a man once lays out a cottage a little neater than his neighbour's, you will see it imitated for ten miles on each side of him down the road.
William Dunlop, *Statistical Sketches,* 1832

O Architect, thrice happy man are you,
Who of all men can make his dreams come true!
Donald A. Fraser, *Realization,* 1930

For architecture, it is unfortunate that the apex of religious zeal coincided with the apex of poor taste.
Arthur R. M. Lower,
Canadians in the Making, 1958

ARCHIVES

The Archives hold the strata of the vanished years
That shaped the minds of men.
M. Eugenie Perry, *The Archives,* 1954

ARGUMENT

We're so much alike that we can't discuss. We can only fight.
Stephen Leacock, *Rebuilding the Cities*

From argument men go to deeds if their heart's in what they say.
Thomas H. Raddall, *Blind MacNair,* 1945

There are three sides to every argument. Yours. The other guy's. And the right side.
Mordecai Richler, *Son of a Smaller Hero,* 1955

ARISTOCRACY

We have no aristocracy but of virtue and talent, which is the only true aristocracy, and is the old and true meaning of the term.
Thomas D'Arcy McGee,
Confederation Debates, 1865

ART

Art resists analysis and classification, and the artist resists it even more.
Patricia Barclay,
Regionalism and the Writer, 1962

To be sincere is one of the first requisites of good art, even of good taste.
Clara Bernhardt, *The Poet's Function,* 1939

Without idealism art cannot exist, and there is no enduring beauty.
Clara Bernhardt, *The Poet's Function,* 1939

For a Puritan a life devoted to one of the arts is a life misused: the aesthetic life is not a form of the good life.
E.K. Brown
The Problem of Canadian Literature, 1943

Any art is just as great as the age that produced it.
Bliss Carman, *The Friendship of Art,* 1904

Art, . . . , is all made of metaphors, — is itself the universal metaphor of the soul.
Bliss Carman, *The Kinship of Nature,* 1904

All art, like life itself, is a compromise — a compromise between what we would and what we can.
Bliss Carman, *The Friendship of Art,* 1904

Art lies in understanding some part of the dark forces and bringing them under the direction of reason.
Robertson Davies, *A Voice from the Attic,* 1960

Art functions on two opposed levels — bohemia and the snob trade.
Louis Dudek, *The Soil,* 1959

Art for art's sake is a retreat from criticism which ends in an impoverishment of civilized life itself.
Northrop Frye, *Anatomy of Criticism,* 1959

Art, ... begins with the world we construct, not with the world we see . . .
Northrop Frye, *The Educated Imagination,* 1963

15

Man in Canadian art is rarely in command of his environment or ever at home in it.
Elizabeth Kilbourn, *The Centennial Art Show,* 1968

Good art does not justify or reclaim a wasted life.
Jack Ludwig, *Portrait of the Double Artist,* 1960

Art generalizes while science itemizes.
Peter McArthur, *To Be Taken with Salt,* 1903

A work of art
is a consistency
among incommensurables,
or it is that
which remains equal
to itself.
W.W.E. Ross, *Garden,* 1969

Today there is no lack of energy and good will where most of the arts in Canada are concerned; what's needed now is more discrimination; and that's not an easy quality to sustain in this small country.
Robert Weaver, *Monkeys on our Backs,* 1959

It is not in life but in art that self-fulfilment is to be found.
George Woodcock, *The Departing God,* 1960

ARTIST

To the truly gifted artist, the particular character of his environment is secondary; it is the use he is able to make of it that counts.
Patricia Barclay, *Regionalism and the Writer,* 1962

I always suspect an artist who is successful before he is dead.
John Murray Gibbon, *Pagan Love,* 1922

You know, there's nothing so comfortable as an established artist.
Hugh Hood, *The Tolstoy Pitch,* 1969

The most successful and effective artists are those who, other things being equal, establish a condition of reciprocity between their audiences and themselves.
Frank Home Kirkpatrick,
"Hints for the Vocal Interpretation of Literature", 1921

An artist has to take life as he finds it. Life by itself is formless wherever it is. Art must give it form.
Hugh MacLennan, *Two Solitudes,* 1945

Suffering is often approved of, for the artist, because it is believed that experience exists to be turned into art — an invitation to exploit one's pain.
John Reid, *Journey Out of Anguish,* 1969

Time uses the man of action, but the artist uses time.
Robert Weaver, *The Canada Council,* 1957

Art is selective, and the artist must be permitted to arrange life to suit his purposes.
E.H. Winter,
Introduction to: "Our Century in Prose", 1966

AUTONOMY

Autonomy almost always breeds chauvinism, and usually brings as an immediate consequence an unwholesome delight in the local second-rate.
E. K. Brown,
The Problem of Canadian Literature, 1943

AUTHORITY

Why will men dressed in a little brief authority try to crush those less fortunate?
H. A. Cody, *The Fourth Watch,* 1911

Wherever there is authority there is a natural inclination to disobedience.
T. C. Haliburton,
Sam Slick's Wise Saws, 1853

AUTHOR

Every author who appeals to the public to purchase and read a new book should have a reason to give for such a demand.
E. H. Dewart,
Introduction to: "Essays for the Times", 1898

Some authors write for fame, some for money, some to propagate particular doctrines and opinions, some from spite, some at the instigation of their friends, and not a few at the instigation of the devil.
William Dunlop, *Statistical Sketches,* 1832

A great poet or author is a greater resource in this country in time of war than a battleship.
Robert J. C. Stead, *in: Canadian Author,* 1943

16

AUTUMN

There in her flaming robes of royal red,
Gay priestess in a land of vivid dreams,
The honey-coloured Autumn softly
gleams,
A veil of mist about her drooping head.
Augusta Barbara Bailey, *Autumn*, 1938

Then fear not my friends, to leave me
In the boding autumn vast;
There are many things to think of.
When the roving days are past.
Bliss Carman, *The Grave-Tree*

Autumn
Is the husk of summer shorn of its kernel
Don Gutteridge, *Coureur de Bois*, 1967

Fall comes quite gradually on the Pacific
Coast of Canada, so gradually that one
scarcely knows when or whether it has
arrived.
Roderick Haig-Brown, *Fall Defined*

Pale memories appear in autumn rains
Like tears of grief;
Robert Norwood, *Bill Boram*, 1921

Autumn is the bite of a harvest apple
Christina Petrowsky, *Autumn*, 1967

BABY

Homes rich or poor that guard a Baby's
smile,
Are surely Bethlehems of God the while!
Donald A. Fraser, *Bethlehems*, 1929

BANFF

In creating Banff, God assumed the role of
a farsighted parks superintendent and
designed the area with a view of tourism in
the future.
Edward McCourt,
"Overland from Signal Hill to Victoria"

BEAUTY

The scenery is to be sure divine, but one
grows weary of mere scenery.
Frances Brooke,
The History of Emily Montague, 1769

Show me where beauty is hiding!
Can you nail her down less abstract
like God from his heaven crucified?
Eddie Clinton, *Keats, You Old Dog*, 1970

Beauty is everywhere; it has only to be
found.
Diane Corrigan, *A Conversation*, 1956

Beauty of character produces beauty of
face. Therefore, a beautiful face means a
beautiful heart within.
Margaret E. Elliott,
The Favours of My Lady Leone, 1926

Not many men and women love beauty for
its own sake. Not many see it. To most of us
it is only an adjunct to comfort or pride.
Basil King, *The Thread of Flame*

Beauty cannot die, because she is eternal
as God is eternal.
Cecil Francis Lloyd, *Sunset and Evening Star*

Give me the loveliness that is undying,
And I will let all other beauty go.
Wilson MacDonald,
The Undying Beauty, 1926

There is no excellent beauty but hath a
strangeness in the proportions.
Hugh MacLennan, *Two Solitudes*, 1945

How many times had closer acquaintance
with things that were beautiful exposed
only worm-eaten ugliness in their hearts?
John Marlyn,
Under the Ribs of Death, 1957

I hope that I may never look on Beauty
With uncaring eyes; nor ever lose
The wonderment of youth, . . .
Jessica E. Money,
To Bring The Heart Repose, 1949

Women are envious, my Magdalene,
Knowing you are more beautiful than they.
Robert Norwood, *The Man of Kerioth*, 1919

Eyes are dead that fail
To look on beauty with that awe which
seeks
Truth in earth's loveliness . . .
Robert Norwood, *Bill Boram*, 1921

Beauty, like male ballet dancers, makes
some men afraid.
Mordecai Richler, *Son of a Smaller Hero*, 1955

Beauty has taken refuge from our life,
That grew too loud and wounding,
D. C. Scott

When Beauty weeps,
Hardware is melted.
Sam Scribble, *The Skating Carnival*, 1865

17

Beauty is the fragile beast,
deliquent,
of each man's invention.
Glen Siebrasse, *Theory*, 1958

You need no backgrounds
No one would see them anyway.
Raymond Souster, *Poem for Her Picture*

You are the joy and the beauty
Of spring in a wintry land!
Mary Woodworth,
Spring on the Shubenacadie, 1941

BELIEF

The harder the work, the harder we study,
the more we accomplish, the surer we are
that we are sons of God.
Ted Allan, *Lies My Father Told Me*

Once let us acquire the habit of free belief
in place of the habit of credulous timidity,
and the borders of wisdom will seem infinite.
Bliss Carman, *The Kinship of Nature*, 1904

I don't like the price of belief
Every god is jealous.
Leonard Cohen

The age of strong belief is over, the good is
no longer always very good.
D. L. Coles, *Poems for Writers II*, 1967

Whether you are really right or not doesn't
matter; it's the belief that counts.
Robertson Davies, *Overlaid*

I appear to have killed myself
By believing in some other God.
John Glassco, *The Death of Don Quixote*

One has to be believed in, or perish!
Dorothy Livesay, *Song and Dance*, 1969

The basis of all religious belief is the child's
fear of the dark.
Hugh MacLennan, *Two Solitudes*, 1945

Non-believers are only fugitives from God.
He is still a factor in their thinking. Worse
still, he becomes a REASON. In order to be
liberated from God one must FORGET him.
But can one forget?
Mordecai Richler, *Son of a Smaller Hero*, 1955

We must all be stubborn in what we
believe or one day find we believe in
nothing.
Norman Williams, *Protest*, 1956

THE BIBLE

The Bible never lies
but it was written
on stones
and by the time
men took it down
some of the words
had worn away.
Alden Nowlan,
First Lesson in Theology, 1968

Anybody who reads the Bible much will
write good English.
P. D. Ross
The Short Word in English Poetry, 1941

BILINGUALISM

We French, we English, never lost our civil
war,
endure it still, a bloodless civil bore.
Earle Birney, *Canadian Literature*, 1962

To the average English Canadian, bil-
ingualism means acquiring a second
language; at the moment, to many French
Canadians it means the likelihood of losing
a first one.
Ronald Sutherland, *The Fourth Separatism*,
1970

BIRDS

The cry of the loon, the strangest and,
perhaps, the most lovely of all woodland
sounds.
Douglas Leechman, *The Loon's Necklace*

No clay born lilies of the world
Could blow as free
As those wild orchids of the sea.
E. J. Pratt, *Sea Gulls*, 1932

BIRTH

Some mistakes
We make in childhood haunt us all life long
Perhaps. But I suspect that we went wrong
Earlier, indeed, in being born.
Daryl Hine,
Letter from British Columbia, 1970

The single function on which Venus
frowned
Was birth; and maybe, life has proved her
right.
Daryl Hine, *Under the Hill*, 1959

Why was I born?
I do not know.
I ask my face a thousand times
a day and find no answer.
Stephen Leacock, *Nonsense Novels*, 1911

Differences of birth are illusions.
W. D. Lighthall, *The False Chevalier*, 1898

God made me on a morning when
he had nothing else to do.
C. F. Lloyd, *Hippopotamus*, 1936

The station in which we are born,
constitutes fate in this world; it is the only
thing pertaining to man over which his will
has no control. We can destroy our own
lives, but our birth is entirely in the hands
of Providence.
Susanna Moodie, *Geoffrey Moncton*, 1855

at times to be born
is enough, to be
in the way is too much —
John Newlove, *Ride Off Any Horizon*, 1969

Husbands don't really count in — in the
miracle of birth, ...
Doug Spettigue, *Edge of Christmas*, 1969

Most adult birthdays, if they ever get
beyond an attenuated ritual, are times of
mild regret or mild relief; regret that
another set of seasons has slipped so
fruitlessly away, relief that it has slipped
away without disaster.
George Woodcock,
Getting Away With Survival, 1969

BLINDNESS

My fingers are my light and eyes—
With them I read and find my way.
Sara Hazen, *My Fingers*, 1954

BODY

The flesh is lonely and its beauty serves
but nuns.
D. G. Jones,
Like One of Botticelli's Daughters, 1961

In these times, the most of people's bodies
cost them more trouble than their souls;
Thomas McCulloch,
"The Letters of Mephibosheth Stepsure", 1822

Gods or men, of bodies absolute, we are
the equivocal prisoners.
Peter Miller, *Zodiac*, 1964

BOHEMIA

Most American Bohemia has lost its
authority: in England it has spread so far as
to be scarcely distinguishable.
Peter Scott, *A Choice of Certainties*, 1958

Such is the life of Bohemia, up and down,
fast and feast; its very uncertainty its
charm.
Robert Service, *Ballads of a Bohemian*, 1921

BOOKS

To know a good book is to know a good
man. To be influenced by a trivial, or
ignoble, or false book, is to associate with
an unworthy companion, and to suffer the
inevitable detriment.
Bliss Carman, *The Friendship of Art*, 1904

A good book has no ending.
R. D. Cumming, *Skookum Chuck Fables*, 1915

There are still a few of us booklovers
around despite the awful warnings of
Marshall McLuhan with his TV era and his
pending farewell to Gutenberg.
Frank Davies, *Typescript into Book*, 1958

Booklovers are thought by unbookish
people to be gentle and unworldly, and
perhaps a few of them are so. But there are
others who will lie and scheme and steal to
get books as wildly and unconsciously as
the dope-taker in pursuit of his drug.
Robertson Davies, *Tempest-Tost*, 1951

We shall find nothing in books which has
no existence in ourselves.
Robertson Davies, *A Voice from the Attic*,
1960

A book arises as much in the mind of the
reader as in that of the writer; and the
writer's art consists above all in creating
response; ...
F. P. Grove, *In Search of Myself*, 1940

You may stop a man's mouth by crammin'
a book down his throat, but you won't con-
vince him.
T. C. Haliburton, *Sam Slick*, 1853

I like prefaces. I read them. Sometimes I do
not read any farther.
Malcolm Lowry, *Preface to a Novel*, 1948

I love old books
Frayed from the searching
Of truth-hungry fingers:
Wilson MacDonald, *I Love Old Things*

Books, like men, are better understood when we know the mental environment from which they have risen.
William H. New,
Introduction to: "Odysseus Ever Returning", 1969

Books are selves;
They should be made to feel like folks at home—
And not like strangers, stacked there on those shelves.
Robert Norwood, *Bill Boram,* 1921

He had consumed the books.
But who knows at what cost?
Mordecai Richler, *Son of a Smaller Hero,* 1955

I study volumes from the shelf,
Producing nothing of myself.
John Wainscott, *So Blank the Verse,* 1967

The more a book is publicly attacked the better it sells.
Milton Wilson, *Callaghan's Caviare,* 1962

BOY

If there is one thing which utterly destroys a boy's character, it is to be needed. Boys are unendurable unless they are wholly expendable.
Robertson Davies, *Tempest-Tost,* 1951

You bad leetle boy, not moche you care
How busy you're keepin' your poor gran'père
William H. Drummond, *Leetle Bateese,* 1897

Probably a little boy is never quite so happy as when he is worshipping and imitating a young man.
Mazo de la Roche, *Explorers of the Dawn,* 1922

The human boy is the most exasperating animal on the surface of the earth.
Lister S. Sinclair, *The Faithful Heart,* 1945

A boy is a terrible
Question mark,
Dropped from immensity,
And only the hound that follows him
Knows what the answer will be.
Michael Wolf, *Only the Hound,* 1953

BRAINS

Brain labour, is hard labor.
Norman Duncan, *Every Man for Himself,* 1908

Brains be a load to carry and happy he that hath none.
John Hunter-Duvar, *The Enamorado,* 1879

People with brains get through life somehow; the rest need instruction.
Frederick P. Grove,
Fruits of the Earth, 1933

Most everybody keeps the body fit nowadays. But not many try to keep the brain fit too.
Fred Jacob, *The Clever One,* 1925

Her mind is like a good leather briefcase
Completely indexed, — in whose zippered space
Events important or irrelevant
Lie in neat arrangement.
Doris Baillie Phillips, *The Old Lady,* 1963

It's hopeless — all the words are vain
To tell the wonder of my brain.
Robert W. Service, *The Wonderer*

BRAVERY

The one predominating passion of the savage nature is bravery.
Agnes C. Laut, *Pathfinders of the West*

A great nation should overcome their enemies like warriors, and not seek to beguile them with their tongues under the edge of the scalping knife.
John Richardson, *Wacousta,* 1833

BRITAIN

The Empire produces a family resemblance, but here and there, when oceans intervene, a different mould of the spirit.
Sara Jeannette Duncan, *The Imperialist,* 1904

Hail Britannia! the ruler of the sea,
Canada to Britain ever true will be.
William Henry Fuller, *H.M.S. Parliament,* 1874

BRITISH

We British folk are so fearfully afraid of showing our feelings. We go along like graven images; the more really stirred up, the more graven we appear.
Ralph Connor, *The Major,* 1917

We are British subjects, and to-day we are face to face with the consequences which are involved in that proud fact.
Wilfred Laurier, *a speech*, 1915

The British are terribly lazy about fighting. They like to get it over and done with and then get up a game of cricket.
Stephen Leacock,
An Apology for the British Empire

Till the Americans came to England the people were an honest, law-abiding race, respecting their superiors and despising those below them.
Stephen Leacock,
My Discovery of England, 1922

BRITISH COLUMBIA

Unkempt great country
How shall I praise you —
Fretted with rivers,
Inlaid with lakes,
Ragged with mountains.
Anne Margaret Angus, *West Coast*, 1938

Life in British Columbia is so pleasant that it seems absurd to waste any part of it trying to improve on nature.
Edward McCourt,
"Overland from Signal Hill to Victoria"

BUILDINGS

A wooden ruin shows rank and rapid decay, concentrates its interest on one family or one man, and resembles a mangled corpse, rather than the monument that covers it.
T. C. Haliburton, *The Ruined Lodge*

Canadian history is short, but our buildings add spice by getting older faster.
Jack Ludwig, *Requiem for Bibul*

The design is grand;
Here is a thousand;
build you now in Edmonton
or in Jerusalem
all that you ever planned.
Eli Mandel,
The President Ordains the Fee to Be, 1960

BULLY

A brave man is sometimes a desperado. A bully is always a coward.
T. C. Haliburton, *Sam Slick*, 1853

Bullies are all cowards, ... they will yield to courage which they feel to be superior to their own.
Susanna Moodie, *Geoffrey Moncton*, 1855

BUSINESS

So the businessman has replaced the warrior and the aristocrat.
Louis Dudek, *Canada: Interim Report*, 1963

Buy from them that has GOT to sell, and SELL to them that is OBLIGED to buy; and cinch 'em all good and hard — that's all the secret there is to business!
M. Allerdale Grainger,
Woodsmen of the West, 1908

The businessman and the man of art in Canada still meet as seldom as possible, and when they do come together they exchange pleasantries with the unnatural politeness of individuals who distrust each other profoundly.
High MacLennan, *The Art of City-Living*, 1954

Merchants are very useful, and we cannot do without them; but they live altogether by the labours of other people; and they usually live well.
Thomas McCulloch,
The Stepsure Letters, 1821

These days everybody's in show business, all trades are riddled with impurities.
Mordecai Richler, *The Uncertain World*, 1969

If everyone would but consume
I'll bet there'd be a business boom!
D.M. Robinson, *Happiness, Preferred*, 1938

Hail to the hucksters! Knight errant of our time!
Proudly he rides to war for the barons of soap,
Perpetually storming the castles of the home.
F.R. Scott, *Social Sonnets II*, 1954

A new gospel shall you learn — one dollar at ten per cent, for one year, yields one dollar and ten cents. This is the law and the prophets!
A.M. Stephen, *Before Pilate*, 1937

BUSY

If you want work well done, select a busy man — the other kind has no time.
Robert C. Edwards, *Annual*, 1922

She is the kind who always carries water from afar with a yoke. She is not the kind who would dig a well near her door. She hasn't time.
Fred Sloman, *Breath of God*, 1936

CALGARY (Alberta)

Video people! Calgarians, hopeless automobile graveyard contractions squasht into steel cubes . . .someboy save them!
George Bowering, *"above calgary"*, 1969

Calgary is one of the two glamour cities of Canada. (The other is, of course, Montreal)
Edward McCourt
Overland from Signal Hill to Victoria

CANADA

A great, white, empty prison. . .
Patrick Anderson

Yes, here are formed the mouldings of a soul,
Too great for ease, too lofty for control.
anonymous, *"Canada"*, 1806

Canada was created by irrational, arbitrary, and necessary mandates of partial exclusiveness.
anonymous, *A Point of View*, 1960

No land illumed by yonder sun
Can more inspiring be than One
Where my far visions roam
O'er prairies wide, o'er mountains grand—
My love is thine, thou lavish land, Dear Canada, my home.
Grant Balfour, *Canada, My Home*, 1910

What people passed to heritage —
To heritage like thine?
Arise and fill thy destiny—
Thy destiny divine.
Grant Balfour, *Canada, Be Strong*, 1910

Here you receive another kind of wisdom,
Bitter and icy and not to everybody's taste .
The wind blows cold from Labrador:
I have a message for you from the ice age.
Walter Bauer, *Canada*, 1970

Ah! Canada, how your champions suffered for your sake! Ah! Canada, how you have also suffered by their deeds.
Alexander Begg, *Dot-It-Down*, 1963

Canada is under such handicaps: it is full of natural disadvantages, like the French and the savages.
Nathaniel A. Benson, *The Paths of Glory*, 1927

O Canada we march
each an individual, together, believing the future
in the light a young, an awkward but a fearless nation
can pass to others here on the globe.
Luella Booth, *The Plains of Abraham*, 1964

Land of a hundred peoples
From far and wide they came
Merged in the mighty cauldron,
One people and one name.
Arthur S. Borrinot
The Canadian Confederation, 1967

There is a spirit here, a response to the new, the natural, the open, the massive — as contrasted with the old artifical, enclosed littleness of Europe — that should eventually, when we rely on it less timidly, become actively creative.
Bertram Brooker,
Yearbook of the Arts in Canada, 1930

Have you loved this land
For what it is — For its wealth
Its freedom
Its northern wind,
And above all,
For its people?
Paul Call, *Canada 1967*, 1967

Canada, great nurse and mother
Of the young sea-roving clan.
Bliss Carman, *The Ships of St. John*

There isn't any one Canada, any average Canadian, any average place, any type.
Miriam Chapin, *They Outgrew Bohemia*, 1960

I am content with Canada and ask
No fairer land than has been given me,
No greater joy, no more inspiring task,
Than to uphold and share her destiny.
Helena Coleman, *Songs and Sonnets*

My country has an unacknowledged civil war
between the minorities
John Robert Colombo,
Canadian Sunset, 1960

How wonderful the power of this country of yours to transform men.
Ralph Connor, *The Foreigner*

Canada! the only country with newly found and lost land!
Pierre Coupey, *Canada*, 1963

Over a century ago settlers were taking possession of this country . . . Let us now take possession of it once again but this time for purposes of beauty, making use of the civil freedom we have for the development of a new cultural vitality.
Alan Creighton, *Conquest by Poetry*, 1942

This is no country for weaklings
Who husband their breath,
Content to wait in aimless existence,
Their dignity in death!
Annie Charlotte Dalton,
I Know a White Kingdom

Sometimes for us in Canada it seems as though the United States and the United Kingdom were cup and saucer, and Canada the spoon, for we are in and out of both with the greatest freedom, and we are given most recognition when we are most a nuisance.
Robertson Davies, *A Voice from the Attic*, 1960

Canada was settled, in the main, by people with lower middle-class outlook, and a respect, rather than an affectionate familiarity, for the things of the mind.
Robertson Davies, *On Stephen Leacock*, 1957

Everybody says Canada is a hard country to govern, but nobody mentions that for some people it is also a hard country to live in.
Robertson Davies, *Fortune, My Foe*, 1949

It's a wilderness between the jungle and the sea.
Louis Dudek, *Canada: Interim Report*, 1963

Canada's history is not only short, it is also disjointed, The country has passed through various phases of growth with amazing rapidity, too fast indeed to establish much in the way of traditions.
Murray D. Edwards, *A Stage in Our Past*, 1968

Canada, if silence is golden, you're an angel.
Doug Emid, *Dialogue with Ginsberg*, 1968

Canadians salute
This fertile soil, this land,
Our own to love, to expand,
Our birthright and our root.
Margaret Fulton Frame, *A Canadian People*, 1947

We vaguely heard the echoes, not the voice;
We know our country's features, not her face. . .
'Till one day we awoke as from a dream
To weld a brave new nation, forge a race.
Margaret Fulton Frame, *Canadians*, 1947

Stand fast, O Canada!
The World is all a-flame
With passionate rebellion;
Dark deeds of blood and shame
Are flaunted in our faces
In Freedom's slandered name!
Donald A. Fraser, *Stand Fast, O Canada*, 1919

There would be nothing distinctive in Canadian culture at all if there were not some feeling for the immense searching distance, with the lines of communication extended to the absolute limit, which is a primary geographical fact about Canada, . .
Northrop Frye, *Letters in Canada*, 1952

Canadians ask themselves whether they have become free of Britain's colonial influence only to fall under the spell of the United States' economic imperialism.
Walter Gordon, *A Choice for Canada*

The union of two races and languages was needed to enable England to do her imperial work. Will not the same union enable Canada to do a like work, and does it not force us to see good, even in those whom our ancestors may have thought enemies?
George Munro Grant, *a speech*, 1893

This country is the granary of a world. To put it to that use for which it was meant is serving God; not to do so is defying God.
Frederick P. Grove, *The Sower*, 1923

In Europe you can't move without going down into history.
Here, all is a beginning.
Ralph Gustafson, *In The Yukon*

This colony is but a crisis-bag,
Trade throating trade, and creed a-cursing
creed.
With sordid passions slinking everywhere.
John Murdoch Harper, *Champlain*, 1908

This rude country they call Canada
Is but a barren waste, and valueless.
John Hunter-Duvar, *De Roberval*, 1888

Canada is a colony, not a COUNTRY; it is
not yet identified with the dearest affections and associations, rememberances,
and hopes of its inhabitants: it is to them
an adopted, not a real mother.
Anna Brownell Jameson,
Winter Studies, 1838

We had a new country but old peoples;
wealth collectively and in the future, but
individual poverty; . . .
Raymond Knister
Introduction to: "Canadian Short Stories",
1928

Our country is still in the house-building,
land-breaking stage, and all its energies
must go to the laying of a foundation of
material prosperity upon which a future
culture may be built.
Archibald Lampman,
Two Canadian Poets, 1891

Where else in the world could you find
another case like ours — three thousand
miles of forts and not a single frontier?
Stephen Leacock, *All Right, Mr. Roosevelt*

In Canada, unless we maintain this British
stock, we are lost.
Stephen Leacock, *Woman's Level*

The day of annexation to the United States
is past. Our future lies elsewhere.
Stephen Leacock,
in: University Magazine, 1907

Our land is a stripling, its bones are mere
but cartilage forming.
Gordon LeClaire,
A Spring With Its Flower, 1947

Canada, Eldest Daughter of the Empire, is
the Empire's completest type. She is the
full-grown of the family — the one first
come of age and gone out into life as a
nation.
W.D. Lighthall
*Introduction to: "Songs of the Great
Dominion",* 1889

God bless our mighty forest land
Of mountain, lake and river:
Thy loyal sons from strand to strand
Sing "Canada Forever"
Agnes Maule Machar,
"Canada Forever", 1899

How Eldorado once again was found
Where stretch Canadian plains forlorn and
rude,
Hard upon the iron-tempered Arctic
solitude.
Tom MacInnes, *Lonesome Bar*

It's an odd thing about this country — it has
few outright villains. It's only their instincts
that are wrong.
Hugh MacLennan, *Two Solitudes*, 1945

But Canada isn't England, and too many
Canadians try to pretend it is.
Hugh MacLennan, *Two Solitudes*, 1945

The trouble with this whole country is that
it's divided up into little puddles with big
fish in each one of them.
Hugh MacLennan, *Two Solitudes*, 1945

Canada at present was called a nation only
because a few laws had been passed and a
railway line sent from one coast to the
other.
Hugh MacLennan, *Barometer Rising*, 1941

Our romantic Canadian story is a mine of
character and incident for the poet and
novelist.
Charles Mair,
the preface to: "Tecumseh", 1886

We will follow our leader to fields far and
nigh,
And for Canada fight, and for Canada die.
Charles Mair, *Tecumseh*, 1886

The country you call Canada, and which
your sons and your children's children will
be proud to know by that name is a land
which will be a land of power among the
nations.
Marquis of Lorne, *Sources of Canadian Power*

When I can hear our young men say as
proudly; "our Federation", or "our Country" or "our Kingdom", as the young men
of other countries do, . . . , then I shall have
less apprehension for the result of

whatever trials the future may have in store for us.
Thomas D'Arcy McGee,
Confederation Debates, 1865

Canada is now synonymous with culture.
John Newton McIlwraith, *Ptarmigan*, 1895

Seems to me it's the only country that let's a nigger be. Some places, they call it democracy, but it ain't the same. In Canada they don't call it nothin'.
Edward Meade, *Remember Me*, 1946

My love for this country has steadily increased from year to year, and my attachment to Canada is now so strong that I cannot imagine any inducement short of absolute necessity, which would induce me to leave . . . .
Susanna Moodie
the preface to: "Roughing It in the Bush", 1871

Canada is no longer a child, sleeping in the arms of nature, dependent for her very existence on the fostering care of her illustrious mother.
Susanna Moodie,
preface to: "Roughing It in the Bush", 1871

Make your children proud of the land of their birth, the land which has given them bread — the land in which you have found an altar and a home; do this, and you will soon cease to lament your separation from the mother country.
Susanna Moodie,
Roughing It in the Bush, 1871

As power steps from the disorganized grasp of the United States, it will fall to Canada as her natural right, making her the first nation on this continent, as she is now the second.
William Norris, *Canadian Nationality*, 1878

There is no part of this continent which has such an heroic past as Canada.
Thomas O'Hagan, *Canadian Essays*, 1901

Canada's youth is in reality an advantage rather than a handicap. Her future is almost certain to be greater than her past, and this is the basis for the perpetual hopefulness which pervades her literature.
Desmond Pacey
in General Introduction to:
"Creative Writing", 1961

Firm stands the red flag battle-war blown,
And we will guard our own.
Our Canada,
From snow to sea,
One hope, one home, one shining destiny.
Marjorie L. C. Pickthall, *Star of the North*

We have two great shrines at which we speak two languages; yet we have but one passionate loyalty — Canada.
Lorne Albert Pierce
Introduction to:
"Our Canadian Literature", 1923

This country — there are so many things I don't know, so many things to learn.
Thomas H. Raddall, *The Wedding Gift*

Awake my country, the hour is great with change.
Charles G. D. Roberts,
Ode for the Canadian Confederacy, 1880

But thou, my country, dream not thou.
Wake, and behold how night is done—
How on thy breast, and o'er thy brow,
Bursts the uprising sun.
Charles G.D. Roberts, *Canada*

Awake my country, the hour of dreams is done.
Doubt not, nor dread the greatness of thy fate.
Charles G.D. Roberts,
Ode for the Canadian Confederacy, 1880

Canada first. May the men of the nation,
Progeny great of two peoples of old,
Find such a motto of true inspiration
Stamped on their hearts with the brightness of gold.
James A. Ross, *Canada First*

One voice, one people, one in heart
And soul, and feeling, and desire.
Charles Sangster, *Hesperus,* 1864

Here is the land of quintessential passion,
Where in a wild throb Spring wells up with power.
Duncan Campbell Scott, *Spring on Mattagami*

We are beginning to realize our position in the world, and it is precarious. We lie between the greatest and grimmest of the Grim Great Powers.
Lister Sinclair, *The Canadian Idiom*

The sacred cow under fire is Canadian life itself, with its determined dullness.
William Solly, *Nothing Sacred*, 1962

Canada is yet in her colonial dawn; but the dawn is one of cheering promise.
Samuel Strickland,
"Twenty-Seven Years in Canada West", 1853

No person need starve in Canada, where there is plenty of work and good wages for every man who is willing to labour, and who keeps himself sober.
Samuel Strickland,
"Twenty-Seven Years in Canada West", 1853

One of the chief mental hazards of the Canadian scene was, and to an extent still is, its land mass, stretching arbitrarily for inconceivable distances in almost every direction.
Michael Tait, *Playwrights in a Vacuum*, 1963

Previous to the discovery of Canada, this Continent... may be said to have been in the possession of two distinct races of Beings, Man and the Beaver.
David Thompson,
Narrative of His Explorations, 1784-1812

Here all is new; time has not yet laid its mellowing touch upon the land. We are but in our infancy; but it is a vigorous and healthy one, full of promise for future greatness and strength.
Catherine Parr Traill,
The Canadian Settler's Guide, 1855

Canada is not the land for the idle sensualist. He must forsake the error of his ways at once, or he will sink into ruin here as he would have done had he staid in the old country.
Catherine Parr Traill,
The Canadian Settler's Guide, 1855

In Canada persevering energy and industry, with sobriety, will overcome all obstacles, and in time will place the very poorest family in a position of substantial comfort that no personal exertion alone could have procured for them elsewhere.
Catherine Parr Traill,
The Canadian Settler's Guide, 1855

Great things may be done if we have faith in ourselves and in our dynamic and creative power as a nation.
Herman A. Voaden,
Introduction to: "Six Canadian Plays", 1930

The most characteristically Canadian thing is the Canadian landscape.
Paul West,
"Earle Birney and the Compound Ghost," 1962

If modern Canada has no legend, then the opportunities for imagism are considerable.
Paul West,
"Earle Birney and the Compound Ghost", 1962

Culturally, as well as economically, Canada is largely dependent on the United States.
George Woodcock,
Away From Lost Worlds, 1964

We have passed from colonial imitativeness into national assertiveness, and now, it seems, we may be ready for the next step when Canada becomes the place where one works, with all that means and nothing more.
George Woodcock,
Sparrows and Eagles, 1969

CANADIANS

I am one and none, pin and pine, snow and slow, America's attic.
Patrick Anderson

Let the Canadian
with glaciers in his hair, straddle the continent,
in full possession of his earth and north.
Patrick Anderson, *Poem on Canada*

Among most Canadians there is little eagerness to explore the varieties of Canadian life, little awareness how much variety exists, or what a peril that variety is, in time of crisis, to national unity.
E. K. Brown,
The Problem of Canadian Literature, 1943

Canadians will buy anything stamped indigenous...
John Carroll, *On Richler & Ludwig*, 1963

let every national distinction cease from among us—
let not the native Canadian
look upon his Irish or Scottish neighbour as an intruder.
John Robert Colombo, *Canadians All*

We are all sorts and classes, high and low, rich and poor, and of all nationalities — but we all shake down into good Canadian citizens.
Ralph Connor, *The Major*, 1917

I am glad I am a Canadian. We are much too busy to think of anything so foolish and useless as war.
Ralph Connor, *The Major*, 1917

We are devil-worshippers, we Canadians, half in love with easeful Death. We flog ourselves endlessly, as a kind of spiritual purification.
Robertson Davies, *Tempest-Tost*, 1951

We are the gardeners of the world in Eden yet to be.
Louis Dudek, *Canada: Interim Report*, 1963

Never has any people been endowed with a nobler birthright, or blessed with prospects of a fairer future.
Lord Dufferin, *a speech*

On you, the founders, faith is laid;
On you, the makers, strength is stayed;
By you, the builders, worlds are made.
Life honours you — "The People"
Nora M. Duncan, *The People*, 1938

Historically, a Canadian is an American who rejects the Revolution.
Northrop Frye, *Letters in Canada*, 1952

Fair these broad meads — these hoary woods are grand;
But we are exiles from our fathers' land.
John Galt, *Canadian Boat Song*, 1829

We come of a race that never counted its foes, nor the number of its friends when freedom, loyalty, or God was concerned.
George Munro Grant, *Ocean to Ocean*

Canadians are a bit like spectators in their solemn land, always partly aware of trespassing on the Eden of Gitchi Manitou.
Elizabeth Kilbourn,
The Centennial Art Show, 1968

Many a Canadian can trace lineage back to a United Empire Loyalist woman who planted the first crop by hand with a hoe and reaped the first crop by hand with a sickle.
Agnes C. Laut, *Canada: The Empire of the North*

Canadians are, for the most part, the descendants of armies, officers and men, and every generation of them has stood up to battle.
W. D. Lighthall,
Introduction to: "Canadian Songs and Poems", 1892

If I were English, Canada
Should love me like the deuce,
But I was born in Canada
So what the hell's the use.
Wilson MacDonald,
Song of a Bloody Canuck, 1931

Rise Canadians! Rise as one man, and the glorious object of our wishes is accomplished.
William Lyon Mackenzie,
a Proclamation, 1837

Sons of the old race, we, and heirs of the old and new;
Our hands are bold and strong, and our hearts are faithful and true;
Kate Seymour Maclean,
The Coming of the Princess, 1881

Nobody understands one damn thing except that he's better than everyone else.
Hugh MacLennan, *Two Solitudes*, 1945

Why do people hate beauty in this country the way they do?
Hugh MacLennan, *Two Solitudes*, 1945

Our hearts they are one, and our hands they are free
From clime unto clime, and from sea unto sea.
Charles Mair, *Tecumseh*, 1886

The trouble with Canadians is they spend half their time convincing the Americans they're not British, and the other half convincing the British they're not Americans — which leaves them no time to be themselves.
from: McGill's Red & White Review,
"My Fur Lady", 1957

Canadians: the conglomerate of Europe's overflow, the inheritors of the rich and powerful land that is Canada.
Edward Meade, *Remember Me*, 1946

The Canadian people are more practical than imaginative. Romantic tales and poetry would meet with less favor in their eyes than a good political article from their newspapers.
Susanna Moodie,
Introduction to: "Mark Hurdlestone", 1853

No longer a colony in the legal sense, Canada still has many citizens who are colonials at heart, and who look either to Great Britain or to the United States not only for cultural leadership, but for all valid cultural performances.
Desmond Pacey,
General Introduction to: "Creative Writing", 1961

The word has only one meaning, only one. Two pronunciations, but only one meaning.
Edwin R. Procunier, *Granite and Oak,* 1962

To us was the Northland given,
ours to stronghold and defend;
Ours till the world be riven in
the crash of the utter end;
Robert Service, *The Pines,* 1907

They've got guts, those Canadians, Jeez, they got guts.
Lionel Shapiro, *The Sixth of June,* 1955

There are as many ways of being Canadian as there are of being French or British, and many more than there are of being American or Irish.
Lister Sinclair, *The Canadian Idiom,* 1960

We are very small in population — (yet) we wish to be influential; we have a small voice, but we wish to make it heard.
Lister Sinclair, *The Canadian Idiom,* 1960

The mosaic which marks so obviously the Canadian heritage has also made it easier for Canadians to work with the contemporary problems of alienation, compassion, and love, which makes up so much a part of the themes of contemporary fiction.
Donald Stephens,
The Writing of the Decade, 1969

We are Canadians to the fullest extent of the word while, on many occasions, you are more British than Canadians.
Israel Tarte, *Willison Papers,* 1900

Far from expanding in untrammeled visions of the future, Canadians have been advancing one step at a time, balancing this gain against that loss, this promise against that threat, the horizontal British attraction against the vertical American one.
R. E. Watters, *Original Relations,* 1959

As a people bent on self-preservation, Canadians have had to forego two luxuries: that of forgetting themselves in gay abandon and that of losing their tempers in righteous wrath.
R. E. Watters, *A Special Tang,* 1960

All through our history, the favourite intellectual game of Canadians has been to measure ourselves against the British on the one hand and the Americans on the other.
R. E. Watters, *A Special Tang,* 1960

We have often been told of our necessary dullness because we had no Revolutionary War, no French Revolution, no War Between the States.
Milton Wilson,
Other Canadians and After, 1958

CAPE BRETON

We're a dispersed people doomed to fight for lost causes.
Hugh MacLennan, *Each Man's Son,* 1951

CAREFREE

He has a kind of easy charm which prevents him from taking himself too seriously.
Keith Harrison, *Poetry Chronicle,* 1967

They got lots of time to talk, but none to work, unless they happen to feel like it. They're rich as long as they got a dollar.
Raymond Knister, *White Narcissus*

CARELESSNESS

There's something rotten in the state — 'tis shocking
To see such carelessness.
Sam Scribble, *Dolorsolatio,* 1865

CATS

Cats are
living adornments
Edwin Lent, *Cats*, 1960

The only thing I envy a cat is its purr... It is the most contented sound in the world.
L. M. Montgomery, *Rilla of Ingleside*, 1921

CAUSES

Everyone's crusading — all the fools of earth are there.
Fred E. Laight, *The Everlasting Trumpets*, 1937

Causes are good or bad as they are ours or our neighbours'.
Gilbert Parker, *The Seats of the Mighty*, 1896

CAUTION

You can't get drown' on Lac St. Pierre
So long as you stay on shore.
William Henry Drummond,
The Wreck of the 'Julie Plante'

We shun the rose, and thus avoid the thorn;
Dorothy Sproule, *Peace Through Pain*, 1938

CENSORSHIP

Just because some creature cannot keep his metabolism under control when he reads passages in a book, does that give him the right to cut out those passages before I may read it.
Martin A. Sherwood, *Sex in Literature*, 1960

Censorship of any kind is morally unjustified and practically self-defeating.
George Woodcock,
Areopagitica Re-Written, 1959

CHANGE

It is dangerous for anyone to try to establish something within a civilization, even though his motives be of the very best.
William S. Annett, *The Relic*

nobody
belongs anywhere,
even the
Rocky Mountains
are still
moving
George Bowering,
Rocky Mountain Poet, 1969

Every day, things changing in this country. Things don't last long, stationary, here.
Austin Clarke,
The Woman with the BBC Voice, 1963

The old's laid by, the new will not last long; Error's the fruit of trial, and all that is is wrong.
Raymond Hull, *All Change*, 1953

Whatever changes come, He is the same yesterday, to-day and forever.
Marian Keith, *Duncan Polite*, 1913

Wisest is he, who, never quite secure,
Changes his thoughts for better day by day.
Archibald Lampman, *The Truth*, 1888

Nothing is ever changed at a single stroke, I know that full well, although a person sometimes wishes it could be otherwise.
Margaret Laurence, *The Stone Angel*, 1964

To move to a new place — that's the greatest excitement. For a while you believe you carry nothing with you — all is cancelled from before, or cauterized, and you begin again and nothing will go wrong this time.
Margaret Laurence, *The Stone Angel*, 1964

When they resisted change, they were resisting the English who were always trying to force it upon them.
Hugh MacLennan, *Two Solitudes*, 1945

Shabby and dull folk and dull entertainment are dropped as soon as possible by the prosperous ones; if this does not happen there will be some strange reason for it.
Suzanne Marny, *The Unhappy House*, 1909

We are not sand, to shift beneath the wind, Showing new contours after every storm.
Naomi Marre, *Inheritance*, 1956

It is now the vogue to consider anything old as suspect. Because great scientific advances have resulted in change, change is often popularly equated with advance.
Vincent Massey, *a speech*, 1965

Let us not be too bewildered by the magnitude of the changes all around us, or of the changes in ourselves.
Vincent Massey, *a speech*, 1965

It isn't enough to drive out the old spirit — we've got to bring in the new.
L. M. Montgomery, *Rilla of Ingleside*, 1921

29

When a man is not great enough to let change and chance guide him he gets convictions and dies a fool.
Gilbert Parker, *The Seats of the Mighty*, 1896

True, a man does not change,
But merely develops
Traits latent within him.
Hilda Ridley, *New Faces*, 1954

I rest upon the shore of Changeless change,
The landscape and horizon of Eternity.
Diana Skala, *By The Sea*, 1952

Times have changed. Places have changed. We must dance to the tune of the stranger.
Adele Wiseman, *The Sacrifice*, 1956

Don't try to bear anything for to-morrow, just bear it to-day, for the changes are on the way; they are only around the corner, and may face us by another dawn — nothing lasts for ever, not even trouble.
Kate Westlake Yeigh, *A Specimen Spinster*

CHARACTER

What a man considers indecent is an important clue to his character.
Robertson Davies,
A Voice from the Attic, 1960

Which is more subversive of peace and Christian fellowship — ignorance of our own character, or of the characters of others?
Susanna Moodie,
Roughing It in the Bush, 1852

Character, . . . , is a private affair; and it is properly studied through its public manifestations.
Hugo McPherson, *The Mask of Satire*, 1960

CHILD

You're a rebuke from God for some sin of my youth.
Morley Callaghan,
Such Is My Beloved, 1934

If a kid gets her way, she has to take some advice. That is part of the unwritten code which governs the dealings between generations.
Robertson Davies, *Tempest-Tost*, 1951

I was a very observant child, old and experienced before my time. I saw and understood many things which even my mother did not know, did not suspect I could understand.
Frederick P. Grove, *Settlers of the Marsh*, 1925

By making a child conscious of weakness I make him weaker; by making him conscious of his power I am kindling the elements that will keep him growing toward the Divine.
James Laughlin Hughes,
Froebel's Educational Laws

Where they have failed the child shall succeed; where they have suffered, the little one shall be happy.
Nina Moore Jamieson,
The Hickory Stick, 1921

Books and older people can never give a child just exactly the same abounding companionship that might be found in another child.
Nina Moore Jamieson,
The Hickory Stick, 1921

The child leans on the future
Slender tree ungainly rooted there by private worlds
Dorothy Livesay,
The Child Looks Out . . ., 1944

The heart is forever naked, unprotected, to the touch of one's child.
Susanne Marny, *A Commonplace Life*, 1909

A child that has a quick temper, just blaze up and cool down, ain't never likely to be sly or deceitful.
L. M. Montgomery,
Anne of Green Gables, 1908

To be childlike is not a complete defect, . . . — to be like a child is to remain very curious.
Henry H. Roth, *Sour Muse*, 1968

The child has an enviable capacity to fall in love with a book.
John Selby,
The Transmutation of History, 1960

Let me put my finger
In your crinkled hand,
Fill me with the passion
Only mothers understand.
Norma E. Smith, *Little Son*, 1934

30

It is only the child who is already emotionally disturbed who will act out his fantasies.
Anthony Storr, *Only Connect:...*, 1970

CHILDHOOD

The childhood world was one of endless summer.
Shelia Burnford, *William*

Happy childhood indeed. Can one ever get one grip of the essence of it in later life?
Anison North, *Carmichael*

The arcana of psychoanalysis have become the password to social conversation, and that man is a failure who admits to a happy childhood.
Edwin R. Procunier,
preface to: A Knife to Thy Throat, 1962

The very genius of childhood lies not in analysis, but in response.
John Selby,
The Transmutation of History, 1960

CHILDREN

From children's mouths and those of fools Wise things are said they never taught in schools.
Laura Bedell, *On Growing Old*, 1938

Twins is like red hair; they run in families.
Janey Canuck, *Open Trails*

Children are like postage-stamps. They've got to be licked sometimes to do the work they were intended to do. But if ye lick 'em too much, ye spile 'em.
H. A. Cody, *The Fourth Watch*, 1911

God, what a lot we hear about unhappy marriages, and how little we hear about unhappy sons and daughters.
Robertson Davies, *Leaven of Malice*, 1954

Children are the best STOCK a farmer can possess.
William Dunlop, *Statistical Sketches*, 1832

I see my children have all my proud faults no changelings.
Phyllis Gotlieb, *Paradigm*, 1959

They were always unintended,
like beauty or like joy,
yet now they are my life
and time and place of being.
David Helwig, *The Children*, 1971

And as for our six brats, why fret and foam?
Do they not prove that I am sometimes home?
A. M. Klein, *Hershel of Ostropol*, 1970

Children are riches in this country.
Susanna Moodie
Old Woodruff and His Three Wives, 1847

These children split each other open like nuts,
break and crack in the small house.
P. K. Page, *Sisters*, 1954

Children are our life, our bread and our clothing,
With their two little arms and legs and their one head
They come toppling shouting out of us to prove we're not dead.
James Reaney, *A Suit of Nettles*

If adults but knew how much kids gather — sponge up — they would be terrorized.
Richard Snyder,
"A Late Decorum for De Koven Street", 1968

Beautiful children
conceived in lust and despair,
beautiful children.
Raymond Souster, *Beautiful Children*, 1964

There is only one thing that is worse than to be left without your parents. And that is to be left without your children.
Adele Wiseman, *The Sacrifice*, 1956

CHOICE

He's all right, he's like us; he can't afford the luxury of choice.
Hugh Hood, *The Tolstoy Pitch*, 1969

The world has many crossroads, the heart has none.
Harford Powel, *Reedville is Everywhere*, 1967

CHRIST

Christ is the sanctuary men must find,
Beyond the chaos of an ageless strife.
Clara Bernhardt,
The Seven Last Words VII, 1941

31

Christ is creative art.
The touch of God that gives existence soul,
Who is identified with every part
Of Nature, and yet crowns, completes the whole.
Robert Norwood, *Bill Boram*, 1921

CHRISTENING

At best it is a race between the parson and the infant, both gathering steam and momentum as the moment of immersion approaches; if the parson is still audible above the outraged screams of the child after this point, I award the victor's palm to him.
Robertson Davies,
The Diary of Samuel Marchbanks, 1947

CHRISTIAN

It's hard to be hungry and be a Christian.
Morley Callaghan, *Such Is My Beloved*, 1934

CHRISTMAS

The average Christmas shopper is a lineal and typical descendant of such Gadarenes as managed to swim to safety after they had taken that historic jump off the cliff.
Peter Donovan, *Christmas Shopping*

Each Christmas, grown apart, we find ourselves 'looking forward'
to meeting again, to 'getting to know your family'
Christopher Levenson, *Old Friend*, 1970

CHURCH

The Church is in the world but not of it.
Morley Callaghan, *Such Is My Beloved*, 1934

The Church must be in with the railway; she must have a hand in the shaping of the country.
Ralph Connor, *Black Rock*, 1900

Church affairs, . . . , tend to put one in contact with all sorts of people whom one would prefer not to know socially.
Brian Moore, *Judith Hearne*, 1955

I went to church the other day
To hear, to worship, and to pray—
A scarlet feather on a hat
In front of me took care of that!
Kathryn Munro, *Young Man at Church*, 1951

They're like great big caterpillars, those churches, they eat up everything.
Duncan Campbell Scott, *Pierre*

CIRCUMSTANCES

We are no more victims of circumstance than circumstance is the shadow of ourselves.
Bliss Carman, *The Kinship of Nature*, 1904

We, too, live in isolation and have problems that have no solutions because of the limitations of our characters or because of circumstances that we are powerless to alter.
E.H. Winter
Introduction to: "Our Century in Prose", 1966

CITY

If a city calls, do not deny it, the future may be there.
Christine Turner Curtis, *Montreal Remembered*, 1952

Old cities keep dead churches — walled from sight
And open ruins, bearing the gray soot-blight
With a bowl outheld and a skeleton smile,
Asking any strangers mite
To keep the bones together in one pile.
Ella Davis, *Young City*, 1952

My city is of the new days
Not for her the waste of old delays —
Ella Davis, *Young City*, 1952

Here on the city street
There is no way to loveliness,
This dry haunt is not an Eden.
Irene G. Dayton
"To a Barberry Thicket Surrounding a Garden", 1951

Under a sour and birdless heaven
TV crosses stretch across a flat Calvary
and plaza store windows give me the blank expressionless stare of imbeciles.
Irving Layton, *Osip Mandelshtam*, 1970

We can't plan to rebuild our cities until we first rebuild ourselves.
Stephen Leacock, *Rebuilding the Cities*

Living in cities is not natural to us. It is an art which has to be learned.
Hugh MacLennan, *The Art of City-Living*, 1954

When folks get city ways, you never know what's comin'.
Nancy Rankin, *The Hardhead,* 1926

CIVILIZATION

Civilization does not reside in all those things which we give our lives so breathlessly to obtain; it is to be found in the hearts of our friends, in the thought and science and art of the day.
Bliss Carman, *The Friendship of Art,* 1904

Only our modern industrial and commercial civilization has produced an elite which has consistently rejected all the reigning values of the society.
Louis Dudek
Absinthe Drinkers or Squares?, 1958

I hear pagan laughter,
Deriding man's "culture"
And civilized hell.
Margaret Fulton Frame, *Image,* 1947

While "wealth" and "civilization" are not synonymous terms, they are related; no wealth, no civilization. And perhaps, the converse: too much wealth, little civilization.
Arthur R.M. Lower,
Canadians in the Making, 1958

Good God, if our civilization were to sober up for a couple of days, it'd die of remorse on the third.
Malcolm Lowry, *Under the Volcano,* 1961

Too much civilization is a stifling thing.
Martha Ostenso, *Wild Geese,* 1925

Civilization, while it enters into the heritage which the pioneers prepared for it, may at least look with gratitude on their lowly graves.
Goldwin Smith, *Canada and the Canadian Question*

CLIMATE

I no longer wonder that the elegant arts are unknown here; the rigour of the climate suspends the very powers of the understanding.
Frances Brooke,
The History of Emily Montague, 1769

That climate changes the complexion, not only of men, but of habits of thoughts and actions.
Ralph Connor, *The Prospector,* 1904

It is said that extreme heat or cold seldom continues in this country beyond seventy hours.
T.C. Haliburton, *The Old Judge,* 1849

CLIQUES

In Canada, we've been rifled by cliques, and we still are . . .
Dorothy Livesay, *a symposium,* 1969

A man does not easily slip out of sight so long as he remains among his own class.
William McLennan and J.N. McIlwraith,
"The Span O'Life", 1899

CLOTHES

This business of good grooming can be carried too far. For real attraction, a girl's clothes should have that lived-in look.
Robertson Davies, *Leaven of Malice,* 1954

Clothes and courage have so much to do with each other.
Sara Jeannette Duncan,
An American Girl in London, 1891

When a man doesn't notice a woman's clothes, he notices her.
Frederick P. Grove, *The Master of the Mill,* 1944

I have a peculiar affection for old clothes, partly because they are more comfortable, and partly because one is never distressed with fears of spoiling them.
J.J. Procter,
The Philosopher in the Clearing, 1897

Good sense is as much marked by the style of a person's dress, as by their conversation.
Catherine Parr Traill,
The Canadian Settler's Guide, 1855

COLD

Cold as the winter light that lies
On the Baie des Chaleurs?
Arthur W.H. Eaton,
The Phantom Light of the Baie des Chaleurs

Cold, like pain,
is a companion,
he puts the blade
in lovingly.
Don Gutteridge,
La Salle: Fragments from a Journal, 1970

The sleep of cold is the sleep of death.
Gilbert Parker, *Little Babiche,* 1895

COLONIST

It is as impossible for a colonist to rise above the surface, as for a stone to float on a river.
T.C. Haliburton, *The Attaché,* 1844

Let whoever comes to tame this land, beware.
Can you put a bit to the lunging wind?
Can you hold wild horses by the hair?
Douglas LePan, *Canoe-Trip,* 1948

COLONIZATION

The French thought building a fortress was colonization, and the English that blowing it up was the right way to settle the country.
T.C. Haliburton, *Nature and Human Nature,* 1855

One of the more happy consequences of traditional colonialism, . . . , has been its complex propagation of cultures.
George Woodcock, *Shoots From An Old Tree,* 1961

COLONY

What the administrators of a colony do in time of peace makes a country, does more for a country's strength than twenty wars.
Nathaniel A. Benson, *The Paths of Glory,* 1927

The romantic life of each Colony also has a special flavour — Australian rhyme is a poetry of the horse; Canadian, of the canoe.
W.D. Lighthall,
Introduction to: "Songs of the Great Dominion", 1889

COMEDIAN

You encourage a comic man too much and he gets silly.
Stephen Leacock

He was like the comedian of very great comic powers whose comedy is in its own way every bit as profound and moving as tragedy, but who never ceases to dream of performing in a tragic part.
C.J. Newman, *An Arab Up North,* 1968

I am no hero, but a common man,
Knowing the chill of fear along the spine,
Dreading the different grisly forms of death,
But thinking oftener of this land of mine.
E. Anne Ryan, *Those About to Die,* 1942

COMMUNITY

It is determined with something like humour that communities very young should occupy themselves almost altogether with matters of grave and serious import.
Sara Jeannette Duncan, *The Imperialist,* 1904

In a place where everyone knows everyone else, . . . , you have to avoid not only evil but the appearance of evil.
Margaret Laurence, *The Stone Angel,* 1964

COMPETITION

The exhilaration of contact makes fools of us all.
Fred Jacob, *The Clever One,* 1925

The biggest things are always the easiest to do because there is no competition.
William Van Horne, *My Canadian Memories,* 1920

COMPROMISE

Middle roads are whimpers whispered in old forests where boles jostle roughly cowards crying: "Compromise"
James Boyer May, *For the Existentialists,* 1954

CONCEIT

Our astronomical conceit
Of bulk and power is anserine.
E.J. Pratt, *The Truant,* 1943

A man's conceit of himself is part and parcel of his very existence which nothing that anybody else can say is able to abate one iota.
J.J. Procter
The Philosopher in the Clearing, 1897

CONCLUSIONS

Conclusions are the inalienable prerogative
Of the inexperienced.
Edwin R. Procunier, *Two Sides of Darkness*, 1962

I have come where there is nothing more to know,
Nothing to say.
F.E. Sparshott, *By the Canal*, 1958

CONDUCT

One is not master of his birth, but of his conduct.
W.D. Lighthall, *The False Chevalier*, 1898

CONFORMITY

We must be conventional or die, after we reach what is supposed to be a dignified age.
L.M. Montgomery, *Rainbow Valley*, 1919

The conventional rules of society have formed a hedge about you, which renders any flagrant breach of morality very difficult, in some cases almost impossible.
Susanna Moodie, *Essay*, 1851

Like a bunch of pistons in an engine
Nobody says anything they're not supposed to
And nobody does anything they're not supposed to.
S.D. Neill, *The Insider*, 1958

CONSCIENCE

A man with a conscience is often provoking, sometimes impossible.
Ralph Connor, *Black Rock*, 1900

Man's conscience may be likened to a plant
Of strong vitality, which dormant lies
Long time, yet oft puts forth new buds and leaves.
John Hunter-Duvar, *De Roberval*, 1888

CONSEQUENCE

We seldom or never learn, until too late, to distinguish which act or word, apparently trifling, is big with consequences we should shrink from — could only we see them.
Francis W. Grey, *The Curé of St. Philippe*, 1899

Is there no courage in delib'rate wisdom?
Is all rank cowardice but fire and fury?
Is it all womanish to re-consider
And weigh the consequences of our actions,
Before we desperately rush upon them?
Robert Rogers, *Ponteach*, 1766

This is the truth; this must you understand.
Accept the consequence of what you choose to do.
Lister Sinclair, *Return to Colonus*, 1955

Nothing finally is final —
every love is a rain
opening the bud to fire
asking and receiving its own Easter.
Phyllis Webb, *Flux*

CONSTITUTION

The constitution has always been on trial, so to speak, because Canadians are prone to be critical of their institutions.
A.H.U. Colquhoun, *The Work of the Fathers*

A written constitution is of necessity an artifical invention — a contrivance, a formula as inelastic as the parchment on which it is written.
Lord Dufferin, *a speech*

Almost every modern constitution has been the child of violence, and remains indelibly impressed with the scars of the struggle which ushered in its birth.
Lord Dufferin, *a speech*

CONTENTMENT

In nature one is content with enough; in civilization one is never content.
Bliss Carman, *The Kinship of Nature*, 1904

I have not been unhappy for ten thousand years.
During the day I laugh and during the night I sleep.
Leonard Cohen
"I Have Not Lingered In European Monasteries", 1961

A person has to get soaked full of sunshine and contented feelings to be able to stand things.
Nellie L. McClung, *The Second Chance*

True Contentment comes from within. It dominates circumstance. It is resignation wedded to philosophy; a Christian quality seldom attained except by the old.
Robert Service, *Ballads of a Bohemian*, 1921

CONTRAST

Poverty and pride, haughtiness and vulgarity, confidence and ignorance go hand in hand.
Nicholas Flood Davin, *The Fair Grit*, 1876

Contrasts are life's delights.
Gilbert Parker, *The Seats of the Mighty*, 1896

But half of me is woman grown;
The other half is child.
But half my heart loves quiet ways;
The other half is wild.
Constance Davies Woodrow, *To A Vagabond*

CONVERSATION

There are two things in ordinary conversation which ordinary people dislike — information and wit.
Stephen Leacock,
Are Witty Women Attractive to Men

CO-OPERATION

One need not approve, in order to co-operate.
Clarke L. Blaise, *The Mayor*, 1967

COUNTRY

The greatest pleasure of country life is in having no neighbours. Why should I tolerate neighbours when I cannot tolerate myself?
Janey Canuck, *In a Monastery Garden*

The town is a very good place for an occasional roost, but it is better far to build one's nest in the country.
Janey Canuck, *In a Monastery Garden*

—country life develops strength.
Nina Moore Jamieson, *The Hickory Stick*, 1921

When night-time comes, I'm always glad I live in the country. We know the real charm of night here as town dwellers never do.
L.M. Montgomery, *Rilla of Ingleside*, 1921

COURAGE

Courage, Courage, timid brother,
Ever onward press;
Tho' you never win the laurel,
Courage is success.
Grant Balfour, *Courage*, 1910

To sing in old measures
and pretend that still there are harps
where do people find the courage?
Walter Bauer.
"This Was Not The Way Men Screamed",
1970

Is not courage, as seen by one, multiplied when seen by many?
J. Gounod Campbell,
The Bleeding Heart of Wee Jon

For we are young, my brothers, and full of doubt, and we have listened too long to timid men.
Bruce Hutchison, *Unknown Country*, 1942

Some men fight their battles inch by inch; some men not at all.
Walter McLaren Imrie, *Rememberance*

True courage always appeals to the heart of the people.
Stephen Leacock, *Nonsense Novels*, 1911

Courage is something you have only when you're young. It's a part of good health and good looks and the feeling that no evil ever can touch you.
Thomas H. Raddall, *A Muster to Arms*, 1954

Go on in bitterness and cowardice, because there was nothing else but going-on.
Sinclair Ross, *A Field of Wheat*, 1968

There are some men who are resourceful only in adversity; there are others in whom rivalry breeds irritation and develops incompetency.
Duncan Campbell Scott, *The Witching of Elspie*

One sword can rarely overcome a score, Though one heart may be braver than a hundred.
Samuel James Watson, *Ravlan*, 1876

COWARD

I would often be a coward but for the shame of it.
Ralph Connor, *Black Rock*, 1900

If there were no cowards there would be no bullies.
George Iles, *Canadian Stories*, 1918

CRAZINESS

Crazy, that's what he is, crazy, and he don't know it.
Raymond Knister, *White Narcissus*, 1929

The great thing about being crazy is to be all crazy together.
Stephen Leacock, *Further Foolishness*, 1916

Sometimes one deliberately thinks insane thoughts, to keep healthy as it were.
Jacob Zilber, *The Prince*, 1960

CREATIVITY

The exercise of creative power inevitably produces instability, conflict, and confusion, for when man is creative he is always in private or open opposition to the established order.
Carlyle King
Joyce Cary and the Creative Imagination, 1959

Does everybody have to be creative? Can't a few people just sort of fill in the gaps, I mean, keep life going on serene and smooth for the rest?
Frances Shelley Wees,
M'Lord, I Am Not Guilty, 1954

CRIME

Crime always seems impossible in retrospect.
Stephen Leacock, *Sunshine Sketches*, 1912

The crimes and passions of most men are alike, with only this difference, that some have greater art of concealing them.
Susanna Moodie, *Geoffrey Moncton*, 1855

CRITICS

The critic is the duenna in the passionate affair between playwrights, actors and audiences — a figure dreaded, and oc-

casionally comic, but never welcome, never loved.
Robertson Davies,
A Voice from the Attic, 1960

The beauty of being a critic is that one can write as if one were infallible and be forever wrong.
Louis Dudek, *Laughing Stalks*

The critic now appears no more competent than a schoolboy practising in the backyard with a couple of balls.
Douglas Grant, *Zhivago and the Law*, 1959

A critic who flies easily into speculation runs the risk of leaving the book which is his ground far below.
Robert J. Gibbs, *The Living Contour*, 1969

The outstanding quality of the average Canadian reviewer might be described as failure of nerve.
Phyllis Grosskurth, *The Canadian Critic*, 1970

Too often the critic is one who has been disappointed in his own efforts to make a name for himself in one of the creative arts.
Mazo de la Roche,
Introduction to: "Northern Lights", 1959

The finely acid or wise or benevolent and instructed pen of a superlatively good critic is the pen of a writer.
Ethel Wilson, *A Cat Among the Falcons*, 1959

Critics of novels, some unkind people say, are disappointed novelists.
Ethel Wilson, *A Cat Among the Falcons*, 1959

CRITICISM

Without adequate criticism poetry grows lush and weak as an unpruned tree.
Mary Elizabeth Colman,
A Poet Speaks to the Critics, 1938

Criticism is to art what history is to action and philosophy is to wisdom.
Northrop Frye, *Anatomy of Criticism*, 1958

A public that tries to do without criticism, and asserts that it knows what it wants or likes, brutalizes the arts and loses its cultural memory.
Northrop Frye, *Anatomy of Criticism*, 1958

As art is to criticism, criticism is to culture.
E.W. Mandel,
"Toward a Theory of Cultural Revolution",
1959

The ultimate task of criticism is to disengage itself from all the buzzing, yelps, murmurs, yowls, and shrieks of both the crowd and the ego so that we can hear that voice and that voice alone.
Eli Mandel, *The Language of Humanity,* 1963

Criticism is beneficial in proportion to its honesty.
J.R. Ramsay,
Introduction to: "French Chaos", 1873

It seems to me that the chief defect of our criticism to-day is that the critics are so ignorant. They have read so little that they have no proper standards of comparison.
Lord Tweedsmuir, *Return to Masterpieces*

Parody is also criticism.
George Woodcock, *The Selective Poet,* 1966

CRYING

A child's first cry is fear of the loneness of self.
John Harney, *Dialectic,* 1959

Then cry, but do not cry my love
for more than Egypt held, or Troy:
for beauty is resolved at last
into an unembodied boy.
James Wreford, *A Song for Time,* 1942

CULTURE

Most Canadians continue to be culturally colonial.
E.K. Brown,
The Problem of Canadian Literature, 1943

The average young Canadian is instilled with the idea that culture is of secondary, or tertiary, importance and can wait until after he has amassed a fortune.
Alan Creighton, *Conquest by Poetry,* 1942

Our best English culture has been conservative, cautious, dead-set on traditional values and the advantages of prestige.
Louis Dudek, *The Two Traditions,* 1962

High culture is not always visionary, and historically high cultures have confirmed as much as they have shattered that distortion with which any tribe sees the world.
Dennis Duffy,
The Too-Well-Tempered Critic, 1968

Culture is the present social ideal which we educate and free ourselves by trying to attain, and never do attain.
Northrop Frye

Morose scrutiny of Canadian culture has in recent years become a national amusement almost on the scale of professional hockey.
Robert Fulford,
A Myth in Every Livingroom, 1958

The only part of North America where French culture survived the eighteenth century with any real vitality, was in the parishes of the St. Lawrence valley.
Alan Gowans,
Architecture in New France, 1960

Power and culture must enrich each other, and . . . the quality of a civilization can be measured by what it does with its spare time.
Hugh MacLennan,
The Art of City-Living, 1954

The current bourgeois view that to be acquainted with the world's culture was a handicap for which a man should apologize.
Hugh MacLennan, *Barometer Rising,* 1941

I might have taken in culture; I might at last have known something about the mysteries of my own existence. But now there's hardly time.
Lister S. Sinclair, *No Scandal in Spain,* 1945

Culture is for those
Whose body's urge is finally at rest.
Lister Sinclair, *Return to Colonus,* 1955

Our culture, like our society, is a river composed of streams that have flowed in across the frontiers; cut off the streams, and the river will die in the desert of isolation.
George Woodcock,
Permutations of Politics, 1970

CURIOSITY

Take care when you lift the little copper bottle.
You do not wake the genie.
Roy Daniells,
Three Lecture Hours Per Week, 1963

Wonder of man out wonders all the rest.
Goodridge MacDonald, *Wonder,* 1954

Answers and questions, if they come at all from the ignorant, come more readily than from the knowing.
J.R. Ramsay,
On the Soft Side of Humanity, 1873

CUSTOM

'Tis the Canadian custom, calculated I suppose for the climate, to visit all the ladies on New-Year's-day, who sit dressed in form to be kissed.
Frances Brooke,
The History of Emily Montague, 1769

Truly, custom is an enemy as dangerous to reverence as it is to love.
Francis W. Grey, *The Curé of St. Philippe,* 1899

When wise men among us, out of their experience, have sifted away all intemperate and selfish courses, there remains that which we set down in the Classics as right behaviour. That is custom.
Norman Williams, *A Battle of Wits,* 1956

DANGER

In periods of great danger we act with remarkable vigor and stupidity.
John Gray,
When Elephants Roost in the Trees, 1957

Through all his veins the sacrament of danger,
Discovering secret fires, runs riot.
Douglas LePan,
Reconnaissance in Early Light, 1963

There is something terribly exciting in beholding a fellow-creature in emminent peril, without having the power to help him.
Susanna Moodie, *Roughing It in the Bush,* 1852

You are dangerous anywhere,
And any one is dangerous here.
Lister Sinclair, *Return to Colonus,* 1955

Danger that warns is never dangerous;
But danger, when it comes unheralded,
Is but another name for destiny.
Samuel James Watson, *Ravlan,* 1876

DAWN

And in that place where night and morning meet
I cast my life, a love-gift, at thy feet.
John Killick Bathurst, *Love's Pilgrim*

Sunrise in a dream is the best there is.
Will R. Bird, *Sunrise for Peter*

The dawn is a nun in a flowing grey wimple.
John Paul Talbot, *Contrast,* 1936

Daybreak at last,
Light lifts only the fears that light can explain.
Fred Jacob, *The Basket,* 1925

DAY

The day was born for walking, born so in the mind of God.
Douglas Harding, *The Last Dying,* 1958

I love the light, I'll have no traffic
With the nigger world of night.
Anne Wilkinson,
The Pressure of Night, 1955

DAY-DREAMS

Day-dreams may be the essence of desire
Born on some primal urge, to recreate
From smouldering ashes the celestial fire,
That burned before the soul was satiate.
Margaret Furness MacLeod, *Cosmic Urges,* 1956

The best seller is the day-dream which leads us into a happy fantasy and rather like the books we read when we were boys — books of adventure; we know we're never going to be let down.
Brian Moore, *an interview,* 1962

There is, to be sure, a comfort and even poetry in day-dreaming of an evening in a warm and cheerful room.
E. W. Nichols, *On Lying Awake,* 1929

DEAD

Ah, I come too late. If he had anything to say
to me it is forever lost. He has taken the secret with him.
Mary Elizabeth Colman, *Death of a Stranger*, 1938

I feel good about the dead; they remind me that all this loneliness will end.
John F. Donnelly, *Solace*, 1967

It is not those who are taken, but those who remain to mourn, that are to be pitied.
T.C. Haliburton, *The Old Judge*, 1849

How great unto the living seem the dead.
Charles Heavysege, *Sonnet XVIII*, 1865

Have you ever noticed
how a dead man's
personal articles
Take on a certain
contentious
air.
Lionel Kearns, *Remains*

The dead don't bear a grudge nor seek a blessing. The dead don't rest uneasy. Only the living.
Margaret Laurence, *The Stone Angel*, 1964

So now you lie in your last long sleep
And I look at you there
And much of me lies with you.
Kenneth Leslie, *Empathy*, 1964

'Tis the land of No Care
Where now he lies,
Fulfilled the prayer
of his weary eyes.
Charles G.D. Roberts, *A Place of His Rest*

He lived in the world, and it is a good world to live in;
It is a good world to die from, and he died.
F.E. Sparshott, *Gandhi*, 1958

DEATH

Death is quite different, I have learnt that
By dying.
Walter Bauer, *One Evening I Was King*, 1970

Death's the friend who never falters,
The only one who never alters.
Arthur S. Bourinot,
Everything on Earth Must Die, 1955

Folk who would believe in Immortality,
Why should they pass in panoply of woe
I would be linked with colour and ecstasy
That day I go.
Louise Morey Bowman, *She Plans Her Funeral*

If there be nothing in this world for me,
I have a friend no priest nor Pope can take,
Whose name is death.
William Wilfred Campbell, *Hildebrand*, 1895

How all that lives dies!
How eras pass. How even in our little world
Death and time are Scaffold and executioner.
MacDonald Coleman, *The Old House*, 1966

Death ... it is a fearful word,
a fearful thing ...
A thing certain to come to every man.
Mary Elizabeth Colman,
Death of a Stranger, 1938

Death is a dark hole.
Freedom is the sky.
Valerie Cooper, *Song*, 1964

When I am gone, if there be grief
Let it be light as a falling leaf:
Let it be brief.
Bonnie Day, *Let it be Thus*, 1967

Smarting of dust in the eyes, A moment's catching of breath,
Sudden, a glad surprise — Death.
Norah Holland, *Episodes*, 1924

It is better to die while struggling like a man, full of hope and energy than to perish in inaction and despair.
K. James De Mille, *A Strange Manuscript*, 1888

Death is the end of being — the one sweet hope and crown and glory of life, the one desire and hope of every living man, The blessing is denied to none.
James De Mille, *A Strange Manuscript*, 1888

'Tis fine t' have nothin' agin you on the books when you comes t' die.
Norman Duncan, *The Fruits of Toil*, 1903

What repose is deeper
Than within earth's breast?
Hyman Edelstein, *Herzl*, 1916

Humans alone imagine death, How comfortable to turn and live with other animals.
R.G. Everson, *Foresight*, 1963

Not so much by age, but the deliberate hardening of mind turns us toward the grave.
Douglas Flaherty, *Ponce de Leon*, 1969

Death's infinite release
Pledges their sure repose; and not in vain
Earth's gentle ministry absolves their pain.
Eric F. Gaskell, *At Leggatt's Point*, 1939

A string is broken in the lute of life
That nevermore shall thrill to joy or pain.
H. Isabel Graham, *The Broken Lute*, 1938

So we long for dusk of the twilight
When, with wealth of no earthly gold,
We shall come where sleep-flowers cluster,
To the shop where dreams are sold.
Jean Graham, *Where Dreams Are Sold*

To find death alone, away from confusion and fear and contempt and hatred. Not to seek it, not to aid it in any way. But to find it.
Roderick Haig-Brown, *On the Highest Hill*, 1949

Happy is youth who shatters soul and body on the heroic gates of death, freedom is his, the prerogative of victory.
Lloyd Haines, *Agonistes*, 1942

Come crush, harsh world, and snuff this life,
And bid my sorrows cease,
Rejected and dejected I
But long for my decease.
Paul Hiebert, *Sarah Binks*, 1947

Death loves a shining mark.
Paul Hiebert, *Sarah Binks*, 1947

In the midst of death we are in life, and should be thankful for't.
John Hunter-Duvar, *The Enamorado*, 1879

He yet is mortal, not
Enduring myth.
D.G. Jones,
"Sketches for a Portrait of F.R.S.", 1960

I don't want to trickle out.
I want to pour till the pail is empty, the last bit going out in a gush, not drops.
Rosemary Kilbourn,
Hundreds and Thousands, 1967

In peace that changeth not, nor knoweth end,
We too shall sleep.
Archibald Lampman, *We Too Shall Sleep*, 1899

Was death a feast-day, that one should have nothing else to look forward to?
Margaret Laurence, *A Gourdful of Glory*, 1960

Why should I contend with anyone?
Surely, death is his enemy as he is mine.
Irving Layton, *The Whole Bloody Bird*, 1969

Death, you know, to the clergy, is a different thing from what it is to us.
Stephen Leacock, *Sunshine Sketches*, 1912

When I am gone, will it be as though I had not been?
Madge Macbeth, *Reason for Living*, 1955

Even loveliest autumn cannot pay the price
For life too soon destroyed.
Wilson MacDonald, *In Howard Park*, 1926

Why should we fear thy shadow at the door,
Oh thou mysterious Death? — art thou not sweet
To the worn pilgrim of life's toilsome day.
Kate Seymour Maclean, *Euthanasia*, 1881

I shall soon finish my dream within time;
And yet I fear not nothingness.
I simply am afraid that I snall die
And cease to be so beautifully alive.
Ian Malcolm, *A Moment of Existence*

He never did a permanent thing
Except in meeting death.
Leslie Mellichamp, *Jake*, 1952

Death has few terrors to a sincere Christian, . . .
Susanna Moodie, *Geoffrey Moncton*, 1855

The death
that surrounds us,
believe that,
but do not love it.
John Newlove, *Show Me a Man*, 1969

Dying
My father took our memories with him.
Padraig O'Broin, *Severance*, 1962

I'd sooner be frightened to death than bored to death.
P.K. Page, *The Woman*, 1947

Here's to you, Death.
We hate you for the mean indignities you heap upon us.
Clair Pratt, *A Toast to Death*, 1967

Life fades! O life fades like a blast wafted thither —
A blast o'er the bloom of a desolate lake.
J.R. Ramsay, *Chatterton*, 1873

Through weed and world, through worm and star,
The sequence ran the same —
Death but the travail-pang of life,
Destruction but a name.
Charles G.D. Roberts,
As Down The Woodland Ways, 1941

I gotta die, — same as anybody else. But I ain't gonna die easy. My conscience won't let me!
George Ryga, *Hungry Hills*, 1970

But death is death, and still lends a sombre dignity to all it touches.
Laura Goodman Salverson, *Queer Heart*, 1936

Go and leave me; I will dream of you and love you when you're gone;
I have served you, O my masters! let me die.
Robert Service, *The Song of the Camp-Fire*, 1912

How many dead do you have to see in a war
Before you know it is Death you are fighting for.
Raymond Souster

All things sublime
Must fall to ordinary death, while time
With neat dispatch and no heroics writes
An epitaph for wholeness and restores
Our partial sight.
Miriam Waddington, *Ordinary Death*, 1957

Death turned me first, will twirl me last
And throw me down beneath the grass.
Anne Wilkinson, *Variations on a Theme*, 1961

This evening, I perceive, we are all dying,
We are all dying, like Wilde, beyond our means,
Dying, as sheep, for our folly rather than sins.
George Woodcock, *Selected Poems*

Death, leaning close, with enigmatic smile
Awhile regarded me: then stayed his hand.
Mary I. Woodworth, *Reprieve*, 1936

DEBT

Debt hangs about the neck of an honest man like a millstone.
Thomas McCulloch, *The Stepsure Letters*, 1821

Of all evils, to borrow money is perhaps the worst. If of a friend, he ceases to be one the moment you feel that you are bound to him by the heavy clog of obligation.
Susanna Moodie, *Roughing It in the Bush*, 1852

DEEDS

We of the young countries must be invited to deeds, not theories, of which we have a restless impatience.
Sara Jeannette Duncan, *The Imperialist*, 1904

By deeds not words the souls of men are taught;
Good lives alone are fruitful . . .
Archibald Lampman, *Deeds*

True sympathy is known by deeds, not words.
J.R. Newell, *Friendship*, 1881

The man who isn't scared by deeds is not afraid of words.
Lister S. Sinclair, *Oedipus the King*, 1946

DEMOCRACY

Democracy is a system of thought even more than a system of government.
Benjamin A. Gould
War Thoughts of an Optimist, 1915

A system devised to keep the man who stands out from the common crowd down to the common level.
Frederick P. Grove, *Fruits of Toil*, 1933

Democracy has already shown that even with men most of them don't want to be bothered with active politics, have better things to do (or worse) than to attend trivial meetings and, on the whole, keep away from the control of public affairs.
Stephen Leacock, *Woman's Level*

Under genuine democracy men must consent to the necessary existence of

social order and the unequal distribution of material goods.
John Daniel Logan,
"Democracy, Education and the New Dispensation"

The Democracy which shall make government the organ of public reason, and not of popular passion or of demagogism which trades upon it, is yet in the womb of the future.
Goldwin Smith,
Schism in the Anglo-Saxon Race, 1887

DESIRE

Where wants are many, joys are few.
Bliss Carman, *The Mendicants,* 1894

A man is foolish to torture himself with longing for that which can never be his.
Nina Moore Jamieson, *The Hickory Stick,* 1921

My teeth are bared, my claws uncurled,
Of the red meat I never tire;
In the black jungle of the World
I am the Tiger of Desire!
Tom MacInnes, *Tiger of Desire*

What does a person want out of life: images?
John Newlove, *Like a Canadian*

He has little, and desires no more.
M. Rossiter, *The Old Man,* 1966

Wanting doesn't seem to get you things.
Arthur Stringer, *The Death Cup,* 1939

DESPAIR

Man comes to judgement in the deed
That forfeits hope of heaven's praise.
Percy Adams, *Flower of Evil,* 1961

Life, which is simple, passionate and cruel
Becomes intolerable,
Now I have cast away a certain care
For a dream I may not know.
Marcus Adeney, *The Twisted Stream,* 1939

People who have been prominently destroyed
Stop looking for their names in the papers.
Charles Black, *Prominent Destruction,* 1969

There is no weather any more,
They say, the springtime never comes,
The summer cannot smile again.
Robert Finch, *Survivors,* 1960

Everything here smells of death, boredom, despair.
Silas N. Gooch, *A Season in Limbo,* 1962

This is the gift that looked like a stone
When the heart hungered for bread.
Verna Loveday Harden, *The Gift,* 1947

Sometimes it happens that a person discovers he has built his house upon an island that is sinking.
Margaret Laurence, *The Perfume Sea,* 1960

Whenever things look dark, I lean up against something and think of Mother. If they get positively black, I stand on one leg and think of Father. After that I can face anything.
Stephen Leacock, *Nonsense Novels,* 1911

Our house is dead.
We shall build it again
But our home is gone.
And the world burns on.
Malcolm Lowry, *A Lament—June,* 1944

I am like the shattered raven
flying eyeless in a raven's dreams.
Bernell MacDonald, *Am Like,* 1970

And love is left upon the earth to starve,
My objects gone, and I am but a shell,
A husk, an empty case, or anything
That may be kicked about the world.
Charles Mair, *Tecumseh,* 1886

How dark is our valley
When the stars die.
Isobel McFadden, *A Dreamer in Moab,* 1951

There is no use in loving things if you have to be torn from them, is there?
L.M. Montgomery, *Anne of Green Gables,* 1908

Matters are never so bad but that they may be worse.
Susanna Moodie, *Roughing It in the Bush,* 1852

A man can only get bothered about anything up to a certain point — the point where he's written off his chances. After that you don't care.
Thomas H. Raddall, *A Muster of Arms,* 1954

There is no hope for such as I on earth, nor yet in Heaven
Unloved I live, unloved I die, unpitied, unforgiven.
Robert Service, *The Harpy,* 1907

43

I and my dreams alike are passed away.
All is as though I had not lived, or thought,
or loved.
Percy H. Wright, *Light,* 1936

Despair is not a feeling which takes deep
root in the youthful breast.
Catherine Parr Traill, *Canadian Crusoes,* 1850

DESTINY

'Tis strange how Destiny guards her
chosen ones
And fits their greatness to heroic hours.
Nathaniel A. Benson, *Britain, 1941 III,* 1941

Destiny. It rides
The sea of life across the wake of right:
Is not this ship the cause of all our strife?
Abraham Hartman, *Destiny,* 1956

DILIGENCE

There is no better training for uncommon
opportunities than diligence in common
affairs.
George Iles, *Canadian Stories,* 1918

I am no romanticist, I have no great admiration for myself, and yet when I set out
to hunt a woman honestly, be sure I shall
never back to kennel till she is mine or I am
done for utterly.
Gilbert Parker, *The Seats of the Mighty,* 1896

DISAPPOINTMENT

Do not the keener disappointments of life
flow from attainment, rather than from
failure?
W.H. Blake, *Brown Waters*

Surely it's the snows of disappointment
that cool a man's head and sometimes his
heart.
D.M. Currie, *And Be My Love*

Many things look well at a distance which
are bad enough when near.
Susanna Moodie, *Roughing It in the Bush,*
1852

It was the face of a woman who had aged
without maturing, that had loved the little
vanities of life, and lost them wistfully.
Sinclair Ross, *The Lamp at Noon*

DISASTER

Horror is a feeling that cannot last long;
human nature is incapable of supporting it.
James de Mille, *A Strange Manuscript,* 1888

Decay can take many forms: denial,
failure, madness, reversals of will.
Dave Godfrey
"Starved in the Hour of our Hoarding", 1968

Blessings, like disasters, have a habit of
coming in pairs.
Frederick P. Grove, *Fruits of the Earth,* 1933

DISCIPLES

Disciples were a vanity
Even Christ could not bring himself to
forgo.
John Grube, *Coteries,* 1967

DISCIPLINE

We hear a great deal nowadays of something that is called "moral persuasion" but in
my opinion a good spanking and no nagging afterwards is a much better thing.
L.M. Montgomery, *Rilla of Ingleside,* 1921

DISCONTENT

It is not being out at heels that makes a
man discontented; it is being out at heart.
Bliss Carman, *The Friendship of Art,* 1904

Many of the ills of life are unavoidable; and
wherever this is the case, a discontented
mind bears the calamity, and has the
grumbling to the bargain.
Thomas McCulloch, *The Stepsure Letters,*
1821

Praise be to glorious Discontent.
The questing soul's own counterpart;
Unsatisfied, insatiate,
Mother of creative art.
Joan Richardson, *In Praise of Discontent,*
1962

DISHONESTY

The crooked ways are best, . . .
The only way a cripple learns to move.
Eli Mandel
"A Castle and Two Inhabitants", 1958

Men do not often violate the law of honesty, unless driven to do so by necessity.

Catherine Parr Traill,
The Canadian Settler's Guide, 1855

DISLIKE

It does people good to have to do things they don't like . . . in moderation.
L.M. Montgomery, *Anne of Avonlea*

How repugnant to a sensitive mind, is a forced association with persons in whom we can find no affinity; and whose sentiments and pursuits are at utter variance with our own.
Susanna Moodie, *Geoffrey Moncton*, 1855

DIVORCE

If you still want marriage to mean anything at all, you must open the door of divorce equally wide.
Frederick P. Grove, *A Search for America*, 1927

DOCTOR

Thers is hardly on the face of the earth a less enviable situation than that of an Army Surgeon after a battle.
William Dunlop,
"Recollections of the American War", 1847

They . . . watched him with the humble, fearful, protective expressions such people nearly always have in the presence of doctors.
Hugh MacLennan, *Each Man's Son*, 1951

Doctors are the only men with power. . . . lords of little bits of life and death.
Alan Phillips, *The Presence in the Grove*

If you ask me, doctors should be taken with a grain of salt. Certain diseases are still a mish-mash to them.
Mordecai Richler, *Son of a Smaller Hero*, 1955

A woman must fall in love with her doctor. Maybe she has to, for everything to go right.
Doug Spettigue, *Edge of Christmas*, 1969

DOGS

A good dog is so much a nobler beast than an indifferent man that one sometimes gladly exchanges the society of one for that of the other.
William Butler, *Wild North Land*, 1872

It makes me sick to think
That man must so exhalt his race
By giving dogs a servile place.
E.J. Pratt, *Carlo*, 1923

DOUBT

Lift not your wise, inquiring lamp too high,
As Psyche did o'er Cupid bent above;
One burning drop of doubt upon your love
Will banish him across the courts of sky.
Katherine Hale, *Cupid and Psyche*, 1938

Doubt is the beginning, not the end of wisdom.
George Iles, *Canadian Stories*, 1918

No drug will clear the clouded state
nor cure a nameless blight—
Can surgery eradicate
the cancer cells of doubt?
Anne Marx, *Recovery Doubtful*, 1966

Still doubting the world can measure
What I dared to hope of you.
O. Tucker, *The Old Flame*, 1959

DRAMA

The drama may be called that part of theatrical art which lends itself most readily to intellectual discussion; what is left is theater.
Robertson Davies, *A Voice from the Attic*, 1960

Though swift be the action and final the conflict,
The drama is silent.
E.J. Pratt, *Silences*, 1937

The function of art, . . . and specifically of dramatic art — is to prompt man to examine the morality that he accepts and practises.
J. Percy Smith, *G.B.S. on the Theatre*, 1960

Is there not a certain national lack of self-confidence, pride, and romance which has refused to allow our drama to develop?
William Solly, *Nothing Sacred*, 1962

Drama like other arts derives its vitality from its dynamic relation with the age in which it is written.
Michael Tait, *Playwrights in a Vacuum*, 1963

DREAMS

Take your facts and give me back my dreams,
My world so true although it only seems.
Myrtle Reynolds Adams,
Slight Protest to Now, 1956

Float now, dead dreams in this native void.
Douglas Barbour, *Christmas: 1968*, 1970

My dreams were many years at sea
While forests held me fast.
Edna Alice Boyd, *Earth-Bound*, 1936

A dream is a frail thing,
Easy to break.
Bonnie Day, *Dreams*, 1967

The people alive in dreams are real.
R.G. Everson, *Immortal in Dreams*, 1966

A people of men who place practical things
above all others become wealthy; but a
people of dreamers must become great.
Frederick P. Grove, *A Search for America*,
1927

Escaping into dreams, all anguished,
Though strangely sweet,
I move slowly upon frail pinions of desire.
Ruth Cleaves Hazelton, *Frail Pinions*, 1949

They taught me how to patch and darn,
And sew a thin fine seam;
But what if I should have to mend
A broken dream?
Eileen Cameron Henry, *Untaught*, 1938

Did anyone ever have a boring dream?
Ralph Hodgson

We dreamed by night and we dreamed by
day,
(Alas, for the dream that ne'er came true!)
Norah Holland, *The Dreamers*, 1924

I have dreamed dreams that wanted but
due time
To grow material and reality;
These for a time must yet remain in sleep.
John Hunter-Duvar, *De Roberval*, 1888

Once I built a house of cards and
It was five storeys high
but one day it collapsed,
And all my dreams expired.
Rendel Kulpas, *Perspectives*, 1968

A kibbutz is an organized dream in-
distinguishable from a nightmare.
Irving Layton,
Some Observations and Aphorisms, 1968

. . . dreams do not reveal they obscure.
Dorothy Livesay, *Making The Poem*, 1967

Fine is the fabric of these dreams of mine—
It fades not with the using, for its thread
Was stained immortal colors in my breast.
Wilson MacDonald, *In Howard Park*, 1926

And caring less how the World esteems
Me or my doing, I go on
With incommunicable dreams —
But I would that I knew where my Lord is
gone!
Tom MacInnes, *Ballad of Faith*

Man's trouble isn't what he does nor
doesn't do, it's what he dreams.
Hugh MacLennan, *Each Man's Son*, 1951

Only a step lies between
The dream and the dreamer.
Margaret Furness MacLeod,
Reach For Your Dream, 1955

It long has been my cherished hope,
Upon my dying day
To lie down on some sunny slope
And dream my life away.
Peter McArthur, *My Friends, the Trees*

My soul puts forth her rapid argosies
To the uncharted ports of summer dream.
Peter McArthur, *Earthborn*

If no man dreams, there will be nothing for
the workers to fulfil.
L.M. Montgomery, *Rilla of Ingleside*, 1921

Dreams are one of the greatest mysteries
in the unsolved problem of life.
Susanna Moodie, *Geoffrey Moncton*, 1855

In later life, are our castles often shattered,
and we seldom understand that the fallen
stones go usually to build a foundation
upon which more stable structures may be
created.
Anison North, *Carmichael*

Sad no man on earth
can hold
a dream
in his hand.
Alden Nowlan, *Dream*, 1968

The same nightmares instruct the evil as inform the good.
Alden Nowlan, *The Genealogy of Morals*

We are all children when we dream
Alden Nowlan, *The Genealogy of Morals*

We are only children till we begin to make our dreams our life.
Gilbert Parker,
When Valmond Came to Pontiac, 1895

Perhaps I lie; perhaps.
Sometimes we dream things, and these dreams are true.
Gilbert Parker, *Pierre and His People,* 1892

Clear, O clear my dreams should be made
Of emerald light and amber shade,
Of silver shallows and golden glooms.
Marjorie Pickthall, *The Pool,* 1913

Dreams are an
inconvenient reminder
of something that is being
overlooked in
the straight-line
rationalistic view
of things.
W.W.E. Ross, *Fall '45,* 1969

What I dream is mine, mine beyond all cavil,
Pure and fair and sweet, and mine for evermore.
Duncan Campbell Scott, *Via Borealis*

How we used to sit at the day's sweet end, we two by the firelight's gleam,
And we'd drift to the Valley of Let's Pretend, on the beautiful river of Dream.
Robert Service, *Son,* 1916

Dreams are dangerous. They waste the time one should spend in making them come true. Yet when we do make them come true, we find the vision sweeter than the reality.
Robert Service, *Ballads of a Bohemian,* 1921

Tear down the Ivory Tower,
For life is greater than dream!
A.M. Stephen, *Bring Torches,* 1937

But the dream, the dream, where did it begin?
In jewels, in stars, in powdery snow
Or sin?
Miriam Waddington, *Night in October,* 1955

What a man does not learn in the books he makes up for in his dreams.
Adele Wiseman, *The Sacrifice,* 1956

In Europe men dreamed of utopias, but in North America they set about creating them as concrete entities.
George Woodcock, *An Absence of Utopias,* 1969

DULLNESS

This would be a dull life if one could not invent artifices of amusement.
Martha Ostenso, *Wild Geese,* 1925

Dullness is a misdemeanour.
Ethel Wilson, *A Cat Among the Falcons,* 1959

DUTY

An unflinching observance of duty, unmodified by any other idea, by mercy, by love, by gentleness, by generosity, might readily lead to almost inhuman hardness.
Bliss Carman, *The Kinship of Nature,* 1904

A man who tries to do his duty is bound to stir up opposition.
H.A. Cody, *The Fourth Watch,* 1911

I will ride with you
and think you handsome
but I must be back
before the evening.
Marquita Crevier, *Lord Gordon,* 1960

I've had a bellyful of duty. I've got something in me that wants more than duty and work.
Robertson Davies, *Overlaid*

Duty is generally the thing a fellow doesn't want to do.
Marian Keith, *Treasure Valley*

Because I did my duty, need they gibe?
Grudge me the bit of happiness I've won?
Margaret Preston,
"The Old Maid Speaks to Her Parrot", 1934

You know love the greatest of things, but you know also duty, the sublimest.
Marshall Saunders, *Rose à Charlotte*

The greatest heroine in life is she who knowing her duty, resolves not only to do it, but to do it to the best of her abilities.
Catherine Parr Traill,
The Canadian Settler's Guide, 1855

EARTH

A wise old alchemist is Mother Earth,
working in time but ever for eternity.
Ralph Connor, *The Major,* 1917

Nowadays the mess is everywhere
And getting worse. Earth after all
Is a battlefield.
Daryl Hine, *The Survivors,* 1969

We constantly deface her, use her as we
will,
but she is always beautiful when spring is
on the hill.
Kathleen Jarvis, *Earth,* 1942

What, you're tired and broke and beaten?
— Why, you're rich — you've got the earth!
Robert Service, *Comfort,* 1907

EAST

In the East one travels in time. One
measures not in miles but in years.
Michael Macklem, *A Book a Mile,* 1970

EASTER

Strange and potent gifts of entrancing, and
of looking into the future, are bestowed
upon Easter children of the female sex by
the fairies.
Theodore Goodridge Roberts,
The Harbormaster, 1911

EDUCATION

Education is the fruit of temperament, not
success the fruit of education.
Lord Beaverbrook, *The Three Keys to Success*

Education imposed from without may be a
hindrance rather than a help.
Lord Beaverbrook, *The Three Keys to Success*

To attempt to educate the mind and heart,
without educating the body, is more foolish
than it would be to give a man all the learning of the ages, and then doom him to
solitary confinement for the term of his
natural life.
Bliss Carman, *The Friendship of Art,* 1904

Education — unsettles a fellow — keeps
him from enjoyin' his life as he finds it.
Dora Smith Conover, *Winds of Life,* 1930

The educated like my work, and the
uneducated like it.

As for the half-educated — well, we can
only pray for them in Canada, as
elsewhere . . .
Robertson Davies, *Fortune, My Fie,* 1949

Get a solid piece of scholarship under your
belt and some diploma-mill will always
want you.
Robertson Davies, *Leaven of Malice,* 1954

Of what use is a University education to a
young man unless he comes under the influence of instructors who can astonish
him?
Robertson Davies, *A Voice from the Attic,*
1960

All education is bad which is not self-
education.
Robertson Davies, *A Voice from the Attic,*
1960

When you educate a woman late in life, it
always sort of upsets her.
Fred Jacob, *Man's World,* 1925

Education, . . . is a wonderful thing. But . . . ,
the riches of it belonged only to great
people who were especially clever,
especially worthy.
John Patrick Gillese, *Especially Worthy*

If French Canada is going to continue to in-
sist that matters of education are ex-
clusively the business of the provinces,
then it will indeed be arguing that the rules
are more important than the game.
Gwethalyn Graham, *Dear Enemy,* 1963

There is no use in trying to train the mind of
a child when his body is starved, or abused,
or diseased.
Nina Moore Jamieson, *The Hickory Stick,*
1921

A college education shows a man how
devilish little other people know.
T.C. Haliburton, *Sam Slick's Wise Saws,* 1853

Educationists have spent lifetimes seeking
salvation for these knights of the class-
room. They found the answer — Examinations.
Abraham Hartman, *Examinations,* 1956

Higher education in America flourished
chiefly as a qualification for entrance into a
moneymaking profession, and not as a
thing in itself.
Stephen Leacock, *My Discovery of England,*
1922

It's all right to talk about education and that sort of thing, but if you want driving power and efficiency, get business men.
Stephen Leacock, *Sunshine Sketches*, 1912

Better far the tom-tom's beating
Than the academic bleating
That retards the spirit's yearning with a soul destroying chart.
Wilson MacDonald, *The Song of the Rebel*, 1926

There is but one hope, one liberation for the poor. It is education.
Laura Goodman Salverson, *The Viking Heart*, 1923

Education's a habit; you've got to start off with it, or it's no real use.
Lister S. Sinclair, *Day of Victory*, 1945

EFFICIENCY

The secret of efficiency is to be well attuned with ourselves and our surroundings.
Bliss Carman, *The Friendship of Art*, 1904

EGOTISM

I am not ignorant, and therefore never deny, that I am a very handsome fellow; and I have the pleasure to find all the women of the same opinion.
Frances Brooke,
The History of Emily Montague, 1769

A man's opinion of himself don't really affect the size of his hat band.
Ralph Connor, *The Prospector*, 1904

Most men without being conscious of the fact, spend a great deal of time and effort in bringing about circumstances which will enable them to support an ideal portrait of themselves which they have created.
Robertson Davies, *Tempest-Tost*, 1951

Your true — your intense egotist, cunningly avoids the use of the first personal pronoun. He is, in fact, an Ille-ist. The man who cares nothing, and is never thinking about himself, is constantly uttering the capital I.
William Dunlop, *Statistical Sketches*, 1832

Tis only when self ponders on self, and is pleased therewith, and sedulously seeks self's satisfaction, that self is selfish.
William Dunlop, *Statistical Sketches*, 1832

Pity those sunk in time,
Meeting only themselves;
The image in which they swim
Traps, but never absolves.
Peter Garvie, *Lemons and Hieroglyphs*, 1959

Nothing will ever unseat this superb imperturbable rider.
Irving Layton, *Oil Slick on the Riviera*, 1967

The only possible basis for organized society is that of every man for himself.
Stephen Leacock,
1935

We, who feel our tables groaning
With their wealth of meat and grain
What care we of gentle children
By the breath of famine slain?
Wilson MacDonald, *Volga*, 1926

It is impossible for any human creature to live for himself alone.
Susanna Moodie, *Roughing It in the Bush*, 1852

There are no histories so graphic as those which people tell of themselves, for self-love is sure to embellish the most common-place occurrences with a tinge of the marvelous.
Susanna Moodie,
Old Woodruff and His Three Wives, 1847

Men are always out for what they can get.
Alice Munro, *Postcard*, 1968

Man's egotism prevails even over his love of death.
Alden Nowlan, *Commonplace Book*, 1967

He loved himself too much. As a child was god.
Thunder stemmed from his whims.
P.K. Page, *Paranoid*, 1954

As a mature adult I recognize that to ensure my own happiness and gratification certain others are bound to suffer pain.
Richard Prybyzerski, *Stuffed Clams*, 1970

You never see beyond a glass
That mirrors your reflection.
Genevieve V. Shantz,
Epigram on Window Shopping, 1939

I think the most of us are idolaters whose chief idol is self!
Minnie Smith, *Is It Just?*

How does one please a vain beautiful man?
Not with love, for one cannot give a gift
greater than his own!
Elizabeth Whealy, *Narcissus,* 1967

EMIGRATION

In most instances, emigration is a matter
of necessity, not of choice.
Susanna Moodie, *Roughing It in the Bush,*
1852

Unlettered race, how few the number tells,
Their only pride a cariole and bells.
Standish O'Grady, *The Emigrant,* 1842

EMOTIONS

There are things in the heart too deep if not
for tears most certainly for words.
Ralph Connor, *The Major,* 1917

So strangely are we made that I must know
Why this small thing doth move me so.
Annie Charlotte Dalton, *The Robin's Egg* '

Follow your heart, and you perish.
Margaret Laurence,
The Drummer of All the World, 1956

He had never been an easy man to love.
There seemed to be a diamond in him in
place of a heart.
Hugh MacLennan, *Each Man's Son,* 1951

It is enough to have a few honest emotions
— very few — and stand by them till all be
done.
Gilbert Parker, *The Trial of the Sword,* 1894

Echoes are in my soul, —
Consonances and broken melodies, —
Survivals frayed and remembrances
Vanished and irretrievable.
Duncan Campbell Scott, *Bells*

END

Well, everything must have an end.
I have had my day
I have come home
I see things as they are.
John Glassco, *The Death of Don Quixote*

Now is the last spike driven,
Now is the last tie riven,
Now is the last speech given —
Let's all go home.
Paul Hiebert, *Sarah Binks,* 1947

Let there be no more of this, no marching,
no colours,
No grandeur, nobility, no more applauding.
Violet Lang,
(no title), 1946

The world is round: there is an end:
We do not vainly toil and roam.
George Allen Mackenzie, *Magellan*

When a man draws near this end, God
often opens the eyes of the soul and
reveals, not only what is — but what shall
be.
Susanna Moodie, *Geoffrey Moncton,* 1855

What will endure, when avid Time and
Tide
That ends all things, ends our proud Em-
pire's sway?
Jean Kilby Rorison, *The Immortals,* 1938

ENDURANCE

Whether it be to failure or success, the first
need of being is endurance, — to endure
with gladness if we can, with fortitude in
any event.
Bliss Carman, *The Kinship of Nature,* 1904

O World of grief and desolation!
Endure, endure. These too shall cease;
From the loud furnace of Creation,
Beauty shall rise, and peace.
Sara E. Carsley, *The Lake in the Rockies,* 1939

There was too much grim endurance in his
nature ever to let him understand the fear
and weakness of a woman.
Sinclair Ross, *The Lamp at Noon*

That's the way
We've got to hang on —
like the last patch of snow
clinging to the hillside
crouching at the wood edge
with April done.
Raymond Souster, *Place of Meeting,* 1961

I was made like the anvil solid
I can take the blows as they come
But the hammer must reel
To my tempered steel
I'll be here when the hammers are done.
R.G. Stewart, *The Anvil,* 1941

ENGLAND

England, breeder of hope and valour and
might
Iron mother of men.
Wilfred Campbell, *England*

England, England, England
Girdled by ocean and skies,
And the power of a world and the heart of a
race,
And a hope that never dies.
Wilfred Campbell, *England*

England is a dangerous country to live in;
you run such risks of growing old.
Sara Jeannette Duncan, *The Imperialist,* 1904

Life in England today is seriously lacking in
passion, purpose or principles.
John Graham, *A Tale of a Stifling Dog,* 1958

Perhaps some scientist of the future, . . .
would be able to analyse the nature of the
chain which bound Canada to England.
Hugh MacLennan, *Barometer Rising,* 1941

The Elizabethan age, our first significant
appearance in the world of great politics
and great literature.
Ivon Owen, *The Enterprise of England,* 1960

ENGLISH CANADIANS

What is the shibboleth of English-speaking Canadians?
M.H. Scargill, *Canadians Speak Canadian*

I doubt if there can be any people in the
world as ignorant of its own language as
we English-speaking Canadians are of
ours.
M.H. Scargill, *Canadians Speak Canadian*

ENGLISH LANGUAGE

English is by nature irregular, and trochaic.
Louis Dudek, *The Two Traditions,* 1962

English is the most simple, direct, and
compact of the languages of modern
civilization.
P.D. Ross,
The Short Word in English Poetry, 1941

The Canadian dialect of English, which
seems roughly to be the result of applying
British syntax to an American vocabulary.
Lister Sinclair, *The Canadian Idiom*

ENGLISH PEOPLE

These English have many queer expressions . . . When they mean serious things
they generally give them flippant names.
Stuart Amour, *The Maid,* 1926

Important as politics and religion were,
however, the chief mark of the colonial
Victorian was his profound veneration for
money.
D.J. Goodspeed, *The Conspirators*

The English have two sorts of niggers —
American colonists, who are free white
niggers; and manufacturers' laborers at
home and they are white slave niggers.
T.C. Haliburton, *The Attaché,* 1844

When you're English it's the same as bein'
Canadian.
John Marlyn, *Under the Ribs of Death,* 1957

Give me a glass. Here's honesty in trade;
We English always drink before we deal.
Robert Rogers, *Ponteach,* 1766

ENGLISH CHANNEL

The English Channel. It is the highway of
the world.
Stephen Leacock, *Nonsense Novels,* 1911

ENJOYMENT

We bring our own light to a dark place.
R.G. Everson, *Report For Northrop Frye,* 1959

The people who enjoy the good things of
this life are the sensible ones, not the
hermits who hold themselves aloof.
Suzanne Marny, *The Unhappy House,* 1909

It's been my experience that you can
nearly always enjoy things if you make up
your mind firmly that you will.
L.M. Montgomery, *Anne of Green Gables,*
1908

I've kind of contracted a habit of enjoying
things.
L.M. Montgomery, *Anne's House of Dreams,*
1908

Wherever I go I find life amusing. It may be
sad for a little but I am soon amused again.
Mazo de la Roche, *The Building of Jalna,* 1927

ENTERTAINMENT

Canadian solo performers generally set a high standard.
Thomas D. Closingchild,
A Letter from Vancouver, 1959

The live entertainment Canadians like most is the intimate review, a collection of songs and sketches, preferably with a satirical bias.
Nathan Cohen
Theatre Today: English Canada, 1959

ENTHUSIASM

Obviously, such unbounded enthusiasm doesn't lend itself to critical study.
Anne Greer,
Confessions of a Thesis Writer, 1969

Enthusiasm is a bad beginning for argument.
William McLennan and J.N. McIlwraith,
The Span O'Life, 1899

ENVIRONMENT

We are moulded, we say, by the conditions and surroundings in which we live; but we too often forget that the environment is largely what we make it.
Bliss Carman, *The Kinship of Nature,* 1904

Decent and comfortable surroundings are an almost essential help in humanizing the spirit.
Bliss Carman, *The Friendship of Art,* 1904

This life that what we call culture, education, breeding is largely a matter of environment, something that it takes very long to acquire but which may, after all, be acquired and, therefore, lost.
Frederick P. Grove, *A Search for America,* 1927

People are easier flattered, less smart, less exacting in a small place where people are not so prosperous.
Suzanne Marny, *The Unhappy House,* 1909

EQUALITY

To grant an ordinary man equality is to make him your superior.
Peter McArthur, *To Be Taken with Salt,* 1903

ESKIMO

Inviolate their law of brotherhood;
Their ancient covenant, the common good.
Kathryn Munro, *Innuit,* 1956

ESTRANGEMENT

Not your's, but one's own
Smell of estrangement
Leads me to silence.
D.G. Jones,
"De Profundis Conjugii Vox et Responsum", 1965

They have been estranged so long that they are really dead to each other, and yet if they were left alone together they would both, she, at least, would die the bodily death as well.
Raymond Knister, *White Narcissus,* 1929

ETERNITY

I am an instrument of God;
My heart is sure; my way is clear.
I press on, to Eternity.
Dorothy Dumbrille, *Destiny,* 1941

Eternity is in the heart,
Infinity is in the mind.
Christine L. Henderson, *Unrest,* 1961

Earthly issues are but small —
Soul with vision lift your eyes!
Constance Fairbanks Piers, *Eventide,* 1939

Will we slowly become aware
Of eternity
After the darkness of the world?
Dorothy Cameron Smith, *The Confinement,* 1967

EVIL

Now, Child Pandora, lift the lid again
And let the clamoring mysteries be dumb.
Margaret Avison, *Rigor Viris,* 1957

Evil is a dissonance not a discord.
Bliss Carman

All philosophy and all religions teach us this one solemn truth, that in this life the evil surpasses the good.
James De Mille, *A Strange Manuscript,* 1888

Whether we view evil as a force possessing permanent reality or whether we regard it as an inconvenience to be handled pragmatically...few adults would deny

that its disorderly presence forces itself upon our horrified attention from time to time.
Phyllis Grosskurth,
"Gabrielle Roy and the Silken Noose", 1969

Ah, me! the wrongs
The devil visits on God's creatures here
Are evenly distributed I fear.
N.W. Hainsworth, *In Lieu of Lyrics*, 1939

When evil triumphs, it is not because the God of the Universe is a fool, but because the powers for the right have not fought valiant as the powers for evil.
A.C. Laut, *Freebooters of the Wilderness*

EXAGGERATION

How fools exaggerate.
M. Allerdale Grainger, *Woodsmen of the West*, 1908

This is a blowhard age
what will happen when our superlatives shrink to fact.
Malcolm Miller, *To be Muttered*, 1962

Wimmen always gotta blow the little things up twicet their size — ain't the stuff in wimmen they is in men.
W.O. Mitchell, *A Voice for Christmas*, 1961

EXAMPLE

May there be something that my Life has said,
That others reading, grow by what they've read.
Donald A. Fraser, *A Lesson*, 1921

Others will follow the path we have taken,
Urged by our daring, our dreams and our dangers,
Winging their way through the leagues of the air.
A.H. Lambden, *Tragedy on the Barrier*, 1941

EXISTENCE

Somewhere shots ring out every night,
laws stop up the breath of freedom,
And yet we awake every morning,
we two, in perfect harmony.
Walter Bauer, *And Yet*, 1970

The vestibules of being — birth and death —
Bear interchanging legends.
George Herbert Clarke,
Hymn to the Spirit Eternal, 1936

Who chopped down the bells that say
the world is born again today
We will feed you all my dears
this morning or in later years.
Leonard Cohen, *In Almond Trees Lemon Trees*

I want my very existence to be justified.
Frederick P. Grove, *The Seasons*

Being is inexhaustible.
Hugh Hood, *It's a Small World*, 1967

I am confused, therefore I am.
Jack Ludwig, *Confusions*, 1960

At times to be born
is enough, to be
in the way is too much —
John Newlove, *Black Night Window*, 1970

Self does not readily accept separation, isolation and silence. These are conditions of non-being.
Warren Tallman, *Wolf in the Snow II*, 1960

I am an old parched lawn,
An area life has sown and mown reluctantly
These futile seasons.
Paul West, *Mr. Venal Puts His Feet Up*, 1959

My name is nothing; I contain all time and all space.
Michael Yates,
The Great Bear Lake Meditations, 1970

EXPERIENCE

The characteristics of innocence are happiness and curosity; the characteristics of experience are knowledge and, most often, regret.
Alan Brown,
"Gabrielle Roy and the Temporary Provincial", 1956

If there were no human experience there would be no art.
Louis Dudek, *The Fallacy of Literalism*, 1964

Each of us has his own circle of experience into which no one else can enter.
W.G. Hardy, *The Czech Dog*, 1944

Reality of experience is the raw material of art, and it can only be revealed to the reader through fidelity to facts.
Henry Kreisel, *"Joseph Conrad"*, 1958

I've often wondered why one discovers so many things too late. The jokes of God.
Margaret Laurence, *The Stone Angel,* 1964

Every experience must be lived through until it is done.
Hugh MacLennan, *The Story of a Novel,* 1960

Experience — wisdom's best counsellor — daily teaches us; and a man must either be very self-conceited or very insensible, who cannot profit by her valuable instructions.
Susanna Moodie, *Geoffrey Moncton,* 1855

Exploring one's experience sounds like such a terrible way to describe a simple thing like writing a poem.
A.W. Purdy, *an interview,* 1967

All men lose faith in women ere they die;
Experience is like science, it lays bare
Those moons our early fancy thought so fair.
J.R. Ramsay, *French Chaos,* 1873

When you've had more experience of life you'll not worry about belonging places.
Mazo de la Roche, *The Building of Jalna,* 1927

EXPLANATION

Never deny; never explain.
That's my guiding rule of life.
Robertson Davies, *Leaven of Malice,* 1954

Any meaning you
Can articulate, fella, I
Can obscure. But I'm damned
If I can articulate your
Obscurities.
C.J. Newman, *Critic,* 1967

EXTREMES

This is an age when Magyar hearts declare Unmeasured Valour and unmatched Despair.
Watson Kirkconnell, *Foreward on Request,* 1956

The wildest enthusiasm brings the greatest distaste, the hottest passion the deadest ashes.
Suzanne Marny, *A Commonplace Life,* 1909

EYES

Words also can be conjured to magnify the woe
And gestures overdo despair;

But eyes, they blazen forth the truth
And helplessly portray the agony.
Lilian S. Auty, *Mirrored Suffering,* 1941

FACADE

No matter what he says publicly a man keeps his own inner eye, he keeps the secret little places in his heart.
Morley Callaghan, *Solzhenitsyn,* 1970

And all his virtues have the same pretence:
Amalgamating vice with innocence.
Robert Finch, *The Collective Portrait,* 1946

Call me an escapist in this shouting hour when tinsel drops from tree and hearts of men.
Joseph Joel Keith, *Christ,* 1949

There is another world besides this one, which you must know. Where you can be all yourself.
Raymond Knister, *White Narcissus,* 1929

Everything is artificial these days, it seems to me. Silks and people have gone out of style, or no one can afford them any more.
Margaret Laurence, *The Stone Angel,* 1964

Half the bodies draped in satin have the inner breed of sluts;
Half our rulers need the sunshine for the poison in their guts.
Wilson MacDonald, *The Song of the Rebel,* 1926

He could make a gesture worthy of a millionaire and borrow the money to do it.
John Marlyn, *Under The Ribs of Death,* 1957

Pomp is one thing, splendour is another, and pageantry plays a reasonable part in life.
Vincent Massey, *a speech,* 1965

Do you think of me solely
As what you can see,
Without ever knowing
The genuine me?
Rita Meredith, *If I Changed My Face,* 1963

The world judges so much by externals, that nothing is to be despised that helps to flatter its prejudices, and ensure popularity.
Susanna Moodie, *Geoffrey Moncton,* 1855

In this gay house, I must be flippant, for I am now of the foolish world. But under all the trivial sparkle a serious heart beats.
Gilbert Parker, *The Seats of the Mighty*, 1896

FACE

Her pancaked face belies a pancaked mind.
Blake Brodie, *On A Bus*, 1960

A sour visage means debauchery of the soul, as truly as other appearances indicate bodily intemperance.
Bliss Carman, *The Kinship of Nature*, 1904

You may look pretty disagreeable and repellent but that's because you can't help it with that face of yours. Try to let people realize that it is only just your face; that behind it you are all right.
Stephen Leacock, *Casting Out Animosity*

I understand
Why just to see some faces is pure gain;
Through them we touch the race that yet may be.
Cecil Francis Lloyd, *The Girl in the Store*, 1938

As a lad, I was taught to think the evil person carried evil in his face, repelling the healthy mind; but long ago I found that this was error.
Gilbert Parker, *The Seats of the Mighty*, 1896

FAILURE

Not a mortal in the universe but has said to himself, "I will". And in the evening we are aware of determinations unfulfilled.
Bliss Carman, *The Kinship of Nature*, 1904

Failure teaches a man nothing except compassion for the failure of others.
Kildaire Dobbs, *Matata*, 1962

The world defeats only him who has already been defeated in his heart.
Frederick P. Grove, *Fruits of the Earth*, 1933

I like the lower towns, the place across the tracks, the poorer streets not far from the river. They represent failure, and for me failure here has a strong appeal.
Norman Levine, *Canada Made Me*, 1970

In his own eyes he was always falling short of an ideal.
Hugh MacLennan, *Each Man's Son*, 1951

Failed!
And Lucifer will rack me for the failure.
Sister Maure, *Via Vitae*, 1923

The loneliest places of earth are not those where man has never set foot, but those from which he has withdrawn defeated.
Edward McCourt,
Overland from Signal Hill to Victoria

The Laws of God and man
Push us down.
We smother ourselves
With negatives.
Barbara Nease, *Suffocation*, 1955

The whole of the world is gain;
The whole of your soul. Too vain
You judge yourself in the cost.
'Tis you — not your soul — is lost.
Albert E.S. Smythe, *Anastasia*, 1923

FAIRY

Fairies are a human inheritance, born of imagination and memory, as ghosts of tradition and fear.
Eileen B. Thompson, *Pan in the New World*, 1922

FAITH

If reasoned faith is a faithless cause
faith unreasoned may be more so.
Myrtle Reynolds Adams, *The Search*, 1968

Faith is not less faith because it fluctuates.
Elizabeth Brewster,
Poem for the Year of Faith, 1968

Only the child-like dare
To walk by faith,
Only the simple-hearted
Take the Almighty at His word.
Mary Elizabeth Colman, *Hunger*, 1937

Faith is the reflection of experience.
Ralph Connor, *The Prospector*, 1904

There are great compensations for all losses; but for the loss of a good conscience toward God, what can make up?
Ralph Connor, *Black Rock*

A mere intellectual assent to a creed may be a fruitless thing; but a living faith in the truths of the Christian religion is not a vain thing.
E.H. Dewart, *Essays for the Times*, 1898

Yours was the gift of a faith
That spread past horizon's edge,
And you might have kept it so
Had you but kept the pledge.
Stella Falk, *Boundless*, 1940

Where knowledge is denied, faith comes in.
Frederick P. Grove, *Fruits of the Earth*, 1933

Faith wanting, all his works fell short.
Charles Heavysege, *Saul*, 1857

O we had a great deal of pleasure
But practically no faith.
George Jonas, *To A Christian*, 1967

Come, child, and Faith will set thee on the way
Of life.
Sister Maure, *Via Vitae*, 1923

For most people any faith is better than no faith.
Brian Moore, *an interview*, 1967

Faith lives not in the earnest word
Soon spoken — haply soon forgot;
But faith will dare, has ever dared,
The touch of time, the sway of thought.
J.R. Newell, *Mizpah*, 1881

It is easy to believe in whatever one knows nothing about. Is not faith founded on finity?
J.R. Ramsay, *One Quiet Day*, 1873

But for the sake of simple goodness
And His laws
We shall sacrifice our all
For The Cause!
Lloyd Roberts, *Come Quietly, England*

Without the consequence of action,
Faith is flattery and self-delusion.
Lister Sinclair, *Return to Colonus*, 1955

the world is getting
dark but I carry
icons.
Miriam Waddington, *Time*, 1970

FAME

She keeps her glory in her soul;
Mine's at midnight between my legs.
Joan Finnigan, *For Monique at Midnight*, 1959

Fame like a drunkard consumes the house of the soul
Exposing that you have worked for only this.
Malcolm Lowry,
after publication of 'Under the Volcano', 1961

A person can never get true greatness by trying for it. You get it when you're not looking for it.
Nellie L. McClung, *The Second Chance*

It is one of the pleasant ironies of history, and cause of hope for all of us, that it is possible for a man to achieve great reputation and even enduring fame by doing something just a little worse than anyone else.
Edward McCourt,
Overland from Signal Hill to Victoria

Fame — witching fame! — by what seductive art
Dost thou subdue creation's mighty heart?
J.R. Newell, *The Times*, 1877

Small minds, when in high places, thirst for fame,
And rob their servitors of all they win.
Samuel James Watson, *Ravlan*, 1876

FAMILY

For a millenium, their ancestors long ago thrived in pristine innocence and peace. The tribes of men lived side by side in Arcadian friendliness.
Marius Barbeau,
The Downfall of Temleham, 1928

A family whose men are gone is no family at all.
Margaret Laurence, *A Bird in the House*, 1964

"Families" no longer flourish in this new world of rampant equality and whirling change than do baronial mansions.
Arthur R.M. Lower, *Canadians in the Making*, 1958

The loss of fortune may have previously afflicted us, but greatly as that is to be deplored, what is it to the lack of breeding?
Blanche Lucile Macdonell,
Diane of Ville Marie, 1898

Blood and breeding will tell every time.
Hugh MacLennan, *Two Solitudes*, 1945

Kindred love and hospitality have decreased with the increase of modern

luxury and exclusiveness, and the sacred ties of consanguinity are now regarded with indifference.
Susanna Moodie, *Geoffrey Moncton*, 1855

No family is complete without its skeleton. It is one of the necessary adjuncts to a peerage.
Geo. W. Pacaud, *Social Idolatry*, 1920

Good-breeding is a charming a trait in a servant as it is in a lady.
Catherine Parr Traill,
The Canadian Settler's Guide, 1855

FARM

To drown one's thought in labour is very difficult on the farm: everything is conducive to contemplation.
Frederick P. Grove, *Settlers of the Marsh*, 1925

Get a farm and thrive!
He's a king upon a throne
Who has acres of his own!
Alexander McLachlan, *Acres of Your Own*, 1874

And this is a country where the young leave quickly
unwilling to know what their fathers know or think the words their mothers do not say.
Alfred Purdy,
The Country North of Belleville

FARMERS

The farmer, born and bred to that estate, is the one type among the world's workers into whose contemplation rest does not enter.
Will E. Ingersol,
The Man Who Slept Till Noon, 1918

Farmers must know something outside of farming. The curse of the calling has been its insularity.
Nina Moore Jamieson. *The Hickory Stick*, 1921

People on a farm, like the men on shipboard in the old days, saw too much of each other.
Raymond Knister, *Mist-Green Oats*, 1923

The farmer's way of saving money: to be owed by someone he trusted.
Hugh MacLennan, *Two Solitudes*, 1945

I never saw a gentleman from the old country make a good Canadian farmer.
Susanna Moodie, *Roughing It in the Bush*, 1852

This thing my duty: ·cleave the clod,
Ploughing the field alone with God.
Robert Norwood, *The Ploughman*

All farmers are gamblers, after a fashion.
M.E. Palmer, *I Shall Return*, 1936

Godlike, he makes provision for mankind.
Charles G.D. Roberts, *The Sower*

Whatever a few "seigneurs" may have done, the farmer, the real producer in Canada, never thought of leaving the country, and remained to keep strong the traditions of old France.
George M. Wrong, *The Fall of Canada*

FARMING

Slow work, the work of the farm! Every step took a year.
Frederick P. Grove, *Fruits of the Earth*, 1933

There's always work waiting outside on a farm.
Raymond Knister, *Mist-Green Oats*, 1923

There's no feeling left after the soil and the livestock have taken their share.
Martha Ostenso, *Wild Geese*, 1925

FASHION

To be out of joint with our own time is to be in bad humour with ourselves.
Bliss Carman, *The Friendship of Art*, 1904

Dead or out of fashion, it's the same thing.
Harry Green, *The Death of Pierrot*, 1926

Man is ever the dupe of novelty,
And always willing from himself to flee:
Thus moved he blends in social intercourse,
Oft making what is bad by union worse.
J.R. Newell, *The Times*, 1877

The moment a trend seems perfectly obvious is the time to watch out for a contrary one.
W.W.E. Ross, *New Directions*, 1960

To plead fashion, is like following a multitude to do evil.
Catherine Parr Traill,
The Canadian Settler's Guide, 1855

FATE

I've tasted my blood too much to love what I was born to.
Milton Acorn, *Jawbreakers*, 1963

Why is this human fate so hard to bear?
William Wilfred Campbell, *The Higher Kinship*

We all believe that if we fret and abuse ourselves sufficiently, Providence will take pity and smile upon anything we attempt.
Robertson Davies, *Tempest-Tost*, 1951

The conditions of a vulgarian is that he never expects anything good or bad that happens to him to be the result of his own personality; he always thinks it's Fate, especially if it's bad.
Robertson Davies, *Tempest-Tost*, 1951

What must come would come; no use trying to fight; no use worrying. Too bad if anything happened; but if it did, it could not be helped.
Frederick P. Grove, *Fruits of the Earth*, 1933

Providence moves more quickly when man aids.
John Hunter-Duvar, *De Roberval*, 1888

And what role does Providence play in your scheme? You have forgotten, in your thesis, to place God.
A.M. Klein, *The Second Scroll*, 1959

Each of us in life is a prisoner. We are set and bound in our confined lot.
Stephen Leacock

When things get started happening, they are quite apt to keep it up for a while, as if events invited events.
Charles G.D. Roberts,
The Prisoners of the Pitcher-Plant

For who shall fight with fate?
And who with destiny?
Man is mortal
And the gods are mighty.
But behind the gods is fate!
Lister S. Sinclair, *Oedipus the King*, 1946

We do not understand but we excuse:
For we know we are not really free to choose.
Lister Sinclair, *Return to Colonus*, 1955

A man is what he makes himself
His passions are the moulds wherein the Fates
Shape all his fortunes.
Samuel James Watson, *Ravlan*, 1876

FATHER

The Fathers of Confederation,
profit and progress all that they could know—
the bourgeois midwives of a newborn nation —
Patrick Anderson
The Country Still Unpossessed, 1946

Your fathers are but silly fools,
Old relics of a past age,
No wonder they can't comprehend,
This go-ahead, this fast age.
Alexander McLachlan, *Young Canada*, 1861

FATHERLAND

The enthusiasm of Fatherland, the attachment to native soil, the love of the name of our country, is one of those generous impulses which have always been a moral necessity and an encouraging help to people who do not live by bread alone.
Archibald Lampman, *Two Canadian Poets*, 1891

For where the soul
Doth dwell and the heart linger, there
Alone can be the native land.
Isabel Ecclestone MacKay
Marguerite de Roberval

FATIGUE

I shall away to rest now, for the many wonders of the day have tired me much.
H.A. Cody, *The Fourth Watch*, 1911

When the body is fatigued with labour, unwonted and beyond its strength, the mind is in no condition for mental occupation.
Susanna Moodie, *Roughing It in the Bush*, 1852

FAULT

Never exaggerate your faults; your friends will attend to that.
Robert C. Edwards, *Calgary Eye Opener*, 1921

I can overlook faults when virtues beckon.
Michael Harnyansky,
Countries of the Mind, 1963

Like most men
My faults are many, but my crimes are few.
John Hunter-Duvar, *The Enamorado,* 1879

Well, well, let us put a merry face on life —
we all have our thousand faults.
Suzanne Marny, *Tales of Old Toronto*

Each of us has a flaw, and when two
people love each other, each seems to expect the other to cure his flaw.
Hugh MacLennan, *Each Man's Son,* 1951

FEAR

Few will seek your help with love, none
without fear.
Margaret Atwood,
Procedures for Underground, 1970

Avoid the garden; shun the dark;
Shadow the suspect in the park.
You may find out that he is you.
Ronald Bates, *Overheard in the Garden,* 1960

In darkness I set out for home,
terrified by the clash of wind on grass,
and the victory cry of weeds and water.
Leonard Cohen, *Prayer for Sunset*

Our bitter needs
Disdain the dictates of our baser fears.
Eric F. Gaskell,
Watch-Night Reflections: 1940

Beware the hairy Sasquatch, oh my child!
Clara Hopper, *The Sasquatch,* 1936

Every age and generation has its special
mysteries, its special terrors, its special
realms of fear.
Stephen Leacock, *Can We Beat Inflation?*

Fear ringed by doubt is my eternal moon.
Malcolm Lowry, 1962

Being frightened of things is worse than
the things themselves.
L.M. Montgomery, *Rainbow Valley,* 1919

Never run from anything, . . . till you've had
a good look at it. Most times it's not worth
running from.
Thomas H. Raddall, *Winter's Tale*

Fear, . . . is an important element in a
certain quality of devotion.
Theodore Goodridge Roberts,
The Harbormaster, 1911

I'm lost again in the city of self, all night I
stared into moving crowds of invisible as-
sailants.
Rose Rosberg, *Night Spectrum,* 1967

It appears
that our fears
are well placed
are well based.
W.W.E. Ross, *Laconics,* 1969

A frightened captain makes a frightened
crew.
Lister S. Sinclair, *Oedipus the King,* 1946

When we start up to walk abroad
Fears work and knead us like a crown.
John Sutherland, *Fears,* 1969

Perhaps because he had no love he had no
fear.
Ethel Wilson, *From Flores*

FEMALE

Though the female always runs away, she
never runs so fast that she couldn't run
faster; and it makes no difference whether
the female has wings or fins, flippers or
feet, it is all the same — the female always
does the courting.
Arthur Heming, *The Drama of the Forests*

By the misconduct of a female, labour and
sorrow have become the portion of man.
Thomas McCulloch, *The Stepsure Letters,*
1821

FENCE

I have always found that good fences make
good friends and safe crops.
Thomas McCulloch, *The Stepsure Letters,*
1821

The wall should be low, as to say,
Not a barrier this, but for beauty.
Arthur L. Phelps, *The Wall*

A fence's purpose is to indicate,
Not to divide — it's only walls do that.
Len G. Selle, *Of Fences and Walls,* 1955

Fences are friendly things — if not too
high.
Len G. Selle, *Of Fences and Walls,* 1955

FICTION

The typical heroes of Canadian fiction are intellectuals who search loquaciously for their own identity or Canada's.
Hugo McPherson, *The Garden and the Cage*, 1959

Fiction, however wild and fanciful,
Is but the copy memory draws from truth.
Susanna Moodie, *Essay*, 1851

Every good work of fiction is a step toward the mental improvement of mankind, and to every such writer we say, God speed.
Susanna Moodie, *Essay*, 1851

The value of fiction is that it seeks to interpret the real world for us and thus furnish us with a keener awareness of the daily miracle of life.
E.H. Winter,
Introduction to: "Our Century in Prose", 1966

FIGHT

To cease to strive is to begin to degenerate.
Bliss Carman, *The Kinship of Nature*, 1904

Fighting is no work for man, but for brute.
Ralph Connor, *The Major*, 1917

I don't suppose anything was ever accomplished without somebody being willing to fight a losing battle.
Agnes Laut, *Freebooters of the Wilderness*

The struggle against conditions must have the same effect as passivity would have, ultimately.
Martha Ostenso, *Wild Geese*, 1925

We're gonna have to fight to win . . . there's no other way!
George Ryga, *The Ecstasy of Rita Joe*, 1970

The man who can fight to Heaven's own height
Is the man who can fight when he's losing.
Robert W. Service, *Carry On*, 1916

FISH

The science of fishing can be had from books; the art is learned by the catching and the losing of fish.
W.H. Blake, *Brown Waters*, 1915

Even the people who don't eat fish
May like the look of them on a dish.
W. Clark Sandercock, *A Fish Story*, 1937

FOLKLORE

A properly – conducted barn-raising contains the excitement of a fire, the sociability of a garden party, and the sentimental delights of a summer resort "hop"
Peter McArthur, *The Barn Raising*

The folk culture sponsored every sort of crude practical joke, as it permitted the cruellest and ugliest prejudices and persecutions.
Wallace Stegner, *Specifications for a Hero*

The folk – song is a kind of local signature.
Paul West, *The Unwitting Elegiac*, 1961

FOOD

No finer compliment can be paid a cook than to eat freely and with relish of his cooking.
Ralph Connor, *The Prospector*, 1904

I'm like a city bus — I'm full inside.
F.A. Dixon, *Fifine, The Fisher-Maid*, 1877

There is nothing like feeding a man if you want to put him in a good humour.
Francis W. Grey, *The Curé of St. Philippe*, 1899

Cooks . . . . were always temperamental. If you flattered them they did better. If you didn't, they wilted. They were like women.
Edward Meade, *Remember Me*, 1946

Sub-stantial foods is like hugs, but fancies might come under the 'ead of kisses.
Mazo de la Roche, *Explorers of the Dawn*, 1922

FOOLS

There is no chance for old fools.
Indian Legend,
in: The Trickster and the Old Witch

A fool exhalted to dignity, is merely a fool more conspicious.
Thomas McCulloch, *The Stepsure Letters*, 1821

FORGETFULNESS

I have been too far
and stayed too long away,
my birth is forgotten;
my memory grey.
Rowland Hill, *Transient*, 1942

Forgetfulness is her protection
Sometimes I wondered, though, how
much could be truly forgotten and what
happened to it when it was entombed.
Margaret Laurence, *The Rain Child*, 1962

Forgetting a thing doesn't rule it out of existence.
Hugh MacLennan, *Each Man's Son*, 1951

Oh! that the mind were pliant to desire,
That deep desire for sweet forgetfulness.
J.R. Newell, *Unrest*, 1881

Is it I who am forgotten, dismembered, escaped, deaf, uncollected?
Already I have lost yesterday and the day
before.
P.K. Page,
Traveller, Conjuror, Journeyman, 1970

And so we work; we play; we fret;
we scurry, hurry, worry — to forget.
Malcolm Wrathell, *The Escapists*, 1956

FORTUNE

When fortune decides to afflict a good man
and rob him of his peace, she often
chooses a fine day to begin.
Robertson Davies, *Leaven of Malice*, 1954

O fickle Fortune! thou dost weave
Thy garlands fair but to deceive
Thy worshippers; thy brightest flower
Oft fades within one fleeting hour.
J.E. Pollock, *Fortune*, 1883

FREEDOM

How common is it for men, when impatient of legal restraint, . . . to plunge
headlong into destruction.
Jacob Bailey, *Journal of a Voyage*, 1779

Freedom is not an acquisition of power; it
is merely the disimprisonment of spirit.
Bliss Carman, *The Kinship of Nature*, 1904

O do not compromise with doubt
Or cage with dust a living thing;
Let your own inborn genius out,
Give your imprisoned power wing!
Helena Coleman, *Brother to Stars*, 1938

Eternal vigilance is the price of freedom.
Ralph Connor, *The Major*, 1917

We instinctively side with a man in his
struggle for freedom; for we feel that
freedom is native to him and to us.
Ralph Connor, *Black Rock*, 1900

The pattern of Freedom on the Loom
Of Time shall yet in all its glory be
Wholly completed for Humanity.
G.L. Creed, *They Shall Not . . .*, 1942

It is not surprising that a man who knows
that he has no mission to fulfil should want
to be rid of it.
Downie Kirk, *More Than Music*, 1961

An obsession with freedom is the
persistent dance of the young.
Margaret Laurence, *Ten Years' Sentence*,
1969

Only the tiniest fraction of mankind wants
freedom. All the rest want someone to tell
them they are free.
Irving Layton,
Some Observations and Aphorisms, 1968

Better far a godless bastard, with his
freedom in his hands,
Than the scion of the ages, bound and
gagged with iron bands.
Wilson MacDonald, *The Song of the Rebel*,
1926

Oh, it was blithesome to roam at will
Over the crest of each westering hill,
Over those dreams, enchanted lands
Where the trees held to us their friendly
hands!
L.M. Montgomery, *On The Hills*

God had been created by man out of necessity. No God, no ethic: no ethic — freedom.
Freedom was too much for man.
Mordecai Richler, *Son of a Smaller Hero*, 1955

There lives and there leaps in me
A love of the lowly things of earth,
And a passion to be free.
Robert Service, *A Rolling Stone*, 1912

Crowd back the hills and give me room,
Nor goad me with the sense of things.
Albert Durrant Watson, *Soul Lifted*

I'm waiting,
like all prisoners of towers,
for the grass to grow high enough
to free me.
Liz Woods, *The Tower Rooms*, 1969

FREDERICTON

The snow has pitied you and made you fair,
O snow-washed city of cold, white Christians,
So white you will not cut a black man's hair.
Fred Cogswell, *Ode To Fredericton*, 1959

FREE-WILL

How stained with mortal ill,
The page of man's free-will!
Kathryn Munro, *Conversation with God*, 1942

A man may choose the sunlight, but he has no right to pass casual judgement on the shadows.
Adele Wiseman, *The Sacrifice*, 1956

FRENCH-CANADA

French Canada is almost without curiosity about the literature and culture of English Canada.
E.K. Brown,
The Problem of Canadian Literature, 1943

This constructive and progressive intellectual ferment in French Canada is a precious and admirable movement of liberation and betterment.
Louis Dudek, *The Two Traditions*, 1962

In Montreal the French outnumber the English three to one. In the province we outnumber them more than seven to one. And yet, the English own everything.
Hugh MacLennan, *Two Solitudes*, 1945

The tragedy of French-Canada is that you can't make up your mind whether you want to be free-choosing individuals or French-Canadians choosing only what you think your entire race will approve.
Hugh MacLennan, *Two Solitudes*, 1945

What a mine if inspiration there is in the history of French Canada! Fit theme indeed for poet, novelist, historian and painter!
Thomas O'Hagan, *Canadian Essays*, 1901

French genius and French taste on the banks of the St. Lawrence differ little from French genius and French taste on the banks of the Loire or the Seine.
Thomas O'Hagan, *Canadian Essays*, 1901

FRENCH CANADIANS

We cannot ask more of them; their sin is one of omission rather than commission.
Roy Daniells,
High Colonialism in Canada, 1969

Dere's no girl can touch, w'at we see e 'ry day,
De nice leetle Canadienne.
William H. Drummond,
De Nice Leetle Canadienne, 1897

Poor people! with hearts so happy, they sang as they toiled away.
William H. Drummond, *Madeleine Vercheres*

The majority of French Canadians remained . . . semi-literate, under the tutelage of a repressive clergy.
Louis Dudek, *The Two Traditions*, 1962

Either we French develop our own resources or the English will do it for us.
Hugh MacLennan, *Two Solitudes*, 1945

French-Canadians in the farmland were bound to the soil more truly than to any human being; with God and their families, it was their immortality.
Hugh MacLennan, *Two Solitudes*, 1945

French-Canadians were always inclined to rely too heavily on politics as a means of exercising influence. They talked too much while the English kept their mouths shut and acted.
Hugh MacLennan, *Two Solitudes*, 1945

I want our people to feel that the whole of Canada is their land — not to grow up with the impression that the Province of Quebec is a reservation for them.
Hugh MacLennan, *Two Solitudes*, 1945

Our good Canadians, as you will find, attach more value to the simple word of a priest — than to the command of any lay authority.
William McLennan and J.N. McIlwraith,
"The Span O' Life", 1899

They have . . . founded a literary microcosm of their own — created a literature with a color, form and flavor all its own, which must be considered in itself a greater marvel than their material preservation.
Thomas O'Hagan, *Canadian Essays*, 1901

We are French-Canadians, but our country is not confined to the territory

overshadowed by the citadel of Quebec; our country is Canada.
Edwin R. Procunier, *Granite and Oak*, 1962

But, after all, one French Canadian more or less in the world does not matter!
Sam Scribble, *The Skating Carnival*, 1865

FRENCH LANGUAGE

The French language in Canada will actually flourish and become great if it is open to the American world. It will retreat and shrink if it refuses this challenge. Let us have courage!
Louis Dudek,
Towards a Brotherhood of Nations, 1963

By the laws of probability, North America ought to speak French, not English, today.
Alan Gowans,
Architecture in New France, 1960

French irregular verbs, . . are almost as unpredictable as French-speaking women.
Leslie Roberts,
article in: The Montreal Star

FRENCH PEOPLE

His habit of gesturing could be discounted because he was French; otherwise it would have given him away as too emotional.
Hugh MacLennan, *Two Solitudes*, 1945

Lord, how we love fighting, we French. And 'tis so much easier to dance, or drink, or love.
Gilbert Parker, *The Seats of the Mighty*, 1896

It is said that every Welshman is a poet; so too is every Frenchman a philosopher.
Edwin R. Procunier, *Voices of Desire*

FRIEND

When you are down you will find
those who were once your friends
but they will be changed and dangerous.
Margaret Atwood,
Procedures for Underground, 1970

What good are your friends if you don't use them? You should go right after them and put it up to them.
Morley Callaghan,
They Shall Inherit the Earth, 1934

'Tis friends and not places that make the world.
Bliss Carman, *The Kinship of Nature*, 1904

Your friends are strangers now
your acquaintances merely acquaintances.
John Robert Colombo, *There Is No Way Out*, 1963

The difference between a friend and an acquaintance is that a friend helps where an acquaintance merely advises.
Robert C. Edwards, *Calgary Eye Opener*, 1921

I've had only one single friend in my life. And now I must lose him.
Frederick P. Grove, *Settlers of the Marsh*, 1925

Fair weather friends have no use for you when there's a storm in your soul.
George V. Hobart, *Experience*, 1914

No one who has a friend can be altogether at war with the world.
Nellie L. McClung, *Sowing Seeds in Danny*, 1911

If we associate long with the depraved and ignorant, we learn to become even worse than they.
Susanna Moodie, *Roughing It in the Bush*, 1852

To have a friend is to tend a fire
That glows or dulls as the wind fans, or the rain darkens.
Doris M. Taylor,
We Are Like Blades of Grass, 1936

FRIENDSHIP

So friendship whereso'er we go is sweet;
Whate'er of loss or triumph we may share;
Whatever we endure or do or dare.
Nicholas Flood Davin, *Friendship*, 1884

The friendship of the selfish is a warm wind from the South when the skies are clear, but when trouble comes it's as cold as the blast of Death.
George V. Hobart, *Experience*, 1914

Right from the start, I either like a person or I don't. The only people I've ever been uncertain about were those closest to me. Maybe one looks at them too much. Strangers are easier to assess.
Margaret Laurence, *The Stone Angel*, 1964

How many times had people held infinitely greater promise of friendship, only to fail him in the end.
John Marlyn, *Under the Ribs of Death,* 1957

Grant me the quiet charm which friendship gives,
Which lives unchanged, and cheers me while it lives.
J.R. Newell, *Friendship,* 1881

Playing the Jesus game
I don't smile at strangers
because that might frighten them
into summoning the police.
Alden Nowlan, *Playing the Jesus Game,* 1969

Befriend me, and I menace you!
Lister Sinclair, *Return to Colonus,* 1955

Mutual responsiveness brings on that gradual blur of familiarity which can cause us to notice least those persons we know best.
Warren Tallman, *Wolf in the Snow,* 1960

We are like blades of grass in a wind-swept meadow,
Our friendships just as brief and little-meaning.
Doris M. Taylor,
We Are Like Blades of Grass, 1936

True friendship hath a thousand eyes, no tongue;
'Tis like the watchful stars, and just as silent.
Samuel James Watson, *Ravlan,* 1876

FURS

Bounties are good even when fur is not.
Ernest Thompson Seton,
Wild Animals I Have Known

FUTILITY

We never rest at journey's end
By tracking an imagined foe.
Charles Edward Eaton,
A Song of Simplicity, 1952

Pleasure's forsaken us, Love ceased to smile;
Youth has been funeralled; Age travels fast.
Sometimes we wonder: is it worth while?
Robert Service, *A Song of Success,* 1912

FUTURE

The world is young, young, young tonight!
What will tomorrow bring?
Louise Bowman, *Young World,* 1922

Life gave you yesterday; I will give you tomorrow.
Audrey Alexandra Brown,
Death of Penelophon, 1936

Who knows but in the centuries to be,
When fool-made wars have hurried all men hence,
These things of beauty, all unconsciously,
Shall play their parts to saner audience?
Merrill H. Cook, *Wasaga in November,* 1937

. . . see
they are lining up already
those avant garde children of the future.
Peggy K. Fletcher,
Let Them Have Their Fling, 1968

The New Year lies ahead —
Untouched — a virgin page
As chaste as tender fall
Of snow on trampled earth.
Margaret Fulton Frame, *To The New Year,* 1947

What must come will come; there is much to follow. Why tremble?
Why hasten it? To be merely alive is joy enough.
Frederick P. Grove, *Settlers of the Marsh,* 1925

Tomorrow is a dream
that rarely, if ever, comes true.
So drink the rum that makes the dreams
that make tomorrow now.
Sandra Kolber, *Flight,* 1969

Now that future was the present, and what had it brought? Only an end to seeing ahead. Not even posterity.
Hugh MacLennan, *Each Man's Son,* 1951

The hope of the future is a greater consolation to Everyman than the dream of the past.
Hugo McPherson, *The Garden and the Cage,* 1959

My time is up. So once again I say,
Watch me impartially from day to day,
If we play fairly, we bespeak fair play.

All that we promise we will perform,
And strive to take society by storm!
George Murray,
speech at the opening of Her Majesty's
Theatre, 1898

Live not only for the present,
Live for days that are to come;
Let the days of youth be pleasant,
Soon enough there will be gloom.
J.R. Newell, *To E—,* 1881

Whither I go I know not, nor the way,
Dark with strange passions, vexed with
heathen charms,
Holding I know not what of life or death.
Marjorie Pickthall, *Père Lalement,* 1913

With the young there is ever a magical
spell in that little word 'to-morrow', — it is
a point which they pursue as fast as it
recedes from them.
Catherine Parr Traill, *Canadian Crusoes,* 1850

Sad indeed is the young heart that does not
look forward with hope to the morrow!
Catherine Parr Traill, *Canadian Crusoes,* 1850

GATINEAU

Gatineau, pride of the lumber-kings, river
that taught the old drivers to ride on the
logs.
Ermina E. Tribble, *River Drivers,* 1965

GENEROSITY

And if I share my crust,
As common manhood must,
With one whose need is greater than my
own,
Shall I not also give
His soul, that it may live,
Of the abundant pleasure I have known?
Bliss Carman, *Pipes of Pan*

What have I to give?
Nothing that you can take.
You have no lips for the bread
Which my hands can make.
Wilson MacDonald, *In the Far Years,* 1926

Oh ye, whose homes are warm and bright,
With plenty smiling at the board,
Remember those whose roofs to-night,
Nor warmth, nor light, nor food afford,

Still make those wants, and woes your
care,
And let the poor your bounty share.
Kate Seymour Maclean, *New Year, 1868,*
1881

Much may come to us through our own ef-
fort, if it be for another.
William McLennan and J.N. McIlwraith,
"The Span O'Life", 1899

Those who give us too much take away
everything that we possess.
Alden Nowlan, *Without Her I Would Die,* 1964

You cannot drive the sap of the tree in upon
itself. It must come out or the tree must die
— burst with the very misery of its
richness.
Gilbert Parker, *The Trail of the Sword,* 1894

GENIUS

Men of genius are the worst possible
models for men of talent.
Murray D. Edwards, *A Stage in Our Past,* 1968

Genius contrives
to stir the heart
of every age.
Mariel Jenkins,
An Exhibition of Modern Art, 1953

Genius is simply salesmanship.
Some artists do it by hiring a claque, some
by financing themselves. Some do it by
cutting down their minds like a piece of
cloth to fit the public.
Alexander Knox, *Old Master,* 1939

The simplicity of genius is achieved only by
much searching and a strenuous discipline.
Lord Tweedsmuir, *Return to Masterpieces,*
1937

Nowadays everybody's a genius until
proven otherwise. In my day, it used to be
the other way around.
William Weintraub, *Uneasy Riders,* 1970

GENTLEMAN

Being a gentleman, I assure you, is a trade
which requires costly tools.
Thomas McCulloch, *The Stepsure Letters,*
1821

Gentlemen can't work like labourers, and if they could they won't — it is not in them, and that you will find out.
Susanna Moodie, *Roughing It in the Bush*, 1852

GHOSTS

Canada is no place for ghosts. The country is too new for such gentry.
Samuel Strickland
Twenty-Seven Years in Canada West, 1853

GIRLS

Better with a street woman than with an innocent young girl or a married woman.
Morley Callaghan, *Such Is My Beloved*, 1934

The beauty of girls of eighteen is rarely of a commanding sort. It is very easy to miss it unless one is in the mood for it.
Robertson Davies, *Tempest-Tost*, 1951

Any girl, before she is married, is a kind of unexploded bomb.
Robertson Davies, *Tempest-Tost*, 1951

A girl's private personal cycle was the holy of holies.
Jack Ludwig, *Shirley*, 1969

She knows no silence
This happy brutal noisy animal
She is bursting at the seams.
James A. MacNeill, *There Is No Silence*, 1960

A girl who has a bright color at sixteen is nearly always pale at twenty.
Suzanne Marny, *The Unhappy House*, 1909

I have hardly ever seen a really plain Canadian girl in her teens; and a downright ugly one is almost unknown.
Susanna Moodie, *Roughing It in the Bush*, 1852

GOD

The God is good to them that fear him.
Carroll Aikins, *The God of Gods*

I saw the infinite behind the man,
And reverent whispered, "Surely God is here!"
Grant Balfour, *Where Is God?*, 1910

Man's spirit can only find release
In the upward love of God.
Clara Bernhardt, *Possession*, 1939

The way to God in our time
Is through the market place.
Elizabeth Brewster,
Lemuel Murray: Contemplation, 1969

Is there a god that rules this tiny world,
Or cares what men may do with their little lives?
F.O. Call, *Sceptic*, 1940

I took a day to search for God,
And found him not.
Bliss Carman, *Vestigia*

It's easier for me to say God than "some unnameable mysterious power that motivates all living things".
Leonard Cohen,
article in: Saturday Night, 1969

Close though He always was
Yet never was, my men, so close as now.
Leo Cox, *Vimy Veteran's Dinner*, 1955

What are the gods of this world but organization, planning, efficiency, regimentation, discipline, and order?
Frank Davey, *Pratt and the Corporate Man*, 1970

Wouldn't it be an awful sell for a lot of us — if God turned out to be the Prime Mover of capitalist respectability?
Robertson Davies, *Leaven of Malice*, 1954

I believe in God; but it isn't the God my father believed in. He's changed.
Frederick P. Grove, *Fruits of the Earth*, 1933

Speak daughter: God is love; none need despair.
Charles Heavysege, *Count Filippo*, 1860

I put away
My dingy, dark theology:
I did not know that God could be so gay.
Ralph Mortimer Jones, *The Public Gardens*, 1934

She had loved God but cursed extravagantly His creatures.
Irving Layton, *Keine Lazarovitch*, 1961

God is love, but please don't mention the two in the same breath.
Margaret Laurence, *The Stone Angel*, 1964

The maker of our Dreams is here,
To bide with us a day.

His steps are like the sounds that cheer
When children are at play.
Wilson MacDonald, *The Maker of Dreams*,
1926

We worship the spirit that walks unseen
Through our land of ice and snow:
We know not His face, we know not His
place,
But His presence and power we know.
Thomas D'Arcy McGee,
The Arctic Indian's Faith, 1858

Never allow yourself to think that the true
service of God is confined within any
particular spot or to any outward form and
manner of life.
William McLennan, *Une Soeur*, 1899

A girl's whole life is centered in the man
who succeeds in winning her affections,
and if he abandons her, he is a coward.
Geo. Pacaud, *Social Idolatry*, 1920

The voice of the people is the voice of God.
Thomas H. Raddall, *The Seige*

Each man creates God in his own image.
Mordecai Richler, *Son of a Smaller Hero*,
1955

And there was silence till God spoke.
Two billion years
Before his monstrous mouth
Pronounced its sharp, atomic NO.
F.R. Scott, *Span*, 1969

The wasted ways of earth I trod:
In vain! In vain! I found not God.
Robert W. Service, *The Quest*

God will help us when we help ourselves.
W.P. Wood, *"Minnie Traill"*, 1871

GOODNESS

Goodness is synonymous with creation
and the very Protestant emphasis on work.
Paul Epstein, *Malcolm Lowry and Jazz*, 1970

And though not Bramins,
Who believe truth to lie beyond where the
everyday happens,
We are sufficiently tired by change to wish
to repose on good.
Douglas Grant, *The Kitchen Table*, 1960

There is no such thing as one's own good.
Goodness is mutual, is communal; is only
gained by giving and receiving.
Arnold Haultain, *Hints to Lovers*

Good's the only warmth against a world
That freezes spring out of the years with
lies.
Malcolm Lowry, *In The Shed*, 1962

Beware the stupid Good.
Who, being stupid, cannot therefore tell
Christ from the thief blaspheming on his
rood.
Robert Norwood, *Bill Boram*, 1921

Corruption's the wormed core of human
creeds,
And goodness is rewarded by a sneer.
J.R. Ramsay, *French Chaos*, 1873

Goodness is a senstive plant which shuts
up when roughly handled.
J.R. Ramsay,
On the Soft Side of Humanity, 1873

you are better than I am
but it is not yours
so you can afford to be.
Sheila Streit,
You See San Francisco, O'Flynn, 1969

GOODS

Goods attach, they master dreams and
change them.
Brian Moore, *Judith Hearne*, 1955

GOSSIP

Rumour, always willing to believe what
flatters the interests of the many.
Frederick P. Grove, *Fruits of the Earth*, 1933

The inmost cranny of one's brain she'll
probe
And flash her findings promptly to the
globe.
Clara Hopper, *The News Hawk*, 1937

My God! Every time a dog breaks wind in
this place the whole parish knows it!
Hugh MacLennan, *Two Solitudes*, 1945

Listen. There are some rooms sticky with
the gut of lies
where spidery ladies squat over the husks
of dead blue reputations.
Eli Mandel, *Entomology*

We do not care what grief we bring your
house
So long as it be news.
Sara Jean McKay, *News Flashes*, 1938

Scandal when conducted on a scientific basis is an art.
Geo. W. Pacaud, *Social Idolatry*, 1920

It is that particular food on which society thrives and grows fat; for it tickles the senses, and whets the appetite for more scandal, and more is always forthcoming.
Geo. W. Pacaud, *Social Idolatry*, 1920

Truly the tongue is a powerful weapon for evil when used by a woman who, in her desire to have something to talk about, does not scruple to tear an innocent woman's reputation to pieces.
Minnie Smith, *Is It Just?*, 1911

GOVERNMENT

Gov'ments are funny things.
They do all their thinkin' in the dark and out o'sight.
Nathaniel A. Benson, *The Leather Medal*, 1930

The only thing a change in government ever changes, . . . is the government.
Merrill Denison, *Marsh Hay*, 1923

With perfect citizens any government is good.
Stephen Leacock,
"The Unsolved Riddle of Social Justice", 1920

The distribution of patronage was the most important single function of the government.
O.D. Skelton, *Life of Laurier*, 1921

Historically the state is an organization of lawyers and priests; it becomes destructive of the creative powers of men when the lawyers decide they are priests or when the priests get control of the law.
Robert Weaver, *The Canada Council*, 1957

GRATITUDE

I don't wear gratitude well. . . .
What should I do with this peculiar furred emotion?
Margaret Atwood,
Letters, Towards and Away, 1968

Gratitude you know, begets love.
Susanna Moodie, *Geoffrey Moncton*, 1855

I am grateful; and to you, who only did what you had to, as you could, as we all must, if we can, gracefully.
Gael Turnbull, *For W.C.W.*, 1959

Ingratitude hath no such votaries
As those she picks from old and pampered servants.
Samuel James Watson, *Ravlan*, 1876

GREATNESS

That's what makes a man great; his flashes of insight, when he pierces through the nonsense of his time, and gets at something that really matters.
Robertson Davies, *Tempest-Tost*, 1951

Great men are God's precious gifts to a world that sadly needs them.
E.H. Dewart, *Essays for the Times*, 1898

He was great as the men of any time, a towering glory to the whole race.
Norman Duncan, *The Fruits of Toil*

Greatness has contained one common trait in all ages and among all people, in not being vain, while, in turn, all that showed vanity has always been small and insufficient.
J.G. Fichte, *The Quality*, 1964

Great men were those who had vision, and for their vision passionate love.
Frederick P. Grove, *A Search for America*, 1927

What would material resources be without a corresponding greatness in man?
W.D. Lighthall,
Introduction to: "Songs of the Great Dominion", 1889

The world is cold to greatness.
Wilson MacDonald, *Three O'Clock*, 1926

All things great are wound up with all things little.
L.M. Montgomery, *Anne of Green Gables*, 1908

Men should not discard the gifts that make them great.
Farley Mowat, *The Riddle of the Viking Bow*

One kind of greatness doesn't point the finger at another.
Alfred W. Purdy, *Aiming Low*, 1968

Peril always is the price of greatness.
Samuel James Watson, *Ravlan*, 1876

GREED

Life has its ugliness. The end
Thereof is often simple greed.
Norman Gregor Guthrie, *Nasturtium*, 1928

Greed is an affliction of the soul.
Margaret Laurence, *The Pure Diamond Man*,
1963

GRIEF

Grief is our birthright, none without it.
Nathaniel A. Benson, *L'Envoi*, 1937

It would be grim
If all joy died
When hearts bereft
Are crucified.
Clara Bernhardt, *After Grief*, 1953

How can the soul support
A grief so vast as this? Each dream is dead,
And not one hope remains as last resort.
Clara Bernhardt, *The Seven Last Words*, 1942

Grief will not stitch the tearing years
Nor anger arch our falling sky.
Jean Boudin, *Kitchen Song*, 1967

Grief turns the heart in upon itself, and
tends to mar the fine bloom of an unselfish
spirit.
Ralph Connor, *The Prospector*, 1904

A strange thing in life is the hopelessness
of a child's grief.
Mary Stewart Durie, *A Skye Woman*, 1913

Grief cannot die, it doth but lightly sleep,
To waken at a touch, by night or day.
Francis W. Grey, *Love's Pilgrimage*, 1931

What would'st thou have for easement
after grief,
When the rude world hath used thee with
despite.
Archibald Lampman, *Comfort of the Fields*,
1895

Grief — 'tis a moment's pure passion — no
more.
Wilson MacDonald, *Graduation Day*, 1926

Seek not to calm my grief, To stay the falling tear;
Have pity on me, ye my friends, The hand
of God is here.
Nora Pembroke, *A Mother's Lament*, 1880

If you have lain in the night
And felt the old tears run

In their channels worn in the heart,
Pity me.
Marjorie Pickthall, *The Woodcarver's Wife*,
1920

Out of unhappiness, out of grief can come
peace and a new beginning.
Edwin R. Procunier,
The Strength of Love, 1962

One half the world live by the grief the
other half endure,
And fine professions fatten on the crimes
they cannot cure.
J.R. Ramsay, *One Hundred Years From Now*,
1873

All grief is done; and never more shall we
Make sail at dawning for the living sea.
Theodore Goodridge Roberts,
Fiddler's Green

Daily, I flagellate myself for sins undone.
The simplest act of living sours in this
instant grief.
Glen Siebrasse, *Pupil*, 1965

Grief has grown old and calm. I weep no
tears, —
To me you have been dead for many years.
Vera Munro Smith, *No Tears*, 1963

GROWING UP

As in any problem of individual growth,
one can shrink into isolation, un-
complicated childhood, or accept the
challenge of adult complexity, the struggle
for reality.
Louis Dudek,
The Future of French Canada, 1964

That's the worst of growing up, and I'm
beginning to realize it. The things you
wanted so much when you were a child
don't seem half so wonderful to you when
you get them.
L.M. Montgomery, *Anne of Green Gables*,
1908

GRUMBLING

There is much more fault-finding and
grumbling in the world than thanksgiving
and praise.
E.H. Dewart, *Essays for the Times*, 1898

Grumblers there will always be; what
community was ever united?
T.C. Haliburton, *The Old Judge*, 1849

Grumbling is the flood-gate to the dam
And carries off the surcharged waters
safely.
John Hunter-Duvar, *De Roberval*, 1888

GUILT

Your very protest doth confirm your guilt.
Francis W. Grey, *Bishop and King*, 1931

American guilt has to be felt for things you
are powerless to control.
Jack Ludwig, *Confusions*, 1960

There had been no passion, no guilt;
therefore there could be no responsibility.
Sinclair Ross, *The Painted Door*, 1939

HABITANT

The Canadian habitant, though sufficiently
courageous, is just and peace-loving,
preferring methods of conciliation to the
fury and violence of open war.
James E. LeRossignol, *Theophile*, 1908

The habitant is the true Canadian for he
has no other country.
Ramsay Traquair, *an article on Canada*, 1923

HALIFAX

Halifax sits on her hills by the sea
In the might of her pride, —
Invincible, terrible, beautiful, she
With a sword at her side.
E. Pauline Johnson,
Guard of the Eastern Gate, 1903

For this was the disgraceful thing about
Halifax, the hurting and humiliating thing
about this town, that here, backed by
millions of acres of space, there should be
slums like these and people dull and docile
enough to inhabit them.
Hugh MacLennan, *Barometer Rising*, 1941

This harbour is the reason for the town's
existence; it is all that matters in Halifax,
for the place periodically sleeps between
great wars.
Hugh MacLennan, *Barometer Rising*, 1941

HALLOWEEN

This is the night of dark powers.
All the old pagan savagery, glossed by a
few callow centuries of civilization,
reappears.
True Davidson, *Hallowe'en*, 1931

HAPPINESS

All men are born in bondage and unequal;
and some are blessed by the fairy god-
mother with happier dispositions than
others.
Bliss Carman, *The Kinship of Nature*, 1904

The wearing of a happy countenance, the
preserving of a happy mien, is a duty, not a
blessing.
Bliss Carman, *The Kinship of Nature*, 1904

Just to be happy, to taste even for a
moment the zest of radiant joy, is to
partake of immortality.
Bliss Carman, *The Kinship of Nature*, 1904

Joy in one's work, pleasure in one's
emotions, and satisfaction in one's
thoughts, go to make up the sum of happiness.
Bliss Carman, *The Kinship of Nature*, 1904

Your happiness is water for the sun to dry.
Fred Cogswell, *In the Morning Cold*, 1964

Pray sing at your work. Draw joy from your
occupation, however lowly the world may
deem it, and give joy to its performances;
and thus you will find the truest happiness.
Robertson Davies, *A Jig for the Gypsy*, 1954

The happiness of man consists not in ex-
ternal surroundings, but in the internal
feelings, and that heaven itself is not a
place, but a state.
James de Mille, *A Strange Manuscript*, 1888

Glory be to the gods; may your servant
again enjoy your gifts, in measured
dosages.
Howard Fink, *At The Film Society*, 1963

The happiness of every country depends
upon the character of its people, rather
than the form of its government.
T.C. Haliburton, *Sam Slick*

We envy the happiness of other people
mainly because we believe in it.
Irving Layton,
Some Observations and Aphorisms, 1968

You're a happy person. You've got joy inside you. For God's sake don't be ashamed
of it. The world is dying for lack of it.
Hugh MacLennan, *Two Solitudes*, 1945

The sum of human happiness remains much the same from age to age, no matter how it may vary in distribution, and all the "many inventions" neither lessen nor increase it.
L.M. Montgomery, *Rilla of Ingleside*, 1921

Happiness lies in the absorption in some vocation which satisfies the soul.
William Osler, *Doctor and Nurse*, 1891

Happiness is a great beautifier, they say.
Mazo de la Roche, *Delight*, 1926

There is happiness and pleasure in the society of the most illiterate men, sympathetically if not intellectually, as well as among the learned.
Alexander Ross, *Red River Settlement*

The happy man is he who knows his limitations, yet bows to no false gods.
Robert Service, *Ballads of a Bohemian*, 1921

Am I not rich? — a millionaire no less, If wealth be told in terms of Happiness.
Robert Service, *My Garret*, 1921

Put a touch of spring in the air, the thought of a woman in the heart — and keep from poetry if you can.
Arthur Stringer, *The Silver Poppy*

HASTE

Let us consider abstractions:
you are hasty and brash,
running rashly before you walk.
Frederick Cameron, *Correspondence*, 1969

To live without madness, one must live without haste.
Bliss Carman, *The Kinship of Nature*, 1904

Delays are dangerous! my advice is haste.
Sam Scribble, *Dolorsolatio*, 1865

HATE

And I learn again how the power of hate can humble
All but the banished faith we were fashioned by.
Charles Frederick Boyle, *Repossession*, 1941

Hate I think I learned mostly from fear.
George Jonas, *To A Christian*, 1967

Hate of myself and of others
Has eaten a hole in my heart.
Paul Halley, *Song Before Suicide*, 1939

The earth affords no corner for my ingle, No pillow for my head but hatred's stone!
Gordon LeClaire, *A Half-Caste Prays*, 1937

Hatred and its concomitant passion, Revenge, are feelings worthy of the dammed.
Susanna Moodie, *Geoffrey Moncton*, 1855

Love and hatred, are great sharpeners of the memory. It is as hard to forget an enemy as a friend.
Susanna Moodie, *Geoffrey Moncton*, 1855

Those who hate are doomed for all time To sadness.
C.J. Newman,
Two Poems about Love and Hate, 1967

It is a time for hardness and for hate;
A time for passion — not for gentle tears.
Robert Norwood, *The Witch of Endor*, 1916

No man can be happy and hate.
Gilbert Parker, *The Trail of the Sword*, 1894

But let silent hate be put away for it feeds upon the heart of the hater.
E.J. Pratt, *Silences*, 1937

hate is like an incoming tide
that fills a bay, and inundates
a shore. Receding, leaves the
bay dry, the shore visible
and impotent.
Dave Solway, *Hate*, 1960

Contempt is a hard thing to bear, especially one's own.
Wallace Stegner,
Specifications for a Hero

HEALTH

We shall never be as happy as angels until we are healthy as animals.
Bliss Carman, *The Friendship of Art*, 1904

Your feet are booted for the trail —
Mine slippered for the dance;
I am too young and frail to go
Where you would still advance.
Alice M.S. Lighthall,
"Helene Boulle to Her Husband Samuel de Champlain", 1948

My hopes, men
That you are healthy
In mind if not in muscle.
Dave Williams, *Pals*, 1964

Just health is a lot to be thankful for, plain,
everyday health; with everything working
together so well you don't even think about
your system at all.
Kate Westlake Yeigh, *A Specimen Spinster*

HEART

A simple human heart has a call to care for
its own greatest needs, and must have
fresh air and a bit of solitude, time to think
and room to breathe.
Bliss Carman, *The Kinship of Nature*, 1904

Heart bonds are the strong bonds.
Ralph Connor, *The Major*, 1917

To admit a sacred visitant into the inner
recesses of the human heart, those
recesses must be neat indeed.
Arnold Haultain, *Hints for Lovers*

A clean hide, . . . is next to a clean heart.
Nellie McClung, *The Runaway Grandmother*

The human heart is a foolish thing —
Plenty of rhyme but little of reason.
Lloyd Roberts, *The Human Heart*, 1937

O human heart that sleeps,
Wild with rushing dreams and deep with
sadness!
Duncan Campbell Scott, *Rapids at Night*

Alas! I wish I had the art
To tell the wonder of my heart.
Robert W. Service, *The Wonderer*

It is a gentle natural (is it I?) who
Visits timidly the big world of
The heart.
A.J.M. Smith, *Poor Innocent*, 1963

HEAVEN

The Dome of Heaven is a speck
a dot, the merest sphere
fading, invisible.
P.K. Page, *The Dome of Heaven*, 1970

HELL

O hell, I come, I come;
I feel the dreadful drawing of my doom.
Charles Heavysege, *Saul*, 1857

HELP

We're too much concerned nowadays with
helping other people we don't do enough
to help ourselves.
Robertson Davies, *A Jig for the Gypsy*, 1954

I'll try by example to lead you aright
Out of the shadows and into the light —
If you'll do as much for me.
Lloyd Roberts, *If I Must*

If you want to have what you do for people
really appreciated, don't do too much.
Alice A. Townley, *Opinions of Mary*

A little help was worth a deal of pity.
Catherine Parr Traill,
The Canadian Settler's Guide, 1855

HERO

When the hero died our luck turned.
Alfred G. Bailey, *The Golden Egg*, 1947

By dreaming heroes, fools see heroes,
and, by seeing heroes, they make them —
or think they do.
Britton Cooke,
The Translation of John Snaith

When a woman wants to believe a man is a
hero, there's no stopping her!
Britton Cooke,
The Transalation of John Snaith

And as for me, unlike the ancient bards,
My idols have been shattered into shards.
A.M. Klein, *The Diary of Abraham Segal*

Acts of heroism are common in the lower
walks of life. Thus, the purest gems are
often encased in the rudest crust, and the
finest feelings of the human heart are
fostered in the chilling atmosphere of
poverty.
Susanna Moodie, *Roughing It in the Bush*,
1852

The hero dead cannot expire:
The dead still play their part.
Charles Sangster, *"Brock"*, 1860

HISTORY

History and biography are open books in
which great lessons for our guidance are
taught by living illustrations.
E.H. Dewart, *Essays for the Times*, 1898

History moves through reconfiguration
from grace to death and on to light
and over the roads to black.
Anne Leaton, *The Body's Soil*, 1968

The modern world abridges all historical times as readily as it reduces space.
Marshall McLuhan,
Culture Without Literacy, 1953

Once discovered, history is not likely to be lost.
Wallace Stegner, *Wolf Willow*

CANADIAN HISTORY

It is due to the French Canadians to say that they have done more to preserve the historical records of Canada than all other Canadians together.
Thomas O'Hagan, *Canadian Essays*, 1901

Much of Canadian history can be interpreted as the effort to invade or to reconcile two compelling pulls from outside — the pull of the colonial tie with Great Britain, and the pull of the continental tie with the United States.
Desmond Pacey,
General Introduction to: "Creative Writing", 1961

Canadian history has provided us with few figures that are heroic in the grand manner, or with anything that might be described as a moving historical legend.
E.H. Winter,
Introduction to: "Our Century in Prose", 1966

HOBBY

It is our hobbies that keep us young.
Robertson Davies, *Tempest-Tost*, 1951

HOCKEY

While hockey is easy to understand, it is possibly the hardest of all sports to master.
David MacDonald,
Canada's Game Scores Ahead

Hockey's king of sports.
This is the thing to come to when you're feeling out of sorts.
W.M. Mackeracher,
The Parson at the Hockey Match

HOME

It is, in some ways, a saddening experience to return as a stranger to a town that once belonged to you, because a stranger sees things differently from a native.
Pierre Berton, *The Mysterious North*, 1956

Men's homes, are patriotism, and hearthstones
Are the foundations of all loyalty.
John Hunter-Duvar, *De Roberval*, 1888

That's how to find out just what home is — go away from it for a while!
Nina Moore Jamieson, *The Hickory Stick*, 1921

There where one was born and has grown up, there one should stay.
James E. LeRossignol, *The Exile*, 1908

Homesickness makes us all young, makes us all little children again.
William McLennan and J.N. McIlwraith, *"The Span O'Life"*, 1899

Whoever finds a HOME, has gained the grand point in the business of life.
Thomas McCulloch, *The Stepsure Letters*, 1821

If you wish to enjoy true comfort yourself, make your husband happy by making his home a home.
Thomas McCulloch, *The Stepsure Letters*, 1821

Firefly of pleasure
has sparked this place
echo of whipporwill
has sounded it for sorrow.
Peter Miller, *Demenagement*

There childhood's brief, bright hours were spent;
There life's serenest visions lent
Their brightest charms; there youth's fond dreams
Of life did gild life's silver streams.
J.E. Pollock, *Home*, 1883

Let us who have wandered afar "arise and go" back to our homestead once more, if we have one to return to; if not, then in remembrance revisit some homestead of the heart.
J.R. Ramsay, *One Quiet Day*, 1873

I have come back again to where I belong;
Not an enchanted place, but the walls are strong.
Dorothy H. Rath, *Again*, 1963

Home without Love is bitterness;
Love without Home is often pain.
No! each alone will seldom do;
Somehow they travel hand in glove:
If you win one you must have two,
Both Home and Love.
Robert Service, *Home and Love,* 1912

My home is my care — if gladness be there,
It's a mightly good world after all.
Robert Service, *Cheer,* 1912

Oh but it is good to be
Foot-loose and heart-free.
Yet how good it is to come
Home at last, home, home!
Robert Service, *The Rover,* 1912

It is a great mistake to neglect those little household adornments which will give a look of cheerfulness to the very humblest home.
Catherine Parr Traill,
The Canadian Settler's Guide, 1855

HONESTY

To name is to begin to admit.
George Bowering,
A Comment on the Singular, 1970

A girl must keep herself to herself and always walk in the light; never creep upstairs in the dusk, or linger for a kiss.
Mary Elizabeth Colman,
Death of a Stranger, 1938

Freedom is not as popular among Angry Young Men as "honesty", but they are allied because in order to be 'honest' you must be 'free'.
John Graham, *A Tale of a Stifling Dog,* 1958

You have got to be straight if you want to make friends with men of less intellectual training than your own.
M. Allerdale Grainger,
Woodsmen of the West, 1908

Honesty is essential to any race that desires to spread and increase and build an Empire; or even to build private fortunes.
Maurice Hutton, *The Englishman*

Better far the fool's digression
Than the rigid Scotch confession,

Smeared with crimson of the sages who obeyed not its commands.
Wilson MacDonald, *The Song of the Rebel,* 1926

HONEYMOON

Honeymoons were surely not events that by their nature were supposed to continue.
Malcolm Lowry, *The Forest Path to the Spring*

HOPE

An old man saw a vision, a young man dreamed a dream: so did they depart into the wilderness to seek in vain, and yet to find, great content.
W.H. Blake, *In a Fishing Country*

This is a time for pretending. This is a time for dreaming. The time for being isn't here yet.
Janet Bonellie, *Why Are the People Staring,* 1967

I shall see more radiant visions
Than all my dreams have brought me through the years.
Frank Oliver Call, *Through Arched Windows*

If only the world could cast out fear and establish hope in its place, the morning of the millennium would be already far advanced.
Bliss Carman, *The Kinship of Nature,* 1904

I promise thee all joyous things
That furnish forth the lives of kings.
Isabella Valancy Crawford,
The Axe of the Pioneer

There is always the search; nothing is ever settled finally; one must be resigned to this.
Christine Turner Curtis,
Montreal Remembered, 1952

We are miserable or we are nothing. Hope is out of fashion.
Robertson Davies, *A Masque of Mr. Punch,* 1962

Enjoy your despair, and don't try to deprive me of my consolation. My hope sustains me, and helps me to cheer you up.
James De Mille, *A Strange Manuscript,* 1888

Hope is ever ready to arise.
James De Mille, *A Strange Manuscript,* 1888

Everything looks bright to glad and hopeful hearts. On the other hand, the desponding and sorrowful clothe all things in the hues of their own sombre spirits.
E.H. Dewart, *Essays for the Times*, 1898

What hopes we cherished in life's gay prime.
What castles we built in the air!
Which the iron hand of pitiless Time
Has covered with shrouds of despair.
E.H. Dewart, *Christmastide*, 1898

I am yet young, for in the beginning of my labour I hope.
Norman Duncan, *Every Man for Himself*, 1908

How long must we wait
for the prophets to come,
to tell us of our awakening?
Gail Fox, *Word for the Nameless*, 1970

O child! never allow your heart to harden
welcome the unicorn into your garden.
Phyllis Gotlieb, *Bestiary*, 1963

Hope is a pleasant acquaintance, but an unsafe friend.
T.C. Haliburton, *Sam Slick's Wise Saws*, 1853

Hope has made a mess of chaos.
John Harney, *I Sit in My Cockleshell*, 1959

Day drops away from us, with all its weight of cares and worries, and our souls long for the impossible.
Nina Moore Jamieson, *The Hickory Stick*, 1921

Wherever a poisonous weed grows, just right beside it, mind ye, you will be finding the herb that cures the poison.
Marian Keith, *Treasure Valley*

All is dark, save the light —
Isabel Le Bourdais, *And Mercy Mild*, 1933

There's a word for the dumb,
There's a hue for the blind,
And he, who despairs not, shall find.
Wilson MacDonald, *Why Not I?*

I study all day and pray all night.
My God, send me a sign of Thy coming
Or let me die.
Jay MacPherson,
Ordinary People in the Last Days, 1957

Nothing happens but the impossible . . . ; and we are no longer in an age that hopes for miracles.
William McLennan and J.N. McIlwraith,
"The Span O'Life", 1899

A dream, a hope, needs no justification in the heart of man; it is its own justification.
Edward Meade, *Remember Me*, 1946

Looking forward to things is half the pleasure of them.
L.M. Montgomery, *Anne of Green Gables*, 1908

The extravagance of youthful hope, is only equalled by youthful vanity.
Susanna Moodie, *Geoffrey Moncton*, 1855

When things come to the worst, they generally mend.
Susanna Moodie, *Roughing It in the Bush*

Hopes of the youthful breast,
Oh! Whither have ye gone?
Where is the promised rest,
To crown the labours done?
J.R. Newell,
Hopes of the Youthful Breast, 1881

Hope's a commodity none of us ever runs out of. But you've got to hope reasonably.
John Peter, *Tom's A-Cold*, 1962

If Hope had fled with summer days,
And Faith had faded with the leaves,
Our poor stark soul must surely freeze
Ere came the sun's reviving rays.
Frederic Philips, *Hope*, 1909

And Hope thou art the magic fan
That flames the embers of the soul;
And inspiration gives to man,
And leads him victor to the goal.
J.E. Pollock, *Hope*, 1883

And then before our voice is dumb,
Before our blood-shot eyes go blind,
The Lord of Love and Life may come
To lead our ebbing veins to find
Enough for the recovery
Of plasma from Gethsemane.
E.J. Pratt, *Cycles*

The child's philosophy is the true one. He does not despise the bubble because it burst; and he immediately sets to work to blow another.
J.J. Procter,
The Philosopher in the Clearing, 1897

Hope is the beginning of faith and faith is the beginning of love.
Edwin R. Procunier, *The Strength of Love,* 1962

Be honest, kindly, simple, true;
Seek good in all, scorn but pretence;
Whatever sorrow come to you,
Believe in Life's Beneficence.
Robert Service, *The World's All Right,* 1912

Quixote
is donkeying to heaven
on a puff of hope
D.P. Thomas, *Quixote,* 1967

the world is getting
dark but I carry
icons I remember
the summer
I will never forget
the light.
Miriam Waddington, *Icons,* 1969

HORSES

As clothes betray a person when his face is not observable, so do horses and sleighs on a country road.
H.A. Cody, *The Fourth Watch,* 1911

Nothing could be more willing than a horse. He'd go until he dropped if the driver hadn't sense enough to pull him up, to keep him from foundering himself.
Raymond Knister, *Mist-Green Oats,* 1923

HOSTILITY

Hostility and agression, like a good cry, did a person a world of good.
Jack Ludwig, *Shirley,* 1969

HOUSE

A house is for sleepin' in — a shack is for livin' in.
H.T. Barker, *The Ice Road*

The knack of building houses which have faces, as opposed to grimaces, is retained by few builders.
Robertson Davies, *Tempest-Tost,* 1951

A man lives best when he's taken root.
Sara Jeannette Duncan, *The Imperialist,* 1904

It is not the house itself but the spirit of contentment and family unity within.
Susan Jackel, *The House on the Prairies,* 1969

The rearing of children in a house fit to rear them in, not an apartment house, is a full-time job, but it is one that we have to get done for us somehow, or else our nation, .. . and our civilization, . . . must go under within a hundred years.
Stephen Leacock, *Woman's Level*

A house isn't much different from people, . . . When one thing starts to go, everything goes.
Edwin R. Procunier, *The Moonless Nights,* 1962

Come and let me make thee glad
In this house that I have made!
Francis Sherman, *The Builder*

HUMAN

My theory is, if anything amuses
Me, it may serve to instruct others.
Daryl Hine,
Letter From British Columbia, 1970

Man — woman — what does it matter? We all eat. We all die.
Margaret Laurence, *A Gourdful of Glory,* 1960

HUMANIST

The true humanist, the individual engagé, is rare in any age, and precious.
Marilyn Davies,
The Bird of Heavenly Airs, 1963

Estranged from me — but yet you are not strange,
I see humanity as the wound you bear
Cleft in your side and mine uniting us.
Douglas Le Pan, *Field of Battle,* 1963

A romantic age stands in need of science, a scientific and utilitarian age stands in need of the humanities.
Goldwin Smith, *The Week,* 1893

HUMAN NATURE

There's a great deal of human nature in the brute creation, or of brute nature in the human creation; which is it?
J.J. Procter,
The Philosopher in the Clearing, 1897

It seems a lingering principle of good in human nature, that the exercise of mercy and virtue opens th heart to the enjoyment of social happiness.
Catherine Parr Traill, *Canadian Crusoes,* 1850

HUMILITY

However elevated man may be, there is much in his condition that reminds him of the infirmities of his nature and reconciles him to the decrees of Providence.
T.C. Haliburton, *The Ruined Lodge*

Where Might doth falter, Beauty enters in; Where Pride shall fail, Humility shall win. And this will be until the heavens are old.
Wilson MacDonald,
February the First on the Prairies, 1926

Allow me, . . . to leave humility to those who enjoy it. The shield of pride is just as strong and a great deal brighter.
L.A. MacKay, *The Freedom of Jean Guichet*

How small am I in thine august regard! Invisible, — and yet I know my worth!
Charles G.D. Roberts,
O Solitary of the Austere Sky

HUMOUR

The great humorist forgets himself in his delighted contemplation of other people.
Douglas Bush, *A Vanished Race*, 1926

The love of truth lies at the root of much humour.
Robertson Davies, *On Stephen Leacock*, 1957

Humour is criticism of life, and criticism will always, at some time and in some quarter, beget resentment.
Robertson Davies, *On Stephen Leacock*, 1957

In our day humour has become as never before, a marketable commodity, created and sold by committees of industrious ulcerous, clever but basically humourless men.
Robertson Davies, *On Stephen Leacock*, 1957

Humour is a civilizing element in the jungle of the mind, and civilizing elements never enjoy a complete or prolonged popularity.
Robertson Davies, *A Voice from the Attic*, 1960

A great sense of humour can only exist in company with other elements of greatness.
Robertson Davies, *A Voice from the Attic*, 1960

Wit in a woman is a dangerous thing, like a doctor's lancet, it is apt to be employed about matters that offend our delicacy, or hurt our feelings.
T.C. Haliburton,
Nature and Human Nature, 1855

A quick sense of humor is surely one of the happiest of mortal possessions.
Archibald Lampman, *Happiness*, 1896

There is no quality of the human mind about which its possession is more sensitive than the sense of humour.
Stephen Leacock, *My Discovery of England*, 1922

The world's humour, in its best and greatest sense, is perhaps the highest product of our civilization.
Stephen Leacock, *Further Foolishness*, 1916

To deny a woman's sense of humour is the last form of social insult.
Stephen Leacock, *Further Foolishness*, 1916

The Englishman loves what is literal . . . . . the American . . . tries to convey the same idea by exaggeration.
Stephen Leacock, American Humour, 1914

Genial humour is fairly rare in literature; it is much more elusive than satiric wit.
W.H. Magee,
Stephen Leacock, Local Colourist, 1969

Humour is the tail to the kite of affection.
Arthur Stringer, *The Silver Poppy*

HUNTING

No life on earth . . . is half as hard, So full of disappointments, as a hunter's.
Robert Rogers, *Ponteach*, 1766

Come let us hunt, for there is glory, now-a-days, even in the slaughter of the noblest of God's, four-footed creatures.
Samuel James Watson, *Ravlan*, 1876

HUSBAND

A good husband should always bore his wife.
Fred Jacob, *The Clever One*, 1925

HYPOCRISY

Do not dress in rags for me
I know you are not poor
Don't love me so fiercely
When you know you are not sure.
Leonard Cohen

Beware the judgment of the just.
the traffickers of truth;
a thief is worthier of trust
a savage has more truth.
Gustav Davidson, *New Testament,* 1949

Every man has his own set of minor hypocrisies.
Robertson Davies, *Tempest-Tost,* 1951

Hypocrisy can be a most sincere homage paid by vice and virtue.
Dennis Duffy,
The Too-Well-Tempered Critic, 1968

Having become democratic by ideology, we are divided into groups which eye each other like dull strangers at a dull party, polite in public and nasty when each other's backs are turned.
Hugh MacLennan, *An Orange from Portugal*

The world rarely improves the heart, but only teaches both sexes more adroitly to conceal its imperfections.
Susanna Moodie, *Geoffrey Moncton,* 1855

IDEAS

An idea, you know, is to some people a rare and valuable asset.
Ralph Connor, *The Prospector,* 1904

The woods of Canada howl with my rank ideas.
James Dougherty, *Perils of an American,* 1967

Ideas alone have power. Action is only a weak and watery reflection of thought. The idea, the idea, is everything.
L.A. MacKay, *The Freedom of Jean Guichet*

It would be bad for us to have too high ideas.
Hugh MacLennan, *Each Man's Son,* 1951

What one man has set up, one man can destroy. Every great idea in the world has started in the mind of some one man.
Lister S. Sinclair, *No Scandal in Spain,* 1945

IDEAL

If one has the patrician spirit, one holds to certain ideals.
Charles G. Booth, *This Man Knew,* 1936

We have scorned the belief of our fathers
And cast their quiet aside;
To take the mob for our ruler
And the voice of the mob for our guide.
Bliss Carman, *Twilight in Eden*

The death of a god in scarlet and glowing leaf is very different from the collapse of a drunkard in a blue café, no matter what underground literature might profess.
Leonard Cohen, *The Favourite Game*

But the body alone could not satisfy need
When greatness and power of thought,
And sweetness of mind and heed for mankind
Were qualities still being sought.
Lois Darroch, *The Unattainable,* 1942

There is no sense in being idealistic — ideals don't necessarily advance the world anyway — some of the most idealistic men have done the worst damage.
Cicely Louise Evans, *Anti Disposition,* 1935

We praise men for worshipping "ideals"; we condemn them for worshipping "idols"
John Daniel Logan,
"Democracy, Education and the New Dispensation".

IDEALISM

He who insists on hunting the unicorn will certainly discover, when at last he is sure that the fabulous creature is in his net, that he has snared a laughing jackass.
Robertson Davies, *A Voice from the Attic,* 1960

This high idealism is the criterion of French poetry in Canada.
Louis Dudek,
Towards a Brotherhood of Nations, 1963

Do you know what it is to have something ever beside you to look up to? — I am never greater than My Rock.
William MacLennan, *Mon Rocher,* 1899

I built myself a citadel of thought
And Reason kept the gate. But nowadays
My own men seem uncertain of their part.
Lister Sinclair, *Return to Colonus,* 1955

IDEALIST

They are the young. Salute their bright formation

To build a new world free of scimitars
On highways unsurveyed in winged gyration
They elbow clouds and mingle with the stars.
Amabel King, *The New Crusaders*, 1943

An idealist is someone who has convinced himself other people are less nasty than he is.
A cynic in the making.
Irving Layton,
Some Observations and Aphorisms, 1968

IDLENESS

False idleness consists in doing nothing, but in doing it with the ill-nature and sloth of discontent; this is criminal.
Bliss Carman, *The Kinship of Nature*, 1904

True idleness consists in doing nothing, with the grace and mastery of an accomplishment; this is an art.
Bliss Carman, *The Kinship of Nature*, 1904

Idleness is the prolific progenitor of crime.
Roderick George Macbeth,
Policing the Plains, 1921

Idleness in Canada, will always cover a man with rags.
Samuel Strickland,
Twenty-Seven Years in Canada West, 1853

IGNORANCE

A man is never astonished or ashamed that he don't know what another does; but he is surprised at the gross ignorance of the other in not knowin' what he does.
T.C. Haliburton, *Sam Slick*, 1936

More rich are men in their ignorance,
For in their not knowing they know much.
Edwin R. Procunier, *Two Sides of Darkness*, 1962

ILLUSIONS

Brush from young women's eyes
Cloud of illusion —
She who in travail lies
She shall in travail rise.
Jessie L. Beattie, *Motherhood*, 1940

Faith is outmoded;
All those illusions I once held so fine
Have long been exploded.
Winnifred A. Hillier, *Frivolity*, 1941

It was no one's fault that life had allowed us a time of illusion, and that the time was now past.
Margaret Laurence,
The Drummer of All the World, 1956

No season swells
like the summer of illusion.
Elizabeth Whealy, *Season of Illusion*, 1967

IMAGINATION

He imagined a thing and straightaway felt it to be true.
Morley Callaghan,
Last Spring They Came Over, 1929

It is the devoted imaginers who have been the benefactors of their race.
Bliss Carman, *The Friendship of Art*, 1904

A failure of imagination has far wider significance than most of those acts which we usually refer to as sins.
Gwethalyn Graham, *Dear Ennemy*, 1963

The worst of imagining things is that the time comes when you have to stop and that hurts.
L.M. Montgomery, *Anne of Green Gables*, 1908

Effective imaginative literature is an amalgam of the new and the strange — whatever taxes credulity and complacency — with what is somehow believable, authentic, and immediate.
Robert Rosenheim,
Children's Reading and Adult's Values, 1970

Those who have Imagination live in a land of enchantment which the eyes of the others cannot see. Yet if it brings marvellous joy it also beings exquisite pain.
Robert Service, *Ballads of a Bohemian*, 1921

Imagination is the great gift of the gods. Given it, one does not need to look afar for subjects. There is romance in every face.
Robert Service, *Ballads of a Bohemian*, 1921

Imagination fools such clowns as thou
When wine lends wings to sober ignorance.
Samuel James Watson, *Ravlan*, 1876

IMMATURITY

The difficulty with immature people was that their own sins were too heavy for them.
Frances Shelley Wees,
M'Lord, I Am Not Guilty, 1954

An inevitable sign of the immature reader is his taste for fiction that takes him out of the real world and into the land of make-believe.
E.H. Winter,
the Introudction to:
"Our Century in Prose", 1966

IMMIGRANT

These people here exist as an undigested mass. They must be taught our ways of thinking and living.
Ralph Connor, *The Foreigner*

The refugee is the everyman of our time.
Henry Kreisel, *The Betrayal,* 1964

A country attracts the kind of immigrants it deserves.
Hugh MacLennan, *The Art of City-Living,* 1954

The immigrant who comes to Canada really sees the country much more as a whole. He doesn't know the nuances which are so important and so dearly beloved by the Torontonian or the Montrealer.
Brian Moore, *an Interview,* 1962

IMMORTALITY

They are not dead, the soldier and the sailor,
Fallen for Freedom's sake;
They merely sleep with faces that are paler
Until they wake.
A.S. Bourinot, *Immortality,* 1915

Perhaps all we need to do, in order to touch immortal happiness and partake of immortal life, is to attain our own ideal once, and once for all.
Bliss Carman, *The Kinship of Nature,* 1904

A man to be remembered must have endeared himself to men.
Bliss Carman, *The Friendship of Art,* 1904

There is a part of me that knows,
Beneath incertitude and fear,
I shall not perish when I pass.
Beyond mortality's frontier.
Bliss Carman, *Non Omnis Moriar,* 1901

Your children grow up, they leave you,
They have become soldiers and riders.
Your mate dies after a life of service
Who knows you? Who remembers you?
Leonard Cohen, *You Have the Lovers,* 1961

If I should fall, give me a place among ye,
And a name will be my children's pride,
For all, — my all — I risk, as ye, to save
My country.
Sarah Anne Curzon,
Laura Secord: The Heroine of 1812, 1887

But his children were all he had been able to give the world, and they were his only continuity.
Hugh MacLennan, *Barometer Rising,* 1941

These are things I have existed for,
To have someone remember me.
Gerard Malanga, *Immortality,* 1967

To come to a place and build. To leave something complete. That was real, substantial.
R.D. Mathews, *The Biggest Bridge,* 1967

My name shall live — despite Death's greedy mew —
Linked with the lovely echo of your name.
Padraig O'Broin, *Escape,* 1961

Some persons refuse to stay dead.
They are in continual resurrection.
Their flesh is indestructible
Their blood still courses through the veins of humanity.
Helmer O. Oleson, *Indestructible,* 1952

Share if you like, and let your thought
Of earth's endurance be
Your surest claim to immortality.
Edna W. Slater, *Made Flesh,* 1954

IMPROVEMENT

If a man is to rise above himself, the cramping influences of wealth as well as poverty, of arbitrary custom, and the audacious tyranny of each generation upon the next must be removed.
Margaret Fairley, *Creative Evolution,* 1921

If a man cannot improve on what his ancestors did he had better have been born before them.

J.J. Procter,
The Philosopher in the Clearing, 1897

INACTION

It's better far to die
Than fade and go to seed!
Norman Gregor Guthrie, *Blue Salvia*, 1928

I perish in this peace
My frustrate being longs
To dance at Fate's caprice
And leap to snarl of thongs.
Gordon LeClaire, *Ingrate*, 1938

Better to die fighting than to freeze in inaction.

Blanche Lucile Macdonell,
Diane of Ville Marie, 1898

When the powers of good are present in the heart, and can find no outlet in action, they turn to evil.

Nellie L. McClung, *Sowing Seeds in Danny*, 1911

INDEPENDENCE

Nature abhors the independence of man.
William Dunlop, *Statistical Sketches*, 1832

I belong to no one; alas, I am my own!
Daryl Hine,
Estrangement and Transformation, 1959

The independent in soul can rise above the seeming disgrace of poverty, and hold fast their integrity, in defiance of the world and its selfish and unwise maxims.

Susanna Moodie, *Roughing It in the Bush*, 1852

Henceforth I stand upon my strength alone,
Regardless of that God who is so hot
Upon the path of baffled souls.
Robert Norwood, *The Witch of Endor*, 1916

We need no gloves,
Our hands englove each other.
We need no scarves,
Our arms that purpose serve.
James Reaney, *A Riddle*, 1963

INDIANS

The Indians of both sexes are the happiest people on earth; free from all care, they en-joy the present moment, forget the past, and are without solicitude for the future.
Frances Brooke,
The History of Emily Montague, 1769

burial ground
for more than bones
an entire race
lies buried here.
Hugh Cook,
Indian Cemetery, Squamish, B.C., 1968

No man who associates with and follows the pursuits of the Indian, for any length of time, ever voluntarily returns to civilized society.
William Dunlop, *Statistical Sketches*, 1832

An Indian is respectable in his own community, in proportion as his wife and children look fat and well fed; this being a proof of his prowess and success as a hunter, and his consequent riches.
Anna Brownell Jameson, *Winter Studies*, 1838

For the Micmacs summer was the good time, the warm time, the easy time.
Thomas H. Raddall, *The Amulet*

I consider the intellect of the Indian above mediocrity — that is, if you compare him with the uneducated peasantry of other lands.
Samuel Strickland,
Twenty-Seven Years in Canada West, 1853

The Indian must also yield to circumstances; he submits patiently. Perhaps he murmurs in secret; but his voice is low, it is not heard.
Catherine Parr Traill, *Canadian Crusoes*, 1850

INDIVIDUAL

In the end, it is upon the quality of individuals that all group movements depend.
Robertson Davies, *A Voice from the Attic*, 1960

The individual cannot live by bread alone; and the true life of the community must reside in those intangibles which derive their chief value from being enjoyed in common.
Hilda Neatby,
The Massey Report: A Retrospect, 1956

That's all the modern world is nowadays. Individuals. Striving and struggling against one another. Each one puffed up with his own importance. Stuffed with all this nonsense about equality. I'll take the old way, when men had the self-respect to know their place.
Norman Williams, *The King Decides*, 1956

INDIVIDUALITY

It is the uncontemporary spirit that is the genius of discovery and art and invention.
Bliss Carman, *The Friendship of Art*, 1904

There is only one way in the world to be distinguished: Follow your instinct! Be yourself, and you'll be somebody. Be one more blind follower of the blind; and you will have the oblivion you desire.
Bliss Carman, *The Friendship of Art*, 1904

I am convinced, . . . that there is nothing in the world so valuable as personality. I mean of course to other people.
Mrs. Everard Cotes, *The Crow's Nest*

I've met a lot of people with what they call "temperament", and I can't see anything in it at all. I think it's mostly a hedge to hide behind!
Nina Moore Jamieson, *The Hickory Stick*, 1921

I am a renegade, laughing at rules and laws,
And my whims are my king and my royal family.
Wilson MacDonald, *Out of the Wilderness*, 1926

Genuine individuality, distinct from egotism, seeks for communication which, in turn, implies community.
Eli Mandel, *The Language of Humanity*, 1963

The powerful are cruel, and we absurd within our frailties,
Clair Pratt, *A Toast to Death*, 1967

Men do not like originality; they are afraid and suspicious of it.
J.J. Procter,
The Philosopher in the Clearing, 1897

Our culture is one which sets a great value on individuality, the preservation of the unique personality. This idea is one of the bases of democracy, of capitalism, and of the Protestant religious ethic.
Stephen Scobie, *Magic, Not Magicians*, 1970

INDUSTRY

Urban industrialism denies satisfaction by inducing servility.
Frank Birbalsingh,
Grove and Existentialism, 1970

The moment you want anything beyond the peasant's needs, you hand yourself over to the industrial machine.
Frederick P. Grove, *The Seasons*

Though wild, indeed, . . .
Yet soon the patient hand of industry
Will turn the mighty woods to fertile fields.
John Hunter-Duvar, *De Roberval*, 1888

INFLUENCE

It's always the woman has more influence on the man than the man on the woman.
L.A. MacKay, *The Freedom of Jean Guichet*

You cannot touch pitch without being soiled, neither can you do anything in which there is the slightest taint of dishonor without a stain upon your soul.
Minnie Smith, *Is It Just?*

INNOCENCE

I am a child
have seen many dawns
but never felt the dew.
Nelson Ball, *A New Dawn*, 1966

Look not to youth for innocence nor to the pure for saint.
Gustav Davidson, *New Testament*, 1949

Scorn and hate — each evil passion flies
Before the beauty of your sinless eyes.
Nicholas Flood Davin, *To "Bay Mi"*, 1884

May God take care of him, for he never could take care of himself.
Susanna Moodie, *Roughing It in the Bush*

To the pure in heart all things are pure.
Susanna Moodie, *Geoffrey Moncton*, 1855

And all that better life that I would lead,
Writ small in this, one childish face, I read.
Arthur Stringer, *On A Child's Portrait*

INSECTS

It has been the luck of lizards and men alike that insect bodies are so tangled up inside with their vital air tubes that they cannot grow to a size that is dangerous to our kind.
N.J. Berrill, *Perfume, Starlight, and Melody*

INSTINCT

The primitive instinct is uppermost, even in man, and when the wild animal is tamed and gentled, it merely loses its defences against man, the killer.
Joseph Gold,
Introduction to:
"King of Beasts" (C.G.D. Roberts), 1967

We pay for our pleasure with pain;
But the dog will return to his vomit, the hog to his wallow again.
Robert Service, *The Black Sheep,* 1907

INTERFERENCE

It's a wise man that knows how much to meddle in other people's business.
L.A. MacKay, *The Freedom of Jean Guichet*

INTELLECTUALS

I cannot understand why it is that men with brains are so seldom successful.
Fred Jacob, *And They Meet Again,* 1925

The intellectuals are not, to my temperament, the most lovable specimens of the human race — the illiterates are more lovable.
Maurice Hutton, *The Englishman*

He was so intellectual that he was, as he himself admitted, a complete eggnostic.
Stephen Leacock, *Sunshine Sketches,* 1912

The true intellectual is a simple person who knows how to be close to nature and to ordinary people.
Dorothy Livesay, *Song and Dance,* 1969

Intellectual beauty. How we are shrunken now.
Eli Mandel, *Metamorphosis,* 1958

There is no other country in the world where intellectuals suffer from such low repute as in Canada.
Hilda Neatby,
The Massey Report: A Retrospect, 1956

The strength of the student of books is to sit still — two or three hours at a stretch.
William Osler, *The Student Life*

We are the encyclopedists,
Fingers on our own pulse
Self conscious and pseudo clever;
Wayfarers outside the blood,
And have forgotten what we are.
Alfred W. Purdy, *Dimensions,* 1960

The more contact I have with the Canadian scene, the more convinced I become that English-Canadian intellectuals rank among the most neurotic people on the continent.
George Sherman, *Purdy's Romans,* 1968

Today's disgruntled intellectual, who wants a place to air his political convictions, automatically thinks of Government as his obvious sponsor.
Maxwell Vos, *The Un-Broken Butterfly,* 1962

Wherever we look, intellectuals are talking away their feelings of impotence, creating a substitute world of ideas and images, and initiating one another into one another's private mythologies.
Paul West, *Canadian Attitudes,* 1963

INTELLIGENCE

If the civilization of the future is thus to harden towards the communal stereotype of an anthill, it will be all the more important to preserve and nourish the things of the spirit for the life of the individual.
Watson Kirkconnell,
Poetry and National Life, 1942

Only in retrospect is intellect transcended.
E.I. Louch, *Emergence of Poetry,* 1951

The intellect does not age, the body dies daily the mind declares its lies
about the soul, about the self
about the body and its ageless cries.
E.W. Mandel, *The Witch of Endor,* 1963

It is not the heart, but the brain, that must decide in questions of right and wrong.
Susanna Moodie, *Roughing It in the Bush,* 1852

Oh what a curse it must be
to be clever, far worse
than to be handsome or good.
C.J. Newman,
On Being Clever, Handsome, or Good, 1967

There is, and always must be activity and unrest where there is the intellectual faculty; and in proportion as it is wanting, there is inactivity and repose.
J.J. Procter,
The Philosopher in the Clearing, 1897

The only true wealth of a nation is mental wealth.
J.R. Ramsay, *Born in the Purple,* 1873

As men cultivate the mind they rise in the scale of creation, and become more capable of adoring the Almighty through the works of his hands.
Catherine Parr Trail,
The Canadian Settler's Guide, 1855

Let the head direct the hand, and the hand, like a well-disciplined soldier, obey the head as chief.
Catherine Parr Traill, *Canadian Crusoes,* 1850

It is a good mind
that can embody
perfection
with exactitude.
Phyllis Webb, *Suite II,* 1963

INTUITION

Intuition is nearer to life than intellect — or science . . . That's why we have the arts isn't it?
W.O. Mitchell, *The Kite,* 1963

What you mean by intuition is hunch, guided largely by mood. . . . whim!
Michael Yates, *The Calling,* 1970

IRISH

We've bowed beneath the chastening rod,
We've had our griefs and pains,
But with them all, we still thank God,
The Blood is in our veins,
The ancient blood that knows no fear,
The Stamp is on us set,
And so, however foes may jeer,
We're Irish yet! We're Irish yet!
William H. Drummond, *We're Irish Yet,* 1897

Ireland, the land of heart's desire, the land of heart's delight!
Norah Holland,
The Fair Hills of Holy Ireland, 1924

These Gaelic people, . . . had lived close together in small places for so long they could somehow communicate with each other in a way no one else could fathom.
Hugh MacLennan, *Each Man's Son,* 1951

IRRESPONSIBILITY

Pass the buck. It's the secret of life. You can't fight every battle and dry every tear. Whenever you're dealing with something that you don't really care about, pass the buck.
Robertson Davies, *Tempest-Tost,* 1951

JEALOUSY

Jealous men are the greatest bores in the world.
Morley Callaghan, *Rigmarole,* 1935

A person feels more critical of a visitor, especially when he's had advantages.
Sara Jeannette Duncan, *The Imperialist,* 1904

Jealousy . . . has always been the explorer's sin.
Hugh MacLennan,
The People Behind This Peculiar Nation

If all my wounds had tongues, they would proclaim
A cursed thing is jealousy.
Samuel James Watson, *Ravlan,* 1876

A jealous woman is a dangerous thing.
Frances Shelley Wees,
M'Lord I Am Not Guilty, 1954

JEWS

If this be a Jew, — where is the crook of his spine?
and the quiver of lip, where?
A.M. Klein, *Greeting On This Day,* 1940

In their songs, Jews like to laugh and cry at the same time.
Miriam Waddington, *The Cloudless Day,* 1967

Who wants a Jew? This is our life, to hammer on doors.
Adele Wiseman, *The Sacrifice,* 1956

JOKES

There are things of deadly earnest that can only be safely mentioned under cover of a joke.
J.J. Procter,
The Philosopher in the Clearing, 1897

JOURNALIST

We are among the last people who are not completely, utterly and damnably respectable.
Robertson Davies, *Leaven of Malice*, 1954

A journalist is not something which just happens. Like poets, they are born. They are marked by a kind of altruistic nosiness.
Robertson Davies, *Leaven of Malice*, 1954

The journalist everywhere is perhaps more accessible to ideas, more susceptible to enthusiasm, than his fellows.
Sara Jeannette Duncan, *The Imperialist*, 1904

JOY

Be merry — many a priest has lied
To comfort all the groaning throngs.
Nathaniel A. Benson,
Ballade of Little Comfort, 1937

Joy is the only thing in the world more inevitable, more universal than sorrow.
Bliss Carman, *The Friendship of Art*, 1904

Joy, mere gladness in living, is the tiny increment which keeps life dominant and sane.
Bliss Carman, *The Friendship of Art*, 1904

What matter if the sun be lost?
What matter though the sky be grey?
There's joy enough about the house,
For Daffodil comes home to-day.
Bliss Carman, *Daffodil's Return*

For neither thoughts nor words can quite preserve
The blood of joy.
Fred Cogswell, *A Letter*, 1966

I predict many, many very happy days for you. You have that beautiful gift of bringing your joy with you.
Ralph Connor, *The Major*, 1917

Joy's an immortal;
She hath a fiery fibre in her flesh
That will not droop or die.
Isabella Valancy Crawford, *in Collected Poems*

Time will transform him,
Make him a man,
But today he is still
The Happy Troll.
D.G. Jones, *North*, 1963

Scattering beauty
And innocent mirth,
Perhaps 'tis a duty
To gladden the earth.
Mary A. Knight, *Lady Light-Heart*, 1934

Some must make merry, or the world would be
Sodden with tears.
Robert Norwood, *The Man of Kerioth*, 1919

Joy and beauty are but hidden souls
Revealed to him who looks on life and laughs.
Robert Norwood, *The Witch of Endor*, 1916

The brightest thought that fills the mind,
The deepest joy that fills the heart,
Is oft the swiftest to depart
And leaves an aching void behind.
J.E. Pollock, *In Memoriam*, 1883

If ever you are sore at heart, I hope someone may bring you such joy as you have given me.
Laura Goodman Salverson, *The Viking Heart*

JUDGMENT

In judging others, folks work overtime for no pay.
Charles Edwin Carruthers,
God-Forsaken, 1930

Who are you, to cast our sins of omission in our teeth, and to stand in judgment upon us?
Robertson Davies, *At My Heart's Core*, 1950

Human judgment being what it is, first thoughts are all too usually fallible.
Alan Gowans, *Architecture in New France*, 1960

Everyone has their cross to bear, and we can't always understand, so it behooves us not to judge others.
Raymond Knister, *White Narcissus*, 1929

Let him who is guiltless among you —
Let him cast a judgment stone!
Ada M. Strachan, *The Released Prisoner*, 1942

JUSTICE

If you look for justice, man, you will not be finding it in this world.
Margaret Laurence, *The Pure Diamond Man*, 1963

Justice is a human, no longer a divine, gift.
Jack Ludwig,
Fiction for the Majors, 1960

Justice in a new country is administered with promptitude and vigour, or else not administered at all.
Gilbert Parker, *Pierre and His People*

KILLING

It is only man who kills wantonly. The beasts that live by killing kill only as hunger bids.
Bliss Carman, *The Kinship of Nature*, 1904

It is murder of the codes to snap the thread of a man's life.
A.M. Klein,
"Upon First Seeing the Ceiling of the Sistine Chapel", 1951

The gods may snip the thread of life at will, perhaps. But if physicians should take up the shears, where would it all end?
Wilder Penfield, *The Torch*, 1961

To kill game birds for food is a justifiable use of the fruits of the earth. But the wanton extermination of a whole species is an expression of human ugliness, a perverse preliminary to man's own suicide.
John Stevens,
Introduction to:
"Last of the Curlews", 1963

Who has to take a life stands alone on the edge of creation.
Adele Wiseman, *The Sacrifice*, 1956

KINDNESS

When people start out to be kind, they don't realize how far they have to go.
Mary Wallace Brooks, *Voices*, 1926

How could I know, engulfed in silent grieving,
That you were waiting for that one kind word;
The understanding look, the kindly greeting
That when withheld would prove a two-edged sword?
Lois H. Gilpin, *Unthinking*, 1938

Even a stone takes on a pulse in a warm hold.
Dorothy Livesay, *Parenthood*, 1969

Tenderness
Was here, in this very room, in this Place, its form seen, cries heard, by you.
Malcolm Lowry, *Delirium in Vera Cruz*

The love of sweetness is an uneducated love.
John Metcalf, *Keys and Watercress*, 1967

Though it's said that time has wings;
There is always time to find
Ways of being sweet and kind.
R.C. Smith, *Lots of Time*, 1960

The young, the old, the deaf, the dumb, the blind, can read this universal language; its very silence is often more eloquent than words.
Catherine Parr Traill, *Canadian Crusoes*, 1850

The kindest words that are spoken,
Of courage, love, and cheer,
Come from the heart that keeps buried
Loneliness, pain, and fear.
Betty Warren, *Recompense*, 1961

KISS

If you will never do worse than kiss a laddie in a game, it's little harm will be coming to you.
Ralph Connor,
The Man from Glengarry, 1901

The first kiss is important because it is the idea of taking from each other.
George Elliot, *The Commonplace*, 1962

True love's kisses, close and warm,
Melt the ice and break the charm.
Norah Mary Holland,
The Awakening of the Lily, 1924

But a kiss is the bond of earthly love —
Yet it links us close with the throne above.
Rhoda Sivell, *Only a Kiss*, 1911

KNOWLEDGE

There was no tree of knowledge to equal that one in her will to know.
Robert Kroetsch, *The Studhorse Man*, 1970

Knowledge is power, whether it be the knowledge of evil or of good.
Susanna Moodie, *Geoffrey Moncton*, 1855

If you know nothing
be pleased to know nothing.
John Newlove, *Otter's Creek*, 1967

He knows the world,
Who knows the human body.
Leila Pepper, *Knowledge,* 1956

Knowledge can wall one in against chasms of ignorance.
John Reid, *Journey Out of Anguish,* 1969

The more we know the less we have to pray for.
Lister Sinclair, *Return to Colonus,* 1955

Knowledge is uncertainty;
Faith alone is error-free.
Lister Sinclair, *Return to Colonus,* 1955

LABOUR

In a great and populous country the division of labour is the source of its wealth.
Samuel Strickland,
Twenty-Seven Years in Canada West, 1853

LADY

A lady will be a lady, even in the plainest dress; a vulgar minded woman will never be a lady, in the most costly garments.
Catherine Parr Traill,
The Canadian Settler's Guide, 1855

LAND

The land which summer yielded to the plow
Lies alien and naked in the winter light.
D.G. Jones,
Soliloquy to Absent Friends, 1959

Land is in the blood of all French-Canadians.
Hugh MacLennan, *Two Solitudes,* 1945

A man without land is nobody.
Mordecai Richler,
"The Apprenticeship of Duddy Kravitz", 1959

LANGUAGE

Swearing's the only vice that gives me pleasure.
Charles Edwin Carruthers,
God-Forsaken, 1930

A tendency to regard people who speak other languages as either peculiar or slightly subhuman is an abiding and disastrous characteristic of the English-speaking peoples.
Gwethalyn Graham, *Dear Ennemy,* 1963

To speak a second language is a lesson in humility, and there is no reason why that lesson should be confined to French Canadians.
Gwethalyn Graham, *Dear Ennemy,* 1963

It is the angry, working-class language of the recent social plays that has shattered the complacency of the English theatre.
Norman Levine, *A Letter from England*

If one knows his neighbours tongue, he possesses the key to his house.
Arthur Maheux, *What Keeps Us Apart?,* 1944

The infinitive is the language of quotations and generalisations.
Lister S. Sinclair, *A Play on Words,* 1944

I have nothing. Nothing but coarse language
to put a hoarse world off.
Wayne Stedingh, *The Prostitute,* 1970

It is through language that the common man recognizes the stature of the hero.
Michael Tait,
Playwrights in a Vacuum, 1963

Language records a person's attempt to say what he means and what he 'sees'.
George Whalley, *a Criticism,* 1958

LAUGHTER

This weary world is a debtor to the man who has learned to laugh at shadows.
Jean Blewett

With all my singing I can never sing
A gay, glad song — an honest song of mirth.
George Frederick Cameron

When a man laughs he's nearer to letting his money go.
Ralph Connor, *The Prospector,* 1904

Laughter wears a lilied gown —
She is but a simple thing;
Laughter's eyes are water-brown,
Ever glancing up and down
Like a woodbird's restless wing.
Isabella Valency Crawford, *Laughter*

Let us have children's hearts, my friends
And pack our woes to Spain:
So that the day begins and ends
In laughter once again!
Norman Gregor Guthrie, *Joy,* 1928

With age, laughter sinks deeper
Into the heart than youth permits.
Doris Hedges, *Tempo,* 1967

Laugh, if you will, at my gay strut
And run from me on your busy feet.
David Helwig, *Harlequin to Columbine*

A good laugh is as good as a prayer
sometimes.
L.M. Montgomery, *Rilla of Ingleside,* 1921

Where laughter dies there is no holiness.
Robert Norwood, *The Man of Kerioth,* 1919

LAW

Medicine and the law are priesthoods,
against which no whisper must be heard.
Robertson Davies, *Leaven of Malice,* 1954

Never go to law for simple vengeance;
that's not what law is for. Redress, yes;
vengeance, no.
Robertson Davies, *Leaven of Malice,* 1954

Law makes long spokes of the short stakes
of men.
William Empson, *Legal Fiction*

Legislation is never needed to guide the
man with vision. But it should protect that
vast majority which is without it.
Frederick P. Grove, *A Search for America,*
1927

Nowhere on earth was a bad lawyer
spotted more quickly than in Quebec.
Hugh MacLennan, *Two Solitudes,* 1945

Of necessity, the law is somewhat vague.
Hugh MacLennan,
The Defence of Lady Chatterley, 1960

Laws in order to be true only required
followers.
Mordecai Richler, *Son of a Smaller Hero,*
1955

LAZINESS

Sloth and superstition equally counter-
work providence, and render the bounty of
heaven of no effect.
Frances Brooke,
The History of Emily Montague, 1769

Let me taste the old immortal
Indolence of life once more.
Bliss Carman, *Spring Song*

When the troubles of life arise out of
idleness, a return to industry is usually the
last shift.
Thomas McCulloch, *The Stepsure Letters,*
1821

LEADER

Who takes the salute has to tire his arches
same as the troops.
R.G. Everson, *Got the Sack,* 1963

He was a leader, and perhaps he knew
what women may do to the hearts of those
who must lead other men.
Farley Mowat, *The Riddle of the Viking Bow*

The dizzy earth is run
By three inebriated witches — Stay!
E.J. Pratt
Puck Reports Back, 1937

LEADERSHIP

Sure, you've no cause to fear when the
pilot knows the way.
Norman Duncan, *Doctor Luke of the Labrador*

Choose the quiet path, and clear it from the
fallen logs, then others will bless you.
S. Frances Harrison (Seranus)
The Forest of Bourg-Marie

LEARNING

For me at least, the craftiness of learning
Has turned upon itself — and I am I!
Sarah Binks, *A Poem*

Learning has become mainly a knowledge
of what others have thought and done,
rather than reading new pages from the
book of nature for ourselves.
E.H. Dewart, *Essays for the Times,* 1898

The great secret of life is to hear lessons,
and not to teach them.
T.C. Haliburton, *Sam Slick,* 1853

We learn our hardest lessons from
unlikeliest masters.
A.C. Laut, *Heralds of Empire*

His chief weakness was his incapacity for
learning anything new and his resentment
of those who did.
Hugh MacLennan, *Each Man's Son,* 1951

A man who is his own teacher is not complete. There must be implanted early the

habits and discipline of learning. Even to think correctly must be taught.
John Marlyn, *Under the Ribs of Death,* 1957

Is it not strange that erudition breeds Truth's springing flowers and falsehood's baneful weeds?
J.R. Newell, *The Times,* 1877

Wisdom learned, but never put to use. Why do we learn only when it's too late to profit us?
Edwin R. Procunier, *A Knife to Thy Throat,* 1962

Want of learning is a great misfortune. Now thankful should we be that we have schools.
Robert Rogers, *Ponteach,* 1766

LEGEND

When legends die,
Men may begin to create again; when institutions
Crumble, much spirit is set free.
C.J. Newman,
On the Death of an Institution, 1967

The story has been told so often that it is now almost in the realm of legend. Legend has been recited as fact for so long that the truth lies buried fathoms deep.
Orlo Miller,
the Foreward to:
"The Donnellys Must Die"

CANADIAN LEGION

In this stale Valhalla
One re-lives the battle of the bottles,
And the wound he caught in action
With a harlot at Versailles.
John Ower, *Edmonton Legion,* 1967

LIBERTY

Eternal vigilance, even against your own servants, is still the price of liberty.
Maxwell Vos, *The Un-Broken Butterfly,* 1962

LIBRARIES

Libraries are to this age, perhaps, what churches and cathedrals were to the Middle Ages.
Bernard K. Sandwell, *The Bibliothecary*

LIE

I do not know if the world has lied
I have lied
I do not know if the world has conspired against love
I have conspired against love.
Leonard Cohen, *Flowers for Hitler*

If you repeat something often enough, someone will believe you.
Margaret Laurence,
The Merchant of Heaven, 1959

Lying may be excusable in a man, but 'tis a terrible bad habit in a boy.
Susanna Moodie, *Roughing It in the Bush,* 1852

I am in that state of mind where even a lie is a comfort, providing it is a cheerful lie.
L.M. Montgomery, *Rilla of Ingleside,* 1921

LIFE

It seems as if I've slept through
Winters and autumns and summers
And now that I'm readmitting myself
There's something of springtime in my head.
Brian Bartlett, *Explanation,* 1970

Ashes! Ashes! Those are all that life leaves us of our hopes and dreams.
Nathaniel A. Benson, *The Paths of Glory,* 1927

Life isn't worth the lovely songs
The lying poets sing about it.
Nathaniel A. Benson,
Ballade of Little Comfort, 1937

Life is itself simple, but the living of life is an infinitely complex experience.
John W. Bilsland, *Vision of Clarity,* 1960

Give us what creed we have for our daily crimes,
for this road that arrives at no future,
for this guilt
in the griefs of the old and the graves of the young.
Earle Birney, *The Road to Nijmegen,* 1945

Never remove anything from a person's life that you cannot replace.
Janet Bonellie,
Why Are The People Staring?, 1967

Another sentence of this dismal story
Comes to a rueful stop. Such paragraphs
And periods illustrate the page
Of this dull book of life.
Thomas Bush, *Santiago*, 1866

My spring is over, all my summer past:
The autumn closes, — winter now
appears.
George Frederick Cameron,
My Spring Is Over, 1885

All life hath been but shaping up to this.
William Wilfred Campbell, *Mordred*, 1895

It is better to live for a purpose than to die
for it, —
Bliss Carman, *The Kinship of Nature*, 1904

Between fancy and fact lies the dilemma
we call life. On the one hand, things as
they are; on the other, things as we would
have them be.
Bliss Carman, *The Kinship of Nature*, 1904

The bare problem of life is so difficult, the
fine art of living so well-nigh impossible,
that surely no man yet can ever have
looked at it with realization without a
sudden terror at heart.
Bliss Carman, *The Friendship of Art*, 1904

Once life was wine to him,
That now is bread.
Sara E. Carsley,
Portrait of a Very Old Man, 1939

Relief — with always someone hungry till
the soul
As well as the body grew shrivelled and
hopeless.
Henriette Clarke, *Soot*

Life is meant to be enjoyed, and whatever
tends to enlarge our children's perspec-
tive, which will give them a love for the
beautiful, will lessen the drudgery of life,
and develop their characters.
H.A. Cody, *The Fourth Watch*, 1911

The years that bring us many ills, and that
pass so stormfully over us, bear away with
them the ugliness, the weariness, the pain
that are theirs, but the beauty, the
sweetness, the rest, they leave untouched,
for these are eternal.
Ralph Connor, *Black Rock*, 1897

His outlook on life is slightly twisted, due to
some unfortunate incident in his childhood
which has left its scar deeply engraved on
his subconscious mind. The poor boy actually believes that life is meant to be enjoyed.
J.K. Conway, *My Ambition*, 1956

Nothing is written right of the granite
hyphens
after the names and birthdates of my
parents.
We always lived by making up as we went
along.
Gregory M. Cook, *Chebogue Cemetery*, 1970

She's got a rotten figure, — Life.
Britton Cooke,
The Translation of John Snaith

What's the good of winning honours and
the good opinion of the world if you can't
live on good terms with yourself?
Robertson Davies, *Leaven of Malice*, 1954

Everybody is trapped, more or less. The
best thing you can hope for is to
understand your trap and make terms with
it, tooth by tooth.
Robertson Davies, *Leaven of Malice*, 1954

Twaddle as we may about free will, some
of us are bound to live in a context of farce,
some in comedy, some in proletarian
realism, some in melodrama, and a few
unhappy wretches — in tragedy.
Robertson Davies, *A Voice from the Attic*,
1960

This world is only a part of life. We may
lose it and yet live on.
James De Mille, *A Strange Manuscript*, 1888

The love of life must necessarily be the
strongest passion of man. We are so made.
We give up everything for life.
James De Mille, *A Strange Manuscript*, 1888

A long life is everywhere considered as the
highest blessing; (and there is no one who
is willing to die no matter what his suffering may be.)
James De Mille, *A Strange Manuscript*, 1888

Forms of life and truth must vary with the
spirit of the years.
E.H. Dewart, *Then and Now*, 1888

Life has more day than night,
More genial summer calms than wintry
storms.
E.H. Dewart, *Lines to a Pessimist*, 1898

The passing sequence of a drama strange,
Where birth and death vie for supremacy.
Elizabeth Donaldson,
The Progress of Time, 1938

Our mortal life is full of sin, it is also full of
the misconception of virtue.
Sara Jeannette Duncan, *The Imperialist*, 1904

Life is a business — we have to work at
ourselves till it is over. So much cut off and
ended it is . . . If space is the area of life and
time is its opportunity, there goes a
measure of opportunity.
Sara Jeannette Duncan, *The Imperialist*, 1904

How many worlds one lives in as the day
goes by with the different people one cares
for — one beyond the other, concentric,
ringing from the heart!
Sara Jeannette Duncan, *The Imperialist*, 1904

Shall I build a tower, knowing it will rend
Crack upon the hour, boys, waiting for the
end?
Shall I pluck a flower, boys, shall I save or
spend?
All turns sour, boys, waiting for the end.
William Empson, *Just a Smack at Auden*

Yes, there's eternity — in which to do
nothing; and years, in which to do
everything.
Cicely Louise Evans, *Antic Disposition*, 1935

We whirl with the dust of our minds newly
forming
among quasars at the speed of light.
Ronald Everson, *The Dark is Not so Dark*,
1969

Although I cannot love the universe,
unfeeling, or rouse it to love, I rise above
my human failure.
R.G. Everson, *Herd of Cattle*, 1963

Delighted at being alive,
I hurry among the generations. I feel sure
I'll make it as far as the other end.
R.G. Everson, *Dominion Square*, 1963

Life is a pulse, life is a breath,
Pulse and breath to be one day ended.
John M. Ewing, *Life and Death*, 1940

This is the place to see clearly, . . . To relish
life — and perceive its unimportance.
D.K. Findlay, *Heroine of an Anecdote*, 1936

If there were only some meaning to all this
pain and longing — one moment when
love spreads its dazzling wings.
D.K. Findlay, *Heroine of an Anecdote*, 1936

Life's every path its secrets will display
To him who has the eyes of Youth retained!
Donald A. Fraser, *The Old Road*, 1933

We must live our lives, simple lives, we are
born, we have children, we work the fields,
we die.
Raymond Fraser, *Legacy*, 1970

Soon I will be old and die, and my children
will live as I have lived, and know what I
have known, and wonder as I wondered.
Raymond Fraser, *Legacy*, 1970

Aye, it is true, when one doth think
thereon,
That life is but a dream, a cloud, a mist,
That passeth fleetly o'er the scythe of time!
John Hutchinson Garnier, *Prince Pedro*, 1877

Life is ever,
Since man was born,
Licking honey
From a thorn.
Louis Ginsberg, *Age-Old Wisdom*

Life of worry! To know when to be
generous and when to refuse!
M. Allerdale Grainger,
Woodsmen of the West, 1908

The highest we can aspire to in this life is
that we feel we leave a gap behind in the
lives of others when we go.
Frederick P. Grove, *Settlers of the Marsh*, 1925

These people here, when they get
anywhere, are rich at best. Their life has
slipped by; they have never lived.
Especially the women.
Frederick P. Grove, *Settlers of the Marsh*, 1925

What was life anyway? A dumb shifting of
forces. Grass grew and was trodden down;
and it knew not why.
Frederick P. Grove, *Settlers of the Marsh*, 1925

Life was useless; there was no meaning in
it . . . no justification.
Frederick P. Grove, *Settlers of the Marsh*, 1925

When the dust's last death-dance is done
What matters what we may have been?
Norman Gregor Guthrie,
A Rowan Tree in October, 1928

But life will find your fortress, call you out
Upon the hills, your reticence forgiving,
And write upon your face, your hands, your heart,
The agony and ecstasy of living.
Verna Loveday Harden, *To a Young Girl*, 1938

Life is a lonely journey if we take
Only our bodies on the road,
And leave our hearts behind.
Doris Hedges, *Ivory Towers*, 1961

Sometimes I've wondered if perhaps 'twere best
Not to have lived, and craved an empty board.
Anna M. Henderson, *Sonnet*, 1939

Life has given me of its best —
Laughter and weeping, labour and rest,
Little of gold, but lots of fun;
Shall I then sigh that all is done?
Norah Holland, *Life*, 1924

(Unlike the Greek girl, six months spent in hell,
Six on earth) I at one time both span.
Alison Hopwood, *Persephone*, 1952

Awake, life is too definite — I wish that I had died.
Annie Campbell Huestis,
"A Shadow, A Thrush, A Flying Wind", 1934

I know
That life is earnest, time is tough,
But me, I'm not.
George Johnston, *The Bargain Sale*, 1962

Life as it confronts the raw consciousness is a chaos of facts and events of nonsense and injustice and bad luck.
Carlyle King,
"Joyce Cary and the Creative Imagination", 1959

The only thing I have done is keep alive. Perhaps in our time that is something to be proud of. But it isn't much.
Henry Kreisel, *The Betrayal*, 1964

Life has no time for nightmares in its endless quest to reproduce itself.
Henry Kreisel, *The Betrayal*, 1964

Brief the span is, counting the years of mortals,
Strange and sad; it passes, and then the bright earth,

Careless mother, gleaming with gold and azure,
Lovely with blossoms.
Archibald Lampman, *Sapphics*

What am I, then, and what are they that pass
Yonder, and love and laugh, and mourn and weep?
Archibald Lampman, *The Largest Life*

What's life worth if you ain't livin' big!
Victor Lauriston, *Chinook Trail*, 1936

You can sing about life or you can try to understand it. You can't do both.
Irving Layton,
Some Observations and Aphorisms, 1968

Give me back . . . the old life of danger and stress, with its hard toil and its bitter chances, and its heartbreaks. I see its value! I know its worth! Give me no rest.
Stephen Leacock, *Nonsense Novels*, 1911

The mingled heritage of tears and laughter . . . is our lot on earth.
Stephen Leacock, *Further Foolishness*, 1916

Life is at most the lover's hard-kept fir,
A wasting candle lifted to a spire.
August Roberts Leisner,
He Points to Mortality, 1940

If death can fly, just for the love of flying,
What might not life do, for the love of dying?
Malcolm Lowry, *For the Love of Dying*

To live one's life all in one class of society, how dull, how chained by convention!
Suzanne Marny, *The Lonely Student*, 1909

The striking thing about "modern living" is not the degree of change but the rate of change.
Vincent Massey, *a speech*, 1965

Let us joy while we may,
Death comes swiftly our way;
Let our brief hours be gay
Before death comes our way.
Sister Maure, *Via Vitae*, 1923

We live by rhythm on this swinging sphere
Of earth and sea and air. Only death
Can quell the joyous rhythm of the heart,
The flying breath.
Sister Maure, *Breath of the Spirit*, 1934

So that is all my tale. I lived, I live
And shall live on, no doubt.
Isabel Ecclestone MacKay,
Margurite de Roberval

Life's much the same everywhere . . .
Water in a cup is not very different from
water in a river.
Isabel Ecclestone MacKay, *The Second Lie*

Life is labour and not dreaming, and I have
my work to do,
Ere within those happy valleys I shall wear
the lilies too.
Kate Seymour Maclean, *Beyond,* 1881

I live — in a conscious dream within time.
Let me imagine that I have come
To the moment of my awakening.
Ian Malcolm, *A Moment of Existence*

As for man his days are as grass; as a
flower of the field so he flourisheth — for it
is soon cut off and we fly away — fly away
where? — where?
Nellie L. McClung,
Sowing Seeds in Danny, 1911

We live in a rickety house
In a dirty dismal street
Where the naked hide from day
and thieves and drunkards meet.
Alexander McLachlan

My life, like the rusting
hulks of abandoned cars
in quarry depths
lies secret
Eugene McNamara,
Living in the Present, 1970

Life makes it own laws and finds its own
justification.
Edward Meade, *Remember Me,* 1946

It is never quite safe to think we have done
with life. When we imagine we have
finished our story, fate has a trick of turn-
ing the page and showing us yet another
chapter.
L.M. Montgomery, *Rainbow Valley,* 1919

Life is rich and full here . . . . everywhere . . .
if we can only learn how to open our hearts
to its richness and fullness.
L.M. Montgomery, *Anne of Avonlea*

This life is a cross we have to bear in order
to store up merit in the next.
Brian Moore, *Judith Hearne,* 1955

Life was the victor, wasn't it?
Going on was the victory.
Brian Moore, *The Luck of Ginger Coffey*

Life is a comb of honey to the taste —
If it be bitter, then the tongue is coated
With gall of anger or the love of self.
Robert Norwood, *The Man of Kerioth,* 1919

Human beings are born with the
instinctive realization that life is good.
Alden A. Nowlan, *A Defense of Obscenity,*
1959

There are but three things in the world
worth doing — loving, roaming and
fighting.
Gilbert Parker, *The Trail of the Sword,* 1894

The world is mad, and all life is a fever.
Gilbert Parker, *The Seats of the Mighty,* 1896

Life is not so incomparable a thing that I
can not give it up without a pother.
Gilbert Parker, *The Seats of the Mighty,* 1896

Merely to walk erect
Denies the miracle of life.
M. Eugenie Perry, *Divine Hunger,* 1953

Oh, what a dream is all this life!
Oh, what an evanescent tide
Enfolds our lives on every side,
With joys and woes alternate rife!
J.E. Pollock, *In Memoriam,* 1883

The plan on which this life is built
Is somewhat like a patchwork quilt.
E.J. Pratt, *The Anomaly,* 1938

Though hate and greed have grown to their
harvest,
Though tolerance, forgiveness and love
are forgotten
Like scars on the body of Christ —
Too soon in the morning for youth
To take the deep draught of your opiate!
E.J. Pratt, *The Impatient Earth,* 1943

Grave and gay, laughter and tears are
inextricably mingled together in this life;
the sweetest waltzes are those that have
an under-harmony of sadness running
through them.
J.J. Procter,
The Philosopher in the Clearing, 1897

And what is life but a long pause between
two unanswerable questions?
Edwin R. Procunier, *Voices of Desire*

Everyone gets gypped sooner or later
by death or disease or what's inside them
because the world is that sort of place.
Alfred Purdy,
Mr. Greenhalgh's Love Poem, 1965

We encounter the entire race of men just
by being alive here.
Alfred Purdy, *Archaeology of Snow,* 1963

Someday, for us, the Wind will stop
And, like kites, we'll listless drop.
James Reaney, *The Two Kites,* 1949

Life takes away and asks us to accept,
Giving all, and for all, in its taking.
Margaret Rempel, *Life*

Drink of the cup of the love that is life;
Drink of the cup that has no bitter strain;
Drink — on the brink — to a life beyond
strife;
Drink! Bid your friends drink — to love's
dear domain!
Helen T.D. Robinson, *Drink,* 1938

Such is the state of men and human
beings;
We weep, we smile, we mourn, and laugh
thro' life,
Here falls a blessing, there alights a curse,
As the good genius or the evil reigns.
Robert Rogers, *Ponteach,* 1766

I was saved for a taste of life — but it came
too late.
George Ryga, *Hungry Hills,* 1970

We cannot live life o'er again
No matter how we try,
So let's make our life worth living
Before it's time to die!
Lily G. Sather, *A Day at a Time,* 1960

Blind fools of fate and slaves of
circumstance,
Life is a fiddler, and we all must dance.
Robert Service, *Quatrains,* 1907

Fight! That's right, I must struggle.
I know that to rest means death!
Robert Service, *Lost,* 1907

It's a mighty good world, so it is, dear lass,
When even the worst is said.
There's a smile and a tear, a sigh and a
cheer,
But better be living than dead!
Robert Service, *Cheer,* 1912

Life is a dream, its wakening,
Death, gentle shadow of God's wing.
Robert Service, *Death in the Arctic,* 1912

That night is speeding on to greet
Your epitaphic rhyme.
Your life is but a little beat
Within the heart of Time.
Robert Service, *Just Think,* 1912

Alas! the road to Anywhere is pitfalled
with disaster;
There's hunger, want, and weariness, yet
O we loved it so.
Robert Service, *The Tramps,* 1907

The picture of life has changed and we
must build for it a new frame; it will not fit
into the old one.
Lister S. Sinclair, *You Can't Stop Now,* 1945

All men are like me really.
All women, too. We play our parts
Upon a stage of flesh.
We have our exits and our entrances
And such is the creation of a man.
Lister Sinclair, *Return to Colonus,* 1955

With every breath, knowing and
unknowing,
I pile high the fire of life.
Diana Skala, *Postscript,* 1951

It's the same way all through this life of
ours. We go and come like autumn leaves
before the blast; here to-day, to-morrow
whither?
Harry James Smith,
Mrs. Bumpstead-Leigh, 1917

But when my flower and I have lived an
hour,
I'll bear it on the wind away to God.
A.E.S. Smythe, *The Forgotten Poet*

Kill or be killed,
that's the law of nature, and the law
of the lawless of the world, with their
inter-continental
missiles, their bombers, their bombs, all
trigger-happy
to prove it.
Raymond Souster

I was alive once, but am now no more
Than a dream that is full of words.
F.E. Sparshott, *Estrangement,* 1958

94

I am not a woman as other women are. I defy traditions; I defy conventions. I claim the right God gave me to live my life as I will, where I will, how I will, with whom I will.
Robert J.C. Stead, *The Bail Jumper*, 1963

All life's empty, when you stop to think about it.
Arthur Stringer,
The Angle of Adventure, 1939

Our life is like that clod deep in the mine;
Through sin and doubt it holds a living gem:
Great Lapidary take, I pray Thee, mine
And shape it fit to grace Thy Diadem.
Ada M. Taylor, *The Jewel*, 1934

If you're on the merry-go-round, you have to go round.
Kent Thompson, *The Death of Comedy*, 1969

Life holds us like the moon and the sea
Far, far apart;
The image of the moon shines in the sea,
Yours in my heart.
Laura Thompson, *Adoration*, 1941

Live and burn
said the Catholic to the Catholic
Live and learn,
said the cynic to the cynic.
Lionel Tiger, *To F.R. Scott*, 1959

Thus is it often in this life: we wander on, sad and perplexed, our path beset with thorns and briars. We cannot see our way clear; doubts and apprehensions assail us.
Catherine Parr Traill, *Canadian Crusoes*, 1850

Sloppy, raggedy-assed old life. I love it. I never want to die.
Dennis Trudell, *View*, 1969

Life does bad things to people.
Frances Shelley Wees,
M'Lord, I Am Not Guilty, 1954

Life, like a wood-path, is a wavering, Love-haunted, changeful, beauty-shadowed thing.
Ethelwyn Wetherald, *A Wish*, 1940

The important thing is not really the life of the senses, but the imprinting of ourselves on the evanescence of existence.
George Woodcock, *The Song of the Sirens*, 1969

I gave to receive, received to give,
Learned at the last instant of life:
It is impossible to live.
J. Michael Yates, *The Cavern*, 1969

LIGHT

Light is like the waving of long grass.
A.J.M. Smith, *Field of Long Grass*

LIMITATIONS

My knowledge of my limitations is one of my chief defects as an artist.
Robertson Davies, *A Masque of Mr. Punch*, 1962

One of the greatest dangers to happiness is in the refusal to accept genially the limitations which society has set to the undue expansion of the individual.
Archibald Lampman, *Happiness*, 1896

They can be among the most valuable cargo one has, those limitations!
Malcolm Lowry, *(in a letter)*, 1951

Those who possess but little are wise to reserve a small portion of what they have.
Susanna Moodie, *Geoffrey Moncton*, 1855

LITERATURE

It is not always in the great master that you read most clearly the character of the time
James Cappon, *Studies in Canadian Poetry*

Literature is, . . . only a glorified form of speech, produced with greater care and skill and forethought.
Bliss Carman, *The Friendship of Art*, 1904

Popular literature demands clear-cut figures, stock issues, and lots of action.
John Robert Colombo,
"Sax Rohner and His Yellow Shadows", 1960

A national literature is an essential element in the formation of national character.
Edward Hartley Dewart,
the Introduction to:
"Selections from Canadian Poets", 1864

The literature of the world is the footprints of human progress.
E.H. Dewart,
the Introduction to:
"Selections from Canadian Poets", 1864

(Sometimes I think life is much too serious for fooling around with mere literature.)
Louis Dudek, *Canada: Interim Report,* 1963

Literature is life or it is not genuine literature.
Donald G. French,
the Foreward to:
"Standard Canadian Reciter", 1918

In literature, it isn't what you say but how it's said that's important.
Northrop Frye, *The Educated Imagination*

Literature is really a refuge or escape from life, a self-contained world . . . a world of play or make-believe. . . .
Northrop Frye, *The Educated Imagination*

Literature must be savoured, not gulped.
Paul Hiebert, *Sarah Binks,* 1947

To study literature is to experience Life at respectable second-hand.
W.J. Keith, *To Study Literature,* 1964

Literature is a product of the imagination.
Frank Home Kirkpatrick,
"Hints for the Vocal Interpretation of Literature", 1921

At present our people are too busy to read, too busy at least to read with discernment, and where there are no discerning readers there will be no writers.
Archibald Lampman, *Two Canadian Poets,* 1891

The theory of literature is primarily concerned with detaching literature from experimental and practical uses of language.
Eli Mandel, *The Language of Humanity,* 1963

Literature, as we know today, is a relatively conservative time-binding medium compared with press, radio, and movies.
Marshall McLuhan,
Culture Without Literacy, 1953

Take the feminine element out of literature, remove the sopranos from our graves, and how dull and flat would be the grand, sweet song of life!
Thomas O'Hagan, *Canadian Essays,* 1901

The early literature of any country will tend to be somewhat naive in expression but interesting to later generations on historical grounds.
Desmond Pacey,
the Preface to:
"Book of Canadian Stories", 1949

Literature is to the nation what memory coupled with intelligence is to the person.
Desmond Pacey,
the Introduction to:
"Book of Canadian Stories", 1962

Great literatures have grown out of the national consciousness of people and have developed around national ideals.
Lorne Albert Pierce,
the Introduction to:
"Our Canadian Literature"

To study the literature of an epoch means to study the spirit of the man of that epoch.
Giose Rimanelli,
the Introduction to:
"Modern Canadian Stories", 1966

Literature is not a mere word, but the individual expression of man's spirit.
Giose Rimanelli,
the Introduction to:
"Modern Canadian Stories", 1966

All genuinely memorable literary experience is, in some measure, an initiation into the previously unknown.
Robert Rosenheim,
Children's Reading and Adult's Values, 1970

Modern literature is full of regressive images, becoming a literature that constantly calls attention to itself.
Peter Stephens,
The Writing of the Decade, 1969

One can learn more about people and society from creative literature than from scientific reports.
Ronald Sutherland, *The Fourth Separatism,* 1971

Contemporary literature has become a dog wagged by the tail of scholarship.
Kent Thompson, *Editorial,* 1970

Literary sex, unlike literary love, is a poor substitute for the real thing.
Miriam Waddington, *The Cloudless Day,* 1967

In the growing universities the study of literature is tending to be increasingly the

bestowal of plasma-units and adoption of pedantic jargon.
Paul West, *Canadian Attitudes,* 1963

Literatures are defined as much by their lacks as by their abundances.
George Woodcock, *An Absence of Utopias,* 1969

Pure literature — that sterile ideal — can never in fact be achieved.
George Woodcock,
The Frontiers of Literature, 1970

CANADIAN LITERATURE

Literature for Canadian readers is all that has been written in English or French.
anon, *Point of View,* 1959

Preoccupation with Canadian literature as a thing-in-itself is the merest narcissism.
anon, *Point of View,* 1959

Canadian literature, ever the stepchild of British and American critics.
Nathaniel A. Benson,
"Famous Poems of the First Great War", 1939

The Canadian literateur must depend solely upon himself and nature. He is almost without the exhilaration of lively and frequent literary intercourse.
W.E. Collin, *Natural Landscape*

Though politically we have achieved nationhood, emotionally we are still colonials — the sooner we outgrow this childish attitude, the sooner will our literature come of age.
Mary Elizabeth Colman,
A Poet Speaks to the Critics, 1938

The Canadian scene more often appears a scene of nature rather than of humanity.
Alan Creighton,
the Foreword to:
"A New Canadian Anthology", 1938

Our French fellow-countrymen are much more firmly united than the English colonists; though their literature is more French than Canadian, and their bond of union is more religious than literary or political.
E.H. Dewart,
the Introduction to:
"Selections from Canadian Poets", 1864

The first qualification of the student of Canadian literature is a thick skin. He must be incapable of being bored.
Kildaire Dobbs, *Miss Crotchett's Muse* 1958

The invention of Canadian letters, as a distinct subject for academic study, has been a blessing only to those scholars who are paid to investigate it.
Kildaire Dobbs, *Miss Crotchett's Muse,* 1958

The literature of this country begins in rotten romanticism.
Louis Dudek, *The Two Traditions,* 1962

A good deal is being said about Canadian literature, and most of it takes the form of question and answer as to whether a Canadian literature exists.
Archibald Lampman, *Two Canadian Poets,* 1891

Until recently, Canada enjoyed the unenviable distinction of being the only civilized country in the world where the study of its own literature was not made compulsory in the schools and colleges.
Lorne Pierce,
the Foreward to:
"An Outline of Canadian Literature", 1927

The way ahead in the academic waters of Canadian lit. is clearly charted. You find yourself a dead and obscure writer and stake a claim to his revival.
Mordecai Richler,
Wally Sylvester's Canadiana, 1960

Canadian literature, when it has not been neglected entirely, has been contemptuously dismissed or extravagantly praised.
A.J.M. Smith,
the Introduction to:
"The Book of Canadian Prose", 1965

When our poets can free themselves from the omnipresence of two powerful and conflicting voices, . . . we shall see the advent of a strong and indigenous Canadian literature.
W.P. Wilgar,
Poetry and the Divided Mind in Canada, 1944

LIVING
It must be great, . . . to live where you kin see won'erful sights all the time.
Will R. Bird,
The Movies Come to Gull Point, 1936

Long toil and small leisure are part of the heavy price we pay for our North American standard of living.
Robertson Davies, *A Voice from the Attic*, 1960

Men live because they're able for it; not because they're coaxed to.
Norman Duncan,
Every Man for Himself, 1908

To live is to go forward and forget.
Joan Finnigan,
Entrance to the Greenhouse, 1970

Only to live and breathe and be
Exalted! Then the world may keep
Its grimy prizes. Give to me
Joy, weariness, and sleep!
Norman Gregor Guthrie, *Ski Maiden*, 1928

Nothing belongs to me;
it's what I learn,
abd how I will repay
the debt of life that counts.
Doris Hedges, *Loan of Life*, 1968

I will sing a little, laugh a little, love a lot, and the flames I fondle will warm my elder years.
Marshall Laub,
"Wei-Ling Makes a Song on the Mountain", 1965

I have known the worst and the worst and the worst, . . . and yet I live. I fear and fear, and yet I live.
Margaret Laurence, *Godman's Master*, 1960

Somehow or other, we've got to get some graciousness back into human life.
Hugh MacLennan, *Two Solitudes*, 1945

He who lives dangerously lives well.
Edward Meade, *Remember Me*, 1946

To each his appointed time; to youth the dawn with its cool caress, and its promise of future glories and joys; to man, the bustle and the fervor of the full day; to old age, the calm and repose of sunset; and to all, night.
J.J. Procter,
The Philosopher in the Clearing, 1897

One learns to live with what one has, or with what one does not have.
Edwin R. Procunier, *Voices of Desire*

Better make haste to help the living than to decorate the dead.
J.R. Ramsay, *Lo!*, 1873

One day the only man who could have hanged me
Died and ever since I have been designing
Swings, devising trapdoors and tying knots.
James Reaney, *The Killdeer*

We can live but one day at a time,
As we tread life's miry way,
For if we live in the morrow,
We have nothing to give today!
Lily G. Sather, *A Day at a Time*, 1960

If Fate should down you, just get up and take another cuff;
You may bank on it that there is philosophy like bluff,
And grin.
Robert Service, *Grin*, 1907

With eager eyes I greet the morn,
Exultant as a boy,
Knowing that I am newly born
To wonder and to joy.
Robert Service, *Each Day a Life*, 1940

There is no greater joy to the truly living thing than the joy of being alive, of feeling alive in every part and power.
Ernest Thompson Seton, *Lives of the Hunted*

Let us rise up and live! Behold, each thing
Is ready for the moulding of our hand.
Francis Sherman, *Let Us Rise Up And Live*

LONDON (England)

London is like a shot in the arm: I come back from it refreshed and impatient to get down to work again.
Norman Levine, *A Letter from England*, 1958

London is a collection of traditions and great houses, and newspaper offices, and shops.
Sara Jeannette Duncan, *The Imperialist*, 1904

LONELINESS

The land he lives in is a lonely one.
Ronald Bates, *The Glass of Form*, 1959

I shall remain in these meadows:
I will not again be lonely.
Doreen Gordon Davis, *Of Ivory Towers*, 1953

I am secure, But O my God!
Against the loneliness there's no defence!
Dennis A. Donovan, *Apart,* 1961

Yes, the loneliness is worst of all: days of it,
years of it,
lying down with emptiness and getting up
with despair.
Armoral Kent, *For Poets—2,* 1968

Men have cried out against poverty and
disease, against tyranny and unbelief; but
surely the greatest affliction of the human
heart is loneliness.
Edwin R. Procunier,
the Preface to:
"A Knife to Thy Throat", 1962

Loneliness of men makes poets.
Raymond Souster, *In Praise of Loneliness,*
1951

There's never a lonelier place than a
throne-chair of silk.
Arthur Stringer,
The King Who Loved Old Clothes, 1940

I crawl into my loneliness
But cannot find a place to hide.
Bernice Larsen Webb, *Fugitive,* 1967

You do not matter anymore, . . . because
you are no longer in touch with any one
and so you do not exist.
Ethel Wilson, *The Window,* 1958

LOSS

All men lose youth, and usually
Ideals, and eventually, life.
I do not think I've lost much more than
most.
Ronald Bates, *Orpheus and Odyseus,* 1952

LOUISBOURG

Louisbourg, a pretentious and costly
fortification, but miserably situated and
falling to decay for want of the most necessary repair.
William McLennan and J.N. McIlwraith,
'The Span O'Life", 1899

LOVE

and I loved her too much to like how she
dragged her days like a sled over gravel.
Milton Acorn, *Jawbreakers,* 1963

So now I walk again through the familiar
with understanding born of a second love.
Myrtle Reynolds Adams, *Shuttle,* 1966

My love is like the lark that sings to waking,
and like to sleep. My love is all the sun-
time and the star time. My love is waking
and sleep.
Carroll Aikins, *The God of Gods*

Aware of limitations they profess
— Despite the warnings of the dull —
Love still has meanings. That is their
success.
Herb Barrett, *A Way of Life,* 1964

In splendid silences
We wove
That consecrated thing
Called love.
Laura Bedell, *Love*

Your love is vain, unwanted. Let it fade.
But now it is my dream, not love, that die.
Anne Begor, *Ballad of Time,* 1967

Only when he restrains his impulse to kill
the white bird, and acts as love directs him
can man hope for happiness.
John W. Bilsland, *Vision of Clarity,* 1960

Love is both the source of life and the law
of living.
John W. Bilsland, *Vision of Clarity,* 1960

I'm a hard person to love. I suffocate
people.
Janet Bonellie,
Why Are The People Staring?, 1968

Still must I mourn, and dream of the joys of
my vanished love.
Charles Frederick Boyle, *Sounds and
Shadows*

Dear, if our love were of the flesh alone,
Life would be long enough.
Audrey Alexandra Brown, *Lammastide,* 1936

I wonder will this love of ours set so,
And all our lives grow dark, and cold, and
drear,
With but a star-beam floating there and
here?
George Frederick Cameron,
Tis Strange, You Think, 1887

Standing on tiptoe ever since my youth
Striving to grasp the future just above
I hold at length the only future — Truth
And Truth is Love.
George Frederick Cameron, *Standing on Tip-
toe*

People who are in love are nearly always unobservant. Their eyes and ears seem to be dulled.
Janey Canuck, *Open Trails*

Yes, the world is growing old,
But the joys it used to hold,
Love and beauty, only grow
Greater as they come and go.
Bliss Carman, *The Pipes of Pan*

Dream as we will of the spread of the kingdom of love, the old custom of bloodshed remains.
Bliss Carman, *The Friendship of Art*, 1904

It is very trite but very true to call love the seed of success.
Bliss Carman, *The Kinship of Nature*, 1904

Love manifests itself in our bodies as instinctive craving, in our souls as devotion, and in our minds as pride.
Bliss Carman, *The Kinship of Nature*, 1904

Where love reigns there is life in all its fulness.
H.A. Cody, *The Fourth Watch*, 1911

There is no flesh so perfect
As on my lover's bone,
And yet it seems so distant
When I am all alone.
Leonard Cohen, *I Long to Hold Some Lady*, 1961

The measure of a man's power to help his brother is the measure of the love in the heart of him, and of the faith that he has that at last the good will win.
Ralph Connor, *Black Rock*

Most girls were afraid, either that you were about to fall in love with them, or that you would not.
Ralph Connor, *The Major*, 1917

Love, you know, seeks to make happy rather than to be happy.
Ralph Connor, *The Major*, 1917

And love is a cord woven out of life,
And dyed in the red of the living heart.
Isabella Valancy Crawford,
The Camp of Souls, 1884

Love is subtly hid
In the fragrant roses,
Blown in gay Madrid.
I.V. Crawford, *Roses in Madrid*

Short love is sweetest, and most love curdles if you keep it.
Robertson Davies, *A Jig for the Gypsy*, 1954

What is love? It is the ardent outflow of the whole being — the yearning of one human heart to lavish all its treasures upon another.
James De Mille, *A Strange Manuscript*, 1888

Unrequited love is anguish beyond expression — anguish so severe that the heart will often break under it.
James De Mille, *The Strange Manuscript*, 1888

Poverty, sickness and death, . . . are evils; but the worst of all evils is unrequited love.
James De Mille, *A Strange Manuscript*, 1888

Isn't it better to wear the love of one man than the admiration of half a dozen?
Sara Jeannette Duncan, *The Imperialist*, 1904

Nobody sees evil in the man she loves.
A.M.D. Fairbairn, *The Tragedy of Tanoo*, 1935

Love hides its struggle as it hides its fruits.
Robert Finch, *Ventures*, 1961

To love is to listen.
Joan Finnigan,
in: "It Was Warm and Sunny", 1955

For us to love each other, my love, would only lead to a dream with consequences beyond the imagination of either one of us.
Joan Finnigan, *"Simon I tell You..."*, 1968

Love sighs and sorrows;
Love laughs and sings:
Love hurls us beggars;
Love thrones us Kings!
Donald A. Fraser, *Arietta*, 1937

Love often drains off its own existence by driving toward some extreme and unhallowed proportion that overreached its very meaning.
Lawrence Garber,
Garner's Tales from the Quarter, 1970

He was a man who loved a woman. Long after all beauty and cleanliness and decency had gone, he still loved her.
Hugh Garner, *Some Are So Lucky*, 1952

Love's pigment is too delicate for salt. Love is too wild to catch.
Dave Godfrey, *Newfoundland Night*, 1962

Love is a red thing forever against the great grey nets of sorrow and the deep baited hooks of age.
Dave Godfrey, *Newfoundland Night*, 1962

One gives up so much when one loves!
Ronald Goodchild, *The Grand Duchess*

Love is no picnic: it's a disease.
John Gray,
When Elephants Roost in the Trees, 1957

Love: it does not engrave the mind with facts but clouds it with memory.
John Gray,
When Elephants Roost in the Trees, 1957

Love is a fleeting thing with me. Desire is not. Love has to be conquered again and again.
Frederick P. Grove, *Settlers of the Marsh*, 1925

O, love passes everyone all the day long
In avenue, alley and park,
And most people miss it in jostling the throng.
Norman Gregor Guthrie, *The Orchestra Leader,*
1928

Love is the last! But who may dam Time's rapids in the flow of days,
Whereon love floats unheeding, calm
Into the great deep.
Norman G. Guthrie, *December Impression,*
1928

Love means to take and to give Soul, body and heart.
Norman G. Guthrie, *A Lonely Woman*, 1928

This is our heart's love, it would seem to say,
Wrought with the ancient tools of our vocation,
Weave we the web of love from day to day.
Katherine Hale, *Grey Knitting*

Thou art my Tower in the sun at noon.
Katherine Hale, *At Noon*

The law of life is love
Nourished in the earth.
Stella Hancock, *Widow*, 1968

O, never believe in death, dear heart,
For love's a year with no December.
Verna Loveday Harden, *The Mother*, 1952

There are those alive who will gather up your love and bless you for a few daily crumbs of it.
S. Frances Harrison, *The Forest of Bourg-Marie*

Never again will I clutch at the edge of your brightness
Love being what it is, aching and cruel.
Elizabeth Hastings,
the Introduction to:
"The Occasion", 1936

To philanderers and flirts, when a great and true love comes, they do not comprehend it, and they cannot appreciate it.
Arnold Haultain, *Hints for Lovers*

When a woman can no longer weep over a man, she no longer loves him.
Arnold Haultain, *Hints for Lovers*

For little as people seem to be aware of it, love requires constant replenishing. No flame can burn without a feeding oil, no pool overflow without a purling brook.
Arnold Haultain, *Hints for Lovers*

I recognize the vanity and scorn,
The fear, the greed, in short the mask of love.
Daryl Hine, *A Vision*, 1960

The eyes of Love are keen and their vision reaches to the distant border-land of Truth.
George V. Hobart, *Experience*, 1914

Oh sorry thing
That true love aye should be anear to death.
John Hunter-Duvar, *The Enamorado*, 1879

Woman must depend on man for fame,
Her only immortality is love.
John Hunter-Duvar, *The Enamorado*, 1879

The fortress of the heart is won,
More oft by escalade than sap or seige.
John Hunter-Duvar, *The Enamorado*, 1879

Because my love asked naught but that you gave
Freely, . . .
. . ., passion remains yet strong.
Patrick James, *Marriage*, 1939

Now let us go
candle in hand softly,
holding in our heart lightly

Love's warming glow
to melt Hate's numbing snow.
Mariel Jenkins, *Christmas 1953*, 1953

I looked for love but I was very young
And even so I did not do it for too long.
George Jonas, *To A Christian*, 1967

And now your gold,
While love is master of your mood.
Archibald Lampman, *The Violinist*

In love-making, as in war, there is no
substitute for victory.
Irving Layton,
Some Observations and Aphorisms, 1968

Love is a gentle plant. You cannot force its
growth.
Stephen Leacock, *Nonsense Novels*, 1911

Love knows no grammar, yet the stiffest
lock,
the dullest door may open to his knock.
Kenneth Leslie, *Cobweb College*, 1938

Drug and dope me, dress me with love's
fine hand —
Till the end of our time.
Dorothy Livesay, *Lullaby*, 1947

Your way of loving is too slow for me.
Dorothy Livesay, *The Difference*, 1932

He loved her not in days of splendor only
But in the gray of fogs, the dark of rain.
Wilson MacDonald,
He Has Kept Faith with Beauty, 1926

Never again will love
Be as it is to-day;
Nothing in earth or heaven
Comes as it came before.
Wilson MacDonald,
A Song of the Unreturning, 1926

In comparison with a loving human being,
everything else is worthless.
Hugh MacLennan, *Each Man's Son*, 1951

The hurt you gave I inward keep,
Hard Love! remembering whose it is.
Jay Macpherson, *Very Sad Song*, 1958

Where is love, where is life — are they only
in books? They are not here.
Suzanne Marny, *Love Among the Ruins*, 1909

It is rare, it must be rare, when there is not
one person to love us.
Suzanne Marny, *The Unhappy House*, 1909

Men often plunge into dissipation when
they are crossed in love.
Nellie L. McClung, *Sowing Seeds in Danny*,
1911

What statelyness of manner can rival the
pretty softness of a gentle girl wholly in
love.
William McLennan and J.N. McIlwraith,
"The Span O'Life", 1899

I am always sorry when I hear of a young
man or woman being desperately in love,
for it generally ends in disappointment.
Susanna Moodie, *Geoffrey Moncton*, 1855

Love that is sincere is a hidden emotion of
the heart; it shrinks from vain laughter,
and is most eloquent when silent, or only
revealed by tears.
Susanna Moodie, *Geoffrey Moncton*, 1855

Love cannot brook long separation from
the object beloved. It withers beneath
neglect, and without personal intercourse
droops and dies.
Susanna Moodie, *Geoffrey Moncton*, 1855

First passion is instantaneous — electrical. It cannot be described, and can only
be communicated through the same
mysterious medium.
Susanna Moodie, *Geoffrey Moncton*, 1855

Love is so scarce in this world that we
ought to prize it, however lowly the source
from which it glows.
Susanna Moodie,
Old Woodruff and His Three Wives, 1847

Love (is) . . . . knowing you and she will care
about each other when sex and
daydreams, fights and futures — when all
that's on the shelf and done with.
Brian Moore, *The Luck of Ginger Coffey*

Full fifteen years her parents poured
Inflammation into the adored
By amorous example and suggestion;
Then thought it weird when flames
appeared
And blamed it on spontaneous com-
bustion.
Mavor Moore, *Who's Who*, 1947

Alas! I have slowly
Found out in my folly,
That love is as real as love is delusive!
J.R. Newell, *Song*, 1881

What has my love availed me?
What boots my anxious care?
When fortune o'er has failed me,
Who did my sorrow share?
J.R. Newell,
What Has My Love Availed Me?, 1881

A man's love is too rough and rude a thing
For God's red flower called a woman's
heart.
Robert Norwood, *The Man of Kerioth*, 1919

Love is the great reward, the sign
Of heaven's most high approval of a soul.
Robert Norwood, *The Man of Kerioth*, 1919

A man in love is always evident,
He sings his secret as he goes.
Robert Norwood, *The Witch of Endor*, 1916

Love is also
my finding this house
emptier than a stranger
ever would.
Alden Nowlan,
For Claudine, Because I Love Her, 1969

Though she has all my love
Mere love is not enough —
How should she bed in hut?
Padraig O'Broin, *Striapachas*, 1962

There is a sadness known as love.
Its name is man. Its name is woman.
They have a house to hold them sad.
Joyce Odam, *Halves*, 1969

Marriage is a serious business, but love
turns the grey of life to gold.
Miriam Osborne, *The Point of View*

It is possible for men to love and not to admire. It is a foolish thing to say that
reverence must go with love.
Gilbert Parker, *The Seats of the Mighty*, 1896

Love should be sound,
Free from the creeping rot of doubt.
M. Eugenie Perry, *Roof Dancers*, 1938

The memory of first love
Flowers perennially in the heart.
M. Eugenie Perry, *Scent of the Thorn*, 1938

If love be death,
Then let love hold us both —
Cimmerian, jealous death —
Forging us one,
Immutable.
Bluebell Stewart Phillips, *If Love Be*, 1961

Also my love was like a bird. It sang
Within my veins an endless song that rang
My bones in harmony, whose fast
vibration
Sent me into a nightmare of concussion.
Errol Pritchard, *The Bird*, 1959

There is nothing so coarse that love cannot
beautify; nothing so low and common that
it cannot ennoble.
J.J. Procter,
The Philosopher in the Clearing, 1897

Love and the spoils of love,
War and the spoils of war.
Neither do we understand,
But both have always been.
Edwin R. Procunier, *Two Sides of Darkness*,
1962

Love us for what we are not
Yet might be.
Lynn Raney, *Love Us Not*, 1955

So love, though measured breath by
breath,
May seem like walking in a summer
dream,
Visiting nowhere but pleasant places;
So love does often lead a filthy way to
Death.
James Reaney, *A Fantasy and a Moral*, 1963

And there I sin, where sin should know no
part,
Your name instead of God's rings through
my heart.
George William Reid, *Peccavi*, 1936

There will be a time for love — time and to
spare.
But we must scar the ground and cast the
seed
While now the flush of spring is on the air.
Allister Reid, *Drought*, 1938

Let is be said of us that we made no plans.
That the others schemed, got money and
position, honours, futures, but that we —
who dissented — ruined ourselves with
loving.
Mordecai Richler, *Son of A Smaller Hero*,
1955

To love is to fear those fears as yet unborn.
Josephine Ryan,
To Love Is to Live With Fear, 1961

It's love that'll make it all wonderful. Find love quickly — today.
George Ryga, *Ballad of a Stonepicker*, 1970

Romantic whims achieve futility.
Lister Sinclair, *Return to Colonus*, 1955

Love is and was my god and king;
But love you never knew at all.
John Smalacombe,
From the Ill-Tempered Lover, 1937

All that I love I kill, and keep
Encapsuled in a word.
F.E. Sparshott, *Midas*, 1960

We mortals are too slow to learn that love
Transcending self, forgetting grief and loss,
Brings peace that is akin to that above.
Dorothy Sproule, *Peace Through Pain*, 1938

What is the use of a beautiful love if it can't be expressed in a beautiful way?
Arthur Stringer, *The Oyster*, 1939

To wear love's brand you must bear love's burn.
Arthur Stringer, *The Silver Poppy*

Such is the strange nature of love, as with the ivy on the stone wall; the hardness and the coldness of the object to which it has fastened its tendrils does not affect the clinging strength of its hold.
Adeline Teskey,
Where The Maple Sugar Grows

Love, it bloweth where it listeth.
Alberta C. Trimble, *Whistling Girl*, 1936

Love such as yours is less than harlots give!
George Walton, *Prognosis*, 1951

'Tis very hard to know a woman's heart,
For when they love thee best they seem the coldest.
Samuel James Watson, *Ravlan*, 1876

O love, teach us to love you, that we may
Through burning Carthage take our way.
Wilfred Watson, *Invocation*, 1960

In this clock-wound human darkness love is the only light.
Elizabeth Whealy,
Time Circles Man and Woman, 1967

While time and space project my life in doubt,

I know of one firm, timeless truth.
This love amidst the chaos still stands out
Supreme, and forms a pattern there.
G.M. Williams, *Perfection*, 1956

I'm not sure it matters the number of people you're loved by,
so long as you are well loved.
Norman Williams, *The Mountain*, 1956

For love is not the getting, but the giving.
Love is in the loving, not the being loved.
Margaret Harvey Wilton,
Love Is of Eternity, 1956

LOVERS

There is no lover so pure and holy in his adoration as a reformed voluptuary.
Robertson Davies, *Tempest-Tost*, 1951

All lovers protestations are built of such artlessness and ostentation. They are formed of words as decorative and vain as a peacock's tail feathers, but their promise is a chimera that begins as truth and only becomes a lie with its unfulfillment.
Hugh Garner, *Some Are So Lucky*, 1952

What are we
Who need no raiment
Nor the help of weavers, hatters,
Tailors, milliners, stitchers, glovers,
To whom not winter matters?
Answer: A pair of very loving lovers.
James Reaney, *A Riddle*, 1963

Lovers are liars, women always dupes,
And on their innocent heads the Fates make fall
The vengeance due their tempter's perjury.
Samuel James Watson, *Ravlan*, 1876

LOVELINESS

All the loveliness of earth
Is doomed the moment of its birth.
Arthur S. Bourinot,
Everything on Earth Must Die, 1955

Loveliness endures, though youth and fame
Disintegrate.
Willis Eberman, *Coins in the Wind*, 1956

True loveliness shall grow till life be finished;

And they alone shall fade who sin or fear.
Wilson MacDonald,
On His Golden-Wedding Day, 1926

No part of loveliness is ever lost.
Maude Rubin, *The Sound Remains,* 1957

I would weave a garland of words
For your loveliness, of my own heart's
coining.
Miriam Simpson, *Inadequacy,* 1936

LOYALTY

Loyalty demands obedience.
Ralph Connor, *Black Rock,* 1900

The loyal to his race
He bends to death — but never to disgrace.
E. Pauline Johnson, *The White Wampum*

If ye break faith with us who die
We shall not sleep, though poppies grow
In Flanders fields.
John McCrae, *In Flanders Fields*

Loyalty is a matter of which a well bred
person does not speak. It is taken for
granted.
Andrew MacPhail, *Essays in Politics,* 1909

Those who should be most grateful when
the hour of adversity dawns on their
benefactor, are often the first to desert
him.
Samuel Strickland,
Twenty-Seven Years in Canada West, 1853

LUCK

Only the pattern of chance has a claim to
validity in this mechanistic maze.
R.A.D. Ford, *I Say Chance,* 1958

The chance is always hiding round a
corner for the man who goes ahead.
A.C. Laut, *Heralds of Empire*

Teach me to navigate the fjords of chance
Winding through my abyssal ignorance.
Malcolm Lowry, *The Pilgrim,* 1963

Chance sometimes lets humble men like
me balance the scales of fate; and I was
humble enough in rank, if in spirit always
something above my place.
Gilbert Parker, *The Seats of the Mighty,* 1896

LUMBERING

The future and its days of payment do not
weigh heavily upon the logger's mind; he
lives much in the present.
M. Allerdale Grainger, *Woodsmen of the
West,* 1908

Rough in manners, and often only half-
civilized, the lumberer, as an individual,
resembles little the woodsman of other
lands.
Samuel Strickland,
Twenty-Seven Years in Canada West, 1853

LUNCH

Lunch at one — how many cheese
sandwiches
Cheerfully eaten entitle one to a martyr's
crown.
Audrey O'Kelly, *Song for an Office,* 1951

LUST

Lust was the defiling of an instinct of
nature: it was sin.
Frederick P. Grove, *Settlers of the Marsh,* 1925

LUXURY

A hard world is soft when fine silk is
smoothing your skin.
Arthur Stringer,
The King Who Loved Old Clothes, 1940

MADNESS

Yet I scarce know anyone in all mankind
who
has not some tang or other of madness.
Michael Malus,
Cassandra and the Lotus-Eaters, 1960

Mad! If I'm mad then you too are mad; but
it's all in the point of view.
Robert Service, *The Ballad of Pious Pete,* 1907

MAJORITY

The rule of the majority may be all right, but
injustice from a majority is just as bad as
injustice from anybody else.
Hugh MacLennan, *Each Man's Son,* 1951

MALICE

It works like a leaven; it stirs, and swells,
and changes all that surrounds it.
Robertson Davies, *Leaven of Malice,* 1954

People will think ill of you no matter what you do. It's human nature.
Mazo de la Roche, *The Building of Jalna*, 1927

MAN

No animal in nature makes so pernicious an improvement of liberty as man.
Jacob Bailey, *Journal of a Voyage*, 1779

The insect world and the world of men never really meet — they interweave in space and make a mutual nuisance of themself.
N.J. Berrill, *Perfume, Starlight and Melody*

Man is the unique creature, the rebel, the thing of illimitable capacity for creation or destruction, the one unpredictable being in a mechanistic cosmos, the truant of the universe.
Earle Birney,
E.J. Pratt and His Critics, 1958

What an inconstant animal is man!
Frances Brooke,
The History of Emily Montague, 1769

The modern man, no hope in anything, no faith in anything. Just immersed in matter.
Morley Callaghan,
They Shall Inherit the Earth, 1934

I am a man! although I doubt all men.
William Wilfred Campbell, *Morning*, 1908

Man is not born of his mother's pains,
But as the Vast Design ordains.
George Herbert Clarke, *Far-Wanderer*

Every man and woman is a mystery, built like those Chinese puzzles which consist of one box inside another, so that ten or twelve boxes have to be opened before the final solution is found.
Robertson Davies,
The Table Talk of Samuel Marchbanks, 1949

It's mankind, not merely Canada, has a long way to go:
an undeveloped planet.
Louis Dudek, *Canada: Interim Report*, 1963

Passionate-compassionate animal man,
Possessed by one appetite
Fear and desire.
Gerald Fulton, *Allotropy*, 1963

It is strange how rarely the work of man will really harmonize with Nature. The beaver builds, and his work will blend.

Man builds, and it jars — very likely because he mostly builds with silly pretensions.
Frederick P. Grove, *Dawn and Diamonds*

The authentic dance
is the wobbly stance
of the living man.
Lionel Kearns, *Pointing*, 1968

Man is not a rational animal, he's a dull-witted animal who loves to torture.
Irving Layton,
the Foreword to:
"A Red Carpet for the Sun"

Man is absurd, not because he kills and couples, but because he feels obliged to invent reasons for doing so.
Irving Layton,
Some Observations and Aphorisms, 1968

More than anyone before him, twentieth-century man has extended his being into the realm of evil.
Irving Layton,
the Foreword to:
"Balls for a One-Armed Juggler", 1963

Although it thus appears that the average man is rather weak on religion, in point of morals the fellow is decidedly strong.
Stephen Leacock,
the Preface to:
"Winnowed Wisdom", 1926

It is the times that have changed, not the man. He is there still, just as greedy and rapacious as ever, but no greedier: and we have just the same social need of his greed as a motive power in industry as we ever had, and indeed a worse need than before.
Stephen Leacock,
My Discovery of England, 1922

What is a man but the tower of a soul?.
W.D. Lighthall, *The False Chevalier*, 1898

I find in mankind everywhere the same tendencies and the same pretensions.
W.D. Lighthall, *The False Chevalier*, 1898

Man is not long to be trusted with the strings of his destiny.
Malcolm Lowry, *Swinging the Maelstrom*

There is an artist, a poet in every man, hence he is a creature easy for anyone to identify themselves with.
Malcolm Lowry, *Letter to Albert Erskine*

Within the ancient castle of sensation
Man is to be found wallowing
In slopping, rolling, swelling viscera.
Ian Malcolm, *A Moment of Existence*

Every man is to his comrade a stranger,
and every man dwells in his own
wilderness.
Edward Meade, *Remember Me*, 1946

Man still remains a half-reclaimed savage;
the leaven of Christianity is slowly and
surely working its way, but it has not yet
changed the whole lump, or transformed
the deformed into the beauteous child of
God.
Susanna Moodie, *Roughing It in the Bush*,
1852

Only man, the builder
Has changed, has greyed, grown older.
Rona Murray, *Co-Existence*, 1951

If on the living, insects are thus fed,
How ill must fare the worms when we are
dead!
Standish O'Grady, *The Emigrant*, 1842

Man is a great humbug. I don't say he is a
hypocrite, because he really believes in
himself; but he is a humbug.
J.J. Procter,
The Philosopher in the Clearing, 1897

Man is a god to the lower creation.
Margaret Marshall Saunders, *Beautiful Joe*

The stars are laughing at the earth; God's
geatest joke is man.
Robert Service, *Laughter*, 1940

Not one man in a dozen, is what a nice
woman would like to think him.
Harry James Smith, *Mrs. Bumpstead-Leigh*,
1917

Man alone among the larger predators
kills when there is no need, kills for the
love of killing.
John Stevens,
the Introduction to:
"Last of the Curlews", 1963

The wind sweeps the hills, the bleak, grey-
brown hills.
Torn up is the Russian Thistle, the young
Wheat, and the rich soil. Man's roots are
deeper.
Ever has he visioned a new season,
And water, and the living green; thus will
He dream and strive while wind and hills
remain.
Christine Van der Mark, *Thorlief*, 1941

MAPLE

Sap is boiling,
Skies are clear,
Maple syrup
Time is here.
Arthur S. Bourinot, *Sugar Bush*, 1951

There is a story written no art can ever
name,
And golden
As of olden
The fiery heralds run.
Across the fields of Canada we trace their
path of flame.
A.M. Stephen,
Scarlet and Gold—The Maples

MARRIAGE

Couples married for twenty years still have
surprises for each other.
Donald Cameron, *Love By The Book*, 1969

No woman can resist the opportunity to
join in that most fascinating of all sport —
man-hunting.
Ralph Connor, *The Major*, 1917

There's more to marriage than four bare
legs in a blanket.
Robertson Davies, *A Jig for the Gypsy*, 1954

Don't expect a wife to help or hinder you.
Don't expect anything.
That is the golden rule of marriage.
Robertson Davies, *A Jig for the Gypsy*, 1954

One may as well have some fun before
marriage, one gets so little after.
Frederick A. Dixon,
The Maire of St. Brieux, 1875

I know we're married, and it's no use kick-
in'
But please remember, ma'am, that you're
no chicken.
F.A. Dixon,
Fifine, The Fisher-Maid, 1877

A man doesn't seem to get any time when
he's married. Need a lot of frills you never
thought of before.
Frederick P. Grove, *Settlers of the Marsh*, 1925

All girls regard marriage as an enviable lot, or as a necessary evil.
T.C. Haliburton, *Nature and Human Nature,* 1855

The burden of creating a happy marriage falls mainly on the wife.
Marion Hilliard,
"A Woman Doctor Looks at Love and Life", 1957

People who have never married have not really lived.
Stephen Leacock, *Woman's Level*

No man can deliberately exclude his wife from the centre of his life and hope to escape the hounds.
Hugh MacLennan, *Each Man's Son,* 1951

Is not the woman who leaves her lonely virgin freedom for marriage forever in someone's toil?
Suzanne Marny, *The West in the East,* 1909

A married man who has no home, is like a stray sheep, ready to go one way as soon as another.
Thomas McCulloch, *The Stepsure Letters,* 1821

Marriage changes states but not dispositions.
Thomas McCulloch, *The Stepsure Letters,* 1821

It is all very well to marry for love, . . . if a fellow can afford it; but a little money is not to be despised; it goes a great way towards making the home comfortable.
Susanna Moodie,
Old Woodruff and His Three Wives, 1847

An old man marries a pretty face and ends up in a room with a monster.
Brian Moore, *Uncle T.,* 1960

Love is made in heaven, but marriages certainly are made on earth.
Marian Osborne, *The Point of View*

To give oneself in marriage without true affection would be an offense in the sight of heaven.
Thomas H. Raddall, *The Wedding Gift*

Who ever got married who didn't need a little push?
Mordecai Richler,
Some Grist for Mervyn's Mill

In no other country on the face of the earth does the torch of wedded love beam brighter than in Canada, where the husband always finds "the wife dearer than the bride".
Samuel Strickland,
Twenty-Seven Years in Canada West, 1853

The wedding was the important thing, not the man.
Barbara Tansey, *The Wedding*

The desire all women hug to death,
The unappeasable desire of marriage.
Samuel James Watson, *Ravlan,* 1876

Marriage is perfectly happy so long as the woman is utterly submissive.
Frances Fenwick Williams, *Which?* 1926

MARTYR

You never catch a martyr in the ranks of the majority; if you want one, you have to hunt him up elsewhere.
J.J. Procter,
The Philosopher in the Clearing, 1897

MARVELOUS

Mankind are fond of the marvelous, it seems to heighten their character by relating they have seen such things.
David Thompson,
Narrative of His Explorations, 1812

THE MASSES

The peasants are ignorant, lazy, dirty, and stupid beyond all belief.
Frances Brooke,
The History of Emily Montague, 1769

Those fairy tales are most amusing. Good for the masses!
J. Gounod Campbell,
The Bleeding Heart of Wee Jon

The multitude are always fickle-minded.
T.C. Haliburton, *Sam Slick,* 1835

Anything that gives power to the masses will please the masses.
T.C. Haliburton, *Sam Slick,* 1838

In point of news, and amusements and pictures, the public always gets what the public wants. This is a pity but this is so.
Stephen Leacock,
Great National Problems, 1926

If you want to please the great mass of mankind you must talk platitudes: when you can't do that, the next best thing to do is to talk nonsense.
J.J. Procter,
The Philosopher in the Clearing, 1897

You can always hide in a herd.
Sheila Watson, *The Double Hook*, 1969

MASS MEDIA

To be a member of the avantgarde used to be a full - time occupation. But today, with the mass media well ahead of most artists, it is well-nigh impossible.
John Robert Colombo, *New Wave Nichol*, 1967

Mass media are magnifiers of personality.
Louis Dudek,
The Writing of the Decade, 1969

One of the main attractions of the modern mass periodical is its ability to stimulate day - dreams.
Robert Fulford, *The Male Mags*, 1958

Perfection of the means of communication has meant instantaneity.
Marshall McLuhan,
Culture Without Literacy, 1953

The monumental appetites of the broadcast arts can be sated only by a steady diet of the mediocre.
George Robertson, *Drama on the Air*, 1959

In Canada — the radio talk has been one of the means of developing a mature standard of literary criticism.
George Woodcock, *an Editorial*, 1963

MATERIALISM

Our works are hideous, because we have no pleasure in them; and we have no pleasure in them because we are slaves to commercialism.
Bliss Carman, *The Kinship of Nature*, 1904

The continued prevalence of a materialistic idealism keeps our national life financially rich but culturally poor.
Alan Creighton, *Conquest by Poetry*, 1942

Banking and insurance have managed to raise themselves almost to the level of religions.
Robertson Davies, *Leaven of Malice*, 1954

That arrivism, opportunism, at best only cloaks the thirst for getting which is rendering barren the lives we see everywhere. Materialism.
Raymond Knister, *White Narcissus*, 1929

Deny it no one, we are in a material world, and he who garners the most material pleasure in a judicious way has the richest sheaf that may be bound up on this earthy earth.
Suzanne Marny, *The Unhappy House*, 1909

Turn where you will, folly and extravagance stare you in the face.
Thomas McCulloch, *The Stepsure Letters*, 1821

MATURITY

That's the fun of being grown up; one has shed so many things which seem desirable to somebody of my age.
Robertson Davies, *Tempest-Tost*, 1951

Maturity involves moving from childhood, . . . and to acceptance of the responsibilities of a social world.
William H. New,.
A Feeling of Completion, 1963

MEDIOCRITY

Evil came on earth when the first man or woman said: "That isn't the best I can do, but it is well enough"
Bliss Carman, *The Friendship of Art*, 1904

The pint-size writer finds pint-size readers.
Robertson Davies, *A Voice from the Attic*, 1960

Prophecies are easy to make: one can predict that the popular will become more mediocre as time goes on.
Louis Dudek,
The Writing of the Decade, 1969

A mediocrity is someone for whom self-transcendence does nothing.
Irving Layton,
Some Observations and Aphorisms, 1968

MEETINGS

What means this gathering tonight?
What spirit moves along
The crowded hall.
William H. Drummond, *We're Irish Yet*, 1897

109

MEMORY

But all my memories, like dear ghosts, come
And paint my past, as I have loved it, grey.
Marion Berquist, *Grey Things*, 1936

The windows of my room
Are dark with bitter frost
The stillness aches with doom
Of something loved and lost.
Bliss Carman, *A Northern Vigil*

Memory, after all, is the sweetest story ever told.
Gregory Clark, *Two Anecdotes*

Nor does her art die, though she cease to be,
For what lives longer than a memory?
Fisher Davidson, *The Actress*, 1960

Like an epic stretch my memories into dim and ever receding pasts.
Frederick P. Grove, *Over Prairie Trails*

And much against my will —
I must remember old, old hopes
Regret cannot fulfil.
Eve Hellyer, *Regret*, 1938

All eternity be but a space
Haunted by ghosts of by-gone Memory.
Norah Holland, *The Rivers*, 1924

Oh, if I may have one memory only to keep
In the days that are lonely, and cruel, and stark,
Let me hold that moment of loveliness
Close in my heart.
Clara Hopper, *Sail from Nanaimo*, 1943

It is in memory, the recollection of things adventitious or episodical, that our deepest and secured pleasure consist.
Archibald Lampman, *Happiness*, 1896

They shall not die nor wither with the hours:
They were and are and they will be again.
Wilson MacDonald, *Immortal*, 1938

Meditation and the aid of the written word will fix these golden days in memory for the enrichment of less happier times to come.
Archibald MacMechan, *Afoot in Ultima Thule*

Ah, memory, like a silver spear
Piercing this aching heart of mine,

Why dream of things no longer here?
Why worship at an empty shrine?
Alice McKay, *Homesickness*, 1934

The mountains dim in grey and misty veiling,
Shouldered the world away.
Sometime, somewhere when fires of life are waning,
I shall recall this day.
Margaret Minaker, *Loganberries*, 1938

O memory, why repeat
These best-forgotten things?
James A.M. Moir, *El Alamein*, 1951

Back thro' the corridors of time,
Back to the regions of the past,
Mem'ry, on fancy's wings sublime,
Ushers afar to the darkling vast.
J.R. Newell, *Retrospection*, 1881

Rememberance lives to chill me —
Memory is wisdom's light.
J.R. Newell, *Despondency*, 1881

But memory, which is thinner than the senses,
is only a wave in grass that the kiss erases.
P.K. Page, *Summer Resort*, 1944

Arise, ye by-gone memories —
Sweet memories of the past,
Return the tuneful melodies
That once were round me cast.
J.E. Pollock, *Memories*, 1883

Memories have to be shared — they're like laughter — they have to be shared or they're nothing.
Edwin R. Procunier, *The Strength of Love*, 1962

Memories are a torture because they tell you what you've lost.
Edwin R. Procunier, *The Strength of Love*, 1962

Let the flames of memory die
On the hearthstones of the mind.
Let the smoke of heartbreak fade away.
Lucia Trent, *Healing Warmth*, 1948

That's the curse of life. Memory.
Norman Williams, *Night of Storm*, 1956

Life keeps truly alive only in the memory and the imagination.
Ethel Wilson,
On a Portuguese Balcony, 1956

MEN

A wolf is an individualist . . .
They kill out of the sheer lust of killing, and they kill without sense. . . If you want it to be clear that a man is ruthless and an enemy of society you call him a wolf.
Morley Callaghan,
They Shall Inherit the Earth

To be young and strong. To have men afraid, move out of the way, that is the way it should always be for a man.
Peter Chobanian,
A Birthday for Panos, 1969

But men are inconsistent things!
Now with new grief my heart is rent.
Masie Nelson Devitt, *Irony,* 1936

Our sex is great
Because we sweat.
Ralph Connor, *Day and Night,* 1958

All men are hunters.
John Hulcoop, *A Fable for James,* 1968

Slaves murmur to one another in their chains. They whisper what they think of their masters. In the same way the generality of men, being enslaved by women, whisper, when in safety, what they think.
Stephen Leacock,
Are Witty Women Attractive to Men

Most men with their average share of personality and attractiveness can be successful in their wooings by the force of the masculine mind.
Suzanne Marny, *The Island in the North,* 1909

Men were such deceivers — they were all smooth as silk, until it came to livin' with 'em.
Nellie L. McClung, *Sowing Seeds in Danny,* 1911

It is the wont of all men to be fools and heartless apes, to run to death after any proud turkey, and never to perceive those of real worth.
Blanche Lucile Macdonell,
Diane of Ville Marie, 1898

I am as firm a believer in having a man about; they are bothersome creatures often, but have their uses at times.
William McLennan and J.N. McIlwraith,
"The Span O'Life", 1899

Oh these men! They think the world can't turn round without their advice!
William McLennan and J.N. McIlwraith,
The Span O'Life, 1899

Give us men to match our mountains,
Give us men to match our plains,
Men with empires in their purpose
And new eras in their brains.
H.T. Miller, *Give Us Men,*

All fellas is the same, they don't care about you, they just want satisfaction.
Brian Moore, *Judith Hearne,* 1955

Men are all alike. They say yours. But they mean mine.
Mazo de la Roche, *Delight,* 1926

Men are the givers. Women are the takers.
Arthur Stringer, *Alexander Was Great,* 1939

You give into a man, . . .
. . . and you're done for, my girl.
Frances Shelley Wees,
M'Lord, I Am Not Guilty, 1954

METALS

Gold — our earliest, latest foe!
Charles Mair, *Tecumseh,* 1886

Without Iron, man is weak, very weak, but armed with Iron, he becomes the Lord of the Earth.
David Thompson,
Narrative of His Explorations, (1784 - 1812)

MEXICO

Mexico, the meeting place of many races, the ancient battleground of social and political conflicts.
Malcolm Lowry, *"Preface to a Novel",* 1948

MIDDLE AGE

Middle age is at the door,
Hovering all too near,
Eyeing Youth with envy
And Old Age with fear.
L.B. Birdsall, *Three Ages,* 1936

When a man doesn't notice that a girl under thirty has any looks, just because she is a little rumpled and doesn't know how to present herself, he is far gone in middle age.
Robertson Davies, *Leaven of Malice,* 1954

111

A man in middle age is like a ship on fire at sea with a gale driving her.
Hugh MacLennan, *Each Man's Son*, 1951

MIDDLE CLASS

A little bourgeois
thinking his little middle-class emotions
and his sentimentality can hold you
and crucify you for ever.
Morley Callaghan, *Father and Son*, 1936

Knocking the bourgeois about has been excellent sport these three hundred years and it still pleases.
Robert McCormack, *Letter From Toronto*, 1962

We are the people of the middle — the middle-class, the middle brow, the middle age — not very mute and quite inglorious averages anxiously scrambling to be aggregates and never quite making it.
S. Warhaft, *The People of the Middle*, 1960

MIND

The mind cannot quarrel with
Nature successfully; so it turns on its own kind.
Leslie Gordon Barnard,
Four Men And A Box, 1947

The intercourse of our minds is wonderful. We stimulate one another's thought.
Stephen Leacock, *Nonsense Novels*, 1911

One's density of mind is like a veil
Between oneself and heaven. And yet a mind
That seeks beyond its scope may cause some indigestion.
Louise Stone, *Housewife*, 1954

MIRACLE

People who believe in miracles do not make much fuss when they actually encounter one.
Alice Munro,
The Dance of the Happy Shades, 1968

MISERY

Alas, what dire and fateful lot is mine.
. . . Oh, the hopeless misery of my condition.
C.F. Newcomb and J.M. Hanks,
"The Fireworshippers", 1882

With few exceptions, the spirit receives its keenest misery from its own kin.
J.R. Ramsay, *One Quiet Day*, 1873

The experience of life proves to a certainty, that some persons are compelled to drink deeper of the cup of adversity than others, nay even to drain it to the dregs.
Samuel Strickland,
Twenty-Seven Years in Canada West, 1853

MISSIONARIES

So, in the footsteps of their patrons came
A group of men asking the hardest tasks
At the outposts of the Huron bounds
Held in the stern hand of the Jesuit Order.
E.J. Pratt, *Brebeuf and His Brethern*, 1940

MISTAKE

He is a perfect contradiction. He always laughs and cries in the wrong place.
Susanna Moodie, *Roughing It in the Bush*, 1852

A false vision was better than none.
Martha Ostenso, *Wild Geese*, 1925

MODERATION

Moderation is the wisdom which never quite exhausts its reservoirs of power; which never permits depletion, and is, therefore, never exhausted.
Bliss Carman, *The Kinship of Nature*, 1904

It is not the safety of moderation but its beauty and power that makes it so excellent and desirable a virtue.
Bliss Carman, *The Kinship of Nature*, 1904

There's such a thing as moderation, even in telling the truth.
Vera Johnson, *The Huckelmeyer Story*, 1953

MONEY

The economists, that confused company of theorists.
Clara Bernhardt, *The Poet's Function*, 1939

All around us there are all kinds of people prostituting their souls and their principles for money.
Morley Callaghan, *Such Is My Beloved*, 1934

If genius means extraordinary energy

allied to extraordinary originality, the great financier is undoubtedly a genius.
Robertson Davies,
the Introduction to: "Moonbeams from the Larger Lunacy" (S. Leacock), 1964

Privilege has always its last little stronghold, and it still operates to admiration on the office stools of minor finance.
Sara Jeannette Duncan, *The Imperialist*, 1904

Make money and the whole nation will conspire to call you a gentleman.
Robert C. Edwards, *Summer Annual*, 1920

People always laugh at the fool things you try to do until they discover you are making money out of them.
Robert C. Edwards, *Calgary Eye Opener*, 1919

There are more fortin's got by savin' than by makin'.
T.C. Haliburton, Sam Slick, 1835

In a world of economic competition you get the treatment your earning power dictates.
Hugh Hood, *It's a Small World*, 1967

You should be willing to purchase my skill, humble as it may be, as you would purchase any other commodity in the market, by what it is worth to you.
Joseph Howe, *The Locksmith of Philadelphia*

The great way to inspire brotherly love all round is to keep on getting richer and richer till you have so much money that every one loves you.
Stephen Leacock, *Further Foolishness*, 1916

Money is a troublesome thing. But it has got to be thought about even by those who were not brought up to it.
Stephen Leacock,
Arcadian Adventures with the Idle Rich, 1914

Today, money speaks in much louder tones, and learning in much humbler, while both law and medicine have cut down their own status by leaning too far towards the cash.
Arthur R.M. Lower, *Canadians in the Making*, 1958

Money is one of the most important elements in modern literature.
Jack Ludwig, *Fiction for the Majors*, 1960

The British are just as keen to make money as the Americans, but they prefer

hypocrisy to a blatantly commercial attitude.
Wendy Michener,
Towards a Popular Theatre, 1959

What's the good of money if you can't have a little fun with it?
Nellie L. McClung, *Sowing Seeds in Danny*, 1911

When money is scarce, man and beasts are very much alike: upon the least alarm, some run like foxes; and others are as familiar and crusty as bears.
Thomas McCulloch, *The Stepsure Letters*, 1822

Your family may increase, and your wants will increase in proportion. Out of what fund can you satisfy their demands?
Susanna Moodie, *Roughing It in the Bush*, 1852

I, with my whimsied past,
spend my father's riches with caresses
and with a nimble swagger
scar the city with dreams.
Michael Ondaatje, *Paris*, 1967

There's too strong a smell of money here. I confess it never bothered me before. Now it does.
Thomas H. Raddall, *A Muster to Arms*, 1954

Life and money — you can't separate them. Not on this planet. Not in the kind of life you have to live.
Thomas H. Raddall, *A Muster to Arms*, 1954

Money only means a lot when you ain't got it.
Arthur Stringer, *Weathered Oak*, 1939

When you impose money on every situation, you destroy man's relations with one another. Everyone is then either employer or employee. Only obligations remain.
Norman Williams, *The Mountain*, 1956

MONTHS of the YEAR

JANUARY

O laughing Maiden, January stands,
Bedecked in all her snowy mantle fair;
The sunlight glints upon her golden hair,
And sleeping branches fill her warm-gloved hands.
Donald A. Fraser, *January*

113

MARCH

March, the earth-shaker;
March, the sea-lifter;
March, the sky-render.
Isabella Valancy Crawford, *March*

APRIL

The fragrant treasure ship of April lies
In Spring's green harbour.
Rose Winters Burns, *Argosy,* 1961

April, the weaver
Of delicate blossoms,
And moulder of red buds.
Isabella Valancy Crawford, *March*

Maid month of sunny peace and sober
gray,
Weaver of flowers in sunward glades that
ring
With murmur of libation to the spring.
Archibald Lampman, *April*

JUNE

June is the time for lovers!
D.K. Findlay, *To Bid You Welcome*

JULY

July is an emerald,
And in its shimmering depths
My winter-weary heart
Finds peace.
Bluebell Stewart Phillips, *In December,* 1955

OCTOBER

There is something in October sets the
gypsy blood astir;
We must rise and follow her,
When from every hill of flame
She calls and calls each vagabond by
name.
Bliss Carman, *A Vagabond Song,* 1896

DECEMBER

Vain is the spring, and summer a care,
All days are December's.
Joan Buckley, *No Memories,* 1936

MONTREAL

City entirely surrounded by sewers, one of
which provides the drinking water.
Louis Dudek, *O Montreal,* 1963

It is an old city, my city,
Hoary with centuries
Of stimulating clash.
Doris Hedges, *My City,* 1956

Two old races and religions meet here and
live their separate legends, side by side. If
this sprawling half-continent has a heart,
here it is.
Hugh MacLennan, *Two Solitudes,* 1945

An imitation of every example of bad taste
in the universe, and as dull and almost as
dirty as Liverpool.
Hugh MacLennan, *Two Solitudes,* 1945

Bleury, a street which runs through Montreal like a frontier, dividing the English
from the French.
Hugh MacLennan, *Two Solitudes,* 1945

Montreal from the river wears a pleasing
aspect, but it lacks the grandeur, the stern
sublimity of Quebec.
Susanna Moodie, *Roughing It in the Bush,*
1852

The ghetto of Montreal has no real walls
and no true dimensions. The walls are the
habit of atavism and the dimensions are an
illusion.
Mordecai Richler, *Son of a Smaller Hero,*
1955

MOON

Craters, and desolate mounds
Mark hidden sepulchres
Of buried aeons.
Elizabeth Donaldson, *The Moon,* 1939

MORALITY

These moralists are growing overnice:
Surely, my friend, some need there is for
spice!
The salt and pepper of impropriety —
I would not call it vice.
Tom MacInnes, *Beauty,* 1918

We can best judge of the moral ideas of a
people by their conceptions of God and
duty.
E.H. Dewart, *Essays for the Times,* 1898

If moral beauty we would wed,
We must, as the Great Master said,
Of little children learn.
Nicholas Flood Davin, *To "Bay Mi",* 1884

Whatever veneer society had applied to her manners, her morals were those of the mink.
John Gray,
When Elephants Roost in the Trees, 1957

The moral structure of our society is based on a complete reversal of natural morality.
Alden A. Nowlan, *A Defence of Obscenity,* 1959

Manners and morals are never at a standstill. Either they rise or they decline. Like empires.
Mazo de la Roche, *The Building of Jalna,* 1927

MORNING

Morning came at me like a flung snowball, the light flaked out of a chalk-blue sky.
Louis Dudek,
Puerto Rican Side Street, 1951

Morning is more still
Than a long pause
Stretching awkwardly across the room.
Anne Wilkinson, *Summer Storm,* 1968

MOTHER

She has a good smile.
She changes diapers. She puts the wash through and comes
Smiling in to ask what she can do.
Jack Crawford (Jr),
She's the Wife of the Butcher, 1969

What is a man's mother but a gateway through which he enters the world, and which he leaves farther behind with every step?
Robertson Davies,
At the Gates of the Righteous

Motherhood is the greatest thing in the world, . . . it is creation itself — that is, in its highest form.
William Alexander Fraser, *The Lone Furrow*

It is a great responsibility to be a mother, and yet how few there be that think of it.
Nellie L. McClung, *Sowing Seeds in Danny,* 1911

Its monstrous strange how having young makes the female wicked.
Mazo de la Roche, *The Building of Jalna,* 1927

MOUNTAINS

The mountains may be your friend, but the sea is your lover.
Bliss Carman, *The Friendship of Art,* 1904

Who rings his heart with mountains
Will never wander far
Over wide and treeless land
Under alien star.
Joy Trail, *Of Mountains and the Sea,* 1962

MUSIC

I made me long ago, a golden harp, . . . : and I the player,
Slept in the wonder of the music's charm,
And life seemed very far — no world of mine.
Hyman Edelstein, *Ideals and Life,* 1916

Of all artists, musicians are most exclusive in devotion to their own art, and in the want of sympathy, if not absolute contempt, for other arts.
Anna Brownell Jameson, *Winter Studies,* 1838

MYSTERY

Some mystery there must be —
Solution is not known.
W.W.E. Ross, *A Death,* 1969

MYTH

Whistling shamans cannot raise a myth
Buried in archives, in old men's graves.
Floris MacLaren, *Northwest Coast*

Romantic myth-making originates with a vision of the universe as being substantiated by a metaphysical principle by which it is rendered both one and alive.
John Ower, *Black and Secret Poet,* 1969

NAME

Nicknames stick to people and the most ridiculous are the most adhesive.
T.C. Haliburton, *Sam Slick,* 1853

Without a name I am nothing.
Unless you can name me I do not exist.
John Hulcoop, *A Fable for James,* 1968

Changing names, as everyone knows, is an important part of my religious tradition.
Jack Ludwig, *Confusions,* 1960

Long habit has made the English names of many places and positions so familiar to many in Canada that to adhere to the French form in all instances would be as unnatural as to Anglicise all names throughout.
William McLennan and J.N. McIlwraith, *The Span O'Life*, 1899

NATIONALISM

Political nationalism has little positively to do with the cultural traditions of peoples.
George Woodcock,
Views of Canadian Criticism, 1966

NATIONALITY

Nationality is of no consequence. In the things of the spirit there is no such barrier.
John Marlyn, *Under the Ribs of Death*, 1957

NATION

Any process of blending implies confusion to begin with; we are here at the making of a nation.
Sara Jeannette Duncan, *The Imperialist*, 1904

Each mountain
its own country
in the way a country
must be
A state of mind.
Sid Marty, *Each Mountain*, 1971

A country too sharply divided against itself may be culturally no more healthy than it is politically.
George Woodcock,
A Commonwealth of Literature, 1963

NATURE

Nature, highly selective in all things, is most selective with death. The weak neither ask for nor obtain mercy.
Fred Bodsworth, *Last of the Curlews*, 1954

Here where the jewels of nature
Are set in the light of God's smile,
Far from the world's wild throbbing,
I will stay me and rest awhile.
William W. Campbell, *Vapour and Blue*

Nature takes very little thought of herself. It is our human minds that are retrospective, brooding, careworn.
Bliss Carman, *The Kinship of Nature*, 1904

The greatest joy in nature is the absence of man.
Bliss Carman, *The Kinship of Nature*, 1904

How marvellous the works of God! How ugly the things man makes!
Ralph Connor, *The Prospector*, 1904

The elements are sometimes kinder than men, and I feel safer here, even in this river of death, than ashore with such creatures as those.
James De Mille, *A Strange Manuscript*, 1888

Nature is neutral to all values.
Louis Dudek, *Nature*, 1966

I sometimes think that the human spirit, as it is set free in these wide unblemished spaces, may be something more pure and sensitive, more sincerely curious about what is good and beautiful.
Sara Jeannette Duncan, *The Imperialist*, 1904

The forest has spells to enchant me,
The mountain has power to enthrall;
Yet the grace of a wayside blossom
Can stir my heart deeper than all.
James D. Edgar, *Saguenay*

The continual contemplation of nature drives some men to commit crimes; of others it makes poets and gentle thinkers.
S. Frances Harrison,
The Forest of Bourg-Marie

Child of the roofless world am I;
Not of those hibernating drones
Who fear the gray of a wintry sky
And the shrieking wind's ironic tones.
Wilson MacDonald, *The Song of the Ski*

Nature has established a relation between male and female, which constitutes a basis for duty; and a feeling of duty produces exertions of energy, which exhalt the mind and give it exhalted pleasures.
Thomas McCulloch, *The Stepsure Letters*, 1821

The wind in the leaves and the roar of the sea,
These are the sounds that are dearest to me.
Laura E. McCully, *Pioneering*

Ah, glorious Nature! beautiful, purest of all that is pure and holy. Thou visible perfection of the invisible God.
Susanna Moodie, *Geoffrey Moncton*, 1855

Nature is the best guide in works of art, why should not our conversation and manners be governed by the same unerring rule?
Sussanna Moodie, *Geoffrey Moncton*, 1855

Mankind unkind breeds hate in his own kind,
Who turns to Nature, only love shall find.
Frederic Philips, *Nature. A Fragment*, 1909

Nature is womanly. She reserves her choicest smiles for the one who appreciates her.
J.R. Ramsay, *One Quiet Day*, 1873

Are you deaf to the note
In the woodland that rings
With the song of the whitethroat,
As crystal as dew?
Theodore Harding Rand, *The Dragon-Fly*

Nature is not always spectacular and bloody, it works by inexorable law — the struggle for survival.
Charles G.D. Roberts,
"The Last Barrier"

You couldn't find anything cleaner than nature or anything dirtier than man when he goes against nature.
Mazo de la Roche, *Come True*, 1926

I have laid my cheek to Nature's, placed my puny hand in hers,
Felt a kindred spirit warming all the life blood of my face.
Charles Sangster, *The St. Lawrence*, 1856

This is God's house — the blue sky is the ceiling,
This wood the soft, green carpet for His feet,
Those hills His stairs, down which the brooks come stealing.
Frederick George Scott, *In The Woods*

There is always some beauty or some usefulness to be found, however lonely the spot.
Catherine Parr Traill, *Canadian Crusoes*, 1850

NEUTRAL

I'm strictly neutral! and my feelings smother!
I hate one side! and can't abide the other!
Sam Scribble, *Dolorsolatio*, 1865

NEW BRUNSWICK

Like all impoverished provinces — this was a land of soldiers.
Alden Nowlan, *His Native Place*, 1969

NEWFOUNDLAND

A Newfoundlander of the upper shore — the child of a grey, solemn waste-place: a land of artifical graveyards.
Norman Duncan, *The Chase of the Tide*

Hurrah for our own native isle, Newfoundland!
Not a stranger shall hold one inch of her strand!
Her face turns to Britain, her back to the Gulf.
Come near at your peril, Canadian Wolf!
(Folklore), *Anti-Confederation Song*

In Newfoundland any water less than a hundred square miles in area is a pond.
Edward McCourt,
Overland from Signal Hill to Victoria

The Newfoundland song has a defensive or reckless quality missing from most English songs.
Paul West, *The Unwitting Elegiac*, 1961

NEW FRANCE

However starved New France may have been for settlers, it never lacked administrators.
Alan Gowans,
Architecture in New France, 1960

NEWS

If you have anything to tell me of importance, for God's sake begin at the end.
Sara Jeannette Duncan, *The Imperialist*, 1904

With us in America the great thing is to get the news and shout it at the reader; in England they get the news and then break it to him as gently as possible.
Stephen Leacock, *My Discovery of England*, 1922

An early messenger brings no good tidings.
Samuel James Watson, *Ravlan*, 1876

NEWSPAPERS

Everybody knows that it is easy work to

edit a daily newspaper; indeed, everybody knows exactly how it should be done.
Robertson Davies,
"The Double Life of Robertson Davies", 1954

The only paper from which a man can really get the news of the world in a shape that he can understand is the newspaper of his own 'home town'.
Stephen Leacock,
My Discovery of England, 1922

Canadian newspapers clearly play little serious part in the literary life of the country.
Donald Stainsby, *The Press and Literature*, 1961

Our love of gossip and our interest in personalities is reflected in the popularity of the newspaper columnist.
E.H. Winter,
the Introduction to:
"Our Century in Prose", 1966

NEW YEAR'S EVE

The year is dead, for Death slays even time.
Nathaniel A. Benson, *Year's End*

Beyond the reach of sound and sight
The living days and nights have rolled:
Another year has died tonight.
Fred Cogswell,
Vilanelle of the Dead Year, 1955

NIAGARA FALLS

There is nothing at hand to compare them with, and a man must see them often, and from every different point of view, to have any proper conception of the nature of them.
William Dunlop, *Recollections*, 1847

Who can behold the mighty
Niagara and say 'there is no God'.
Samuel Strickland,
Twenty-Seven Years in Canada West, 1853

NIGHT

In the dead of night
the hours drop lifeless.
William Conklin, *Night Shadows*, 1953

Night presses always to still and close eyes or flowers or dancing feet.
Phyllis Gotlieb, *Bestiary*, 1963

Thou art my friend, my comrade
O night! who bendest low
To strike the eyes of dullness
With blindness. Let us go
Into thy purpled chambers
And lose and leave behind
The moribund procession
Of blind who lead the blind.
Norman Gregor Guthrie,
Love and Darkness, 1928

Night! The abhorred magician Night!
The black astrologer Night!
Kate Seymour Maclean,
Night — A Phantasy, 1881

People walking amid trees after night always draw closer together instinctively and involuntarily, making an alliance, physical and mental, against certain alien powers around them.
L.M. Montgomery, *Rainbow Valley*, 1919

Infold us with thy peace, dear moon-lit night,
And let thy silver silence wrap us round,
Till we forget the city's dazzling light,
The city's ceaseless sound.
Virna Sheard, *Nocturne*

NON-CONFORMITY

I am many reprehensible things, in the eyes of the bourgeoisie, because I am unlike them. But therein lies my defence.
Robertson Davies, *Leaven of Malice*, 1954

The non-conformist conscience, however secularized and diluted by culture is a bitter thing.
Millar Maclure, *English Notes*, 1959

Were not people suspicious because he was unable immediately to conform?
William McConnell, *The Alien*

You are not of their world, you are strangers, you are the enemies, the hated, Because you laugh at their money, their women, the cheapness of their lives.
Raymond Souster, *The Enemies*, 1944

THE NORTH

Hoho! hoho! for the glistering North!
With her gold that is locked in ice;
She calls to the sons of men "Come forth!"
Come! buy my gold at a price.
Frederick Philips, *The Klondike*, 1909

The North is for the strong,
for those who, . . .
have named the dismal lakes,
who've sowed their names upon the floods
and tides.
Clair Pratt, *The North,* 1967

Somewhere behind us we have left our
gold and our jewels;
They are without meaning in this land of
pensive trees.
Elfreida Read, *The Meeting Point,* 1955

This is the Law of the Yukon, that only the
Strong shall survive;
That surely the Weak shall perish, and only
the Fit survive.
Robert Service, *The Law of the Yukon,* 1907

Here's to the Land of the rock and the pine!
Here's to the Land of the raft and the river!
Here's to the Land where the sunbeams
shine,
And the night that is bright with the North -
Light's quiver!
William Wye Smith, *Here's To the Land!*

In the North he who travels not, starves.
Alan Sullivan, *The Salving of Pyack*

NOVELS

The characteristic hero of the contemporary English novel is a young man
educated beyond his station, resolved to
find a comfortable niche for himself within
an existing, although shrinking, class
structure.
Nathan Cohen,
Heroes of the Richler View, 1958

The best of novels are only scenarios, to be
completed by the reader's own experience.
Robertson Davies, *A Voice from the Attic,*
1960

The modern novel must convey a message,
or else it must paint a picture, or remove a
veil, or open a new chapter in human
psychology. Otherwise it is no good.
Stephen Leacock,
Moonbeams from the Larger Lunacy, 1916

A novel should concern people, not ideas,
and yet people had become trivial.
Hugh MacLennan, *Two Solitudes,* 1945

The novel is still a popular form, nourished
intravenously by the paper-back
publishers.
Millar MacLure, *Two First Novels,* 1958

To read novels is to gain impressions.
Warren Tallman, *Wolf in the Snow II,* 1960

Until sociologists made a profession of
social observation and a science out of
case histories, no one doubted the sociality
of the novel.
Miriam Waddington, *New Year's Eve,* 1968

Novels are the holidays of poets, gallant
excursions into the workaday lands of
other men from which they either return in
triumph with strange, outlandish cargoes,
or, just as often, come back dashed and dejected by the rains of an alien shore.
George Woodcock, *The Comic Novelist,* 1963

NOVELIST

The novelists' business, . . . is to explore
the territories of his experience . . . and
then to map his discoveries, give them
clear, coherent and accurate shape.
Michael Hornyansky,
Countries of the Mind, 1963

A familiar figure in Canadian literature is
the novelist who races down to the shore
of Lake Experience, strips to the buff, and
strikes out with lemming - like
determination for 'the depths'.
Hugo McPherson, *Three Canadian Novels,*
1958

NOVA SCOTIA

Let's away to New Scotland, where Plenty
sits queen
O'er as happy a country as ever was seen.
Anon, *Nova Scotia: A New Ballad,* 1750

The whole province is a sort of railway
station, where crowds are perpetually
arriving and departing.
T.C. Haliburton, *The Old Judge,* 1849

The evergreen forests . . . cover most of
Nova Scotia like a shaggy hide.
Hugh MacLennan, *Two Solitudes,* 1945

OATH

No one need fear oaths that are properly
enunciated, for they belong to the

inheritance of just men made perfect, and, for all we know, of such may be the Kingdom of Heaven.
E.J. Pratt, *Silences,* 1937

My oaths are empty; I can swear to everything.
The scholar too scrupulous to swear to anything
Was you. Much good it did you. Trouble, Trouble!
Lister Sinclair, *Return to Colonus,* 1955

OBEDIENCE

When a man's too tired to eat or speak he's still willing to obey.
Hugh MacLennan, *Barometer Rising,* 1941

Obedience is the best sacrifice!
Robert Norwood, *The Witch of Endor,* 1916

Horse, or man, or dog aren't much good till they learn to obey.
Marshall Saunders, *Beautiful Joe*

OBSOLESCENCE

Obsolescence was a thing we had never heard about in those days. Things just wore out and were patched or repaired into new usefulness until they vanished.
Harry Boyle, *Homebrew and Patches*

OLD AGE

You can feel his thoughts
As he slips so easily into reverie
As only old and lonely people do.
Marjorie Blanchard,
After Thoughts on "Early March", 1967

Strange old man . . . a failure
by any standard you can name,
yet that hoar head held high
speaks not defeat.
Mary Elizabeth Colman, *Death of a Stranger,* 1938

Only the young have song, but the old have knowledge.
Kathleen Earle, *Laughter,* 1940

I have known toil and pain and anxious hours.
Glad should I be that now my task is o'er.
And yet, oh God! how much I long to hear
The rush of eager footsteps at my door.
Edith B. Henderson, *Empty Hands,* 1938

The summer's past
As my old bones do know. When you grow
As old as I, the current runs but slow,
And the frost bites.
Norah Mary Holland, *When Half Gods Go,* 1924

'Tis old men should be brave, their time is short.
John Hunter-Duvar, *The Enamorado,* 1879

Old age with nothing to look back upon, nothing to lean upon, is poor stuff as compared with the old age that renews its youth and life and interests in its children and grandchildren.
Stephen Leacock, *Woman's Level*

At seventy-five you can feel warm, sweet, girlish even, but an old, old face has trouble expressing soft feelings.
Jack Ludwig, *A Woman of Her Age,* 1962

Youth is a fine adventure,
But it's rare to be old.
Wilson MacDonald, *Oaks,* 1926

In the old of my age Life's basement bargain booth
Has marked me down from dollar tab to dime.
Tom MacInnes, *In The Old of my Age*

When everything is done, old men can rejoice, being old.
Eli Mandel, *An Idiot Joy,* 1968

What a span it is, what a little span it seems, when our griefs and ecstasies are faded and shrivelled and held up to the reminiscent vision of old age!
Suzanne Marny, *The Footstool,* 1909

The very best thing an old man can do, to keep himself warm and comfortable, and to prolong his days upon the earth, is to take a young wife.
Susanna Moodie,
Old Woodruff and His Three Wives, 1847

If you live to be old, you can't help commiting a lot more sins.
Brian Moore, *A Vocation,* 1956

Old people do not really forget more readily than young; they have more things to remember.
E.W. Nichols, *On Lying Awake,* 1929

Our carefree youth has crossed its stage;
We fear the ills from colds and spills, —

We've reached our winter of old age!
Doris E. Baillie Phillips, *Winter*, 1961

Let others sing of Youth and Spring, still will it seem to me
The golden time's the olden time, some time round sixty-five.
Robert Service, *A Song of Sixty-Five*, 1921

He has reached the dusk of all his loneliness.
His sun of ecstasy has lost its gleam!
Lucia Trent, *Old Man Passes*, 1952

She was old; not so old in years, perhaps, but in struggle.
Alberta C. Trimble, *Mrs. Balcom's Hat*

ONTARIO

I've had enough of this inert
Ontario, this eunuch sea
And pastured fenced nonentity.
Earle Birney, *Eagle Island*, 1941

Away!
Let's away from the Pandora's Box of Western Ontario!
Joan Finnigan, *Saga of Number Seven*, 1962

Ontario the beautiful, whose streams
Are fitting mirrors for Canadian daughters
To dwell beside and bathe within their beams.
J.R. Ramsay, *"I.O.G.T."*, 1873

Ontario! we speak thy name with awe!
Home of Draconic (and Druidic) law;
In conference defended by thy pride
Are ways provincial — and exemplified.
William Robbins, *Canadiad*, 1947

Ontario? There's more vitality
In one D.P. than in all the prosperous burghers
Of that fat land.
Fred Swayze, *The Great Canadian Novel*, 1952

OPINION

Nations are just like people. They see things solely from their own point of view.
Ralph Connor, *The Major*, 1917

A public servant has no right to an opinion on any subject that's got two sides to it.
Robertson Davies, *A Voice from the Attic*, 1960

Things never look the same from the outside as they do from the inside.
Margaret Laurence, *The Stone Angel*, 1964

What do I care now what people say? I cared too long.
Margaret Laurence, *The Stone Angel*, 1964

Society is a huge tyrant. Few care to face the great bugbear, and that is why so many follow opinion or fashion instead of principle
J.R. Ramsay, *One Quiet Day*, 1873

OPPORTUNITY

When the violins play, then is the time to dance.
Blanche Lucile Macdonell,
Diane of Ville Marie, 1898

ORGANIZATION

Today we are technicians, and the more progressive among us see no reason why love and hope should not be organized in a department of the government, planned by a politician and administered by trained specialists.
Hugh MacLennan, *An Orange from Portugal*

OTTAWA

Ottawa is a city where nobody lives, though some of us may die there.
Michael Macklem, *A Book a Mile*, 1970

Hail! to the city sitting as a queen
Enthroned, a cataract on either hand,
The voice of many waters in her ears,
And the great river tranquil at her feet.
Nora Pembroke, *Ottawa*, 1880

When the croon of a rapid is heard on the breeze,
With the scent of a pine-forest gloom,
Then my heart hurries home to the Ottawa hills,
Wherever I happen to be.
Edward William Thomson, *A Canadian Abroad*

Before you grow
too tall,
And have outgrown
All your quaint old ways, dear city remember.
Ermina Tribble, *To Ottawa*, 1967

The Ottawa river flows out of Protestant Ontario into Catholic Quebec.
Hugh MacLennan, *Two Solitudes*, 1945

OVERPOPULATION

We must decrease or crowded starve;
Our earth a living tomb.
Val Haigh, *Explosions*, 1961

PAIN

They tell me it is spring again,
And who am I to say they're wrong,
But in my heart is bitter pain,
And no bird song.
Helen Fitzgerald Doughter, *Indifference* 1942

Pain was your vocation and achievement,
The restless sea your anthemed citadel.
Douglas Le Pan, *A Fallen Prophet*, 1963

If I am fire, and you are always rain,
We know a different quality of pain.
Tom Marshall, *If I am Free*, 1965

Who can borrow
Joy or sorrow,
Light or darkness
Without pain?
Robert Norwood, *The Witch of Endor*, 1916

Why inflict pain on one's self when so many others are ready to save us the trouble?
Geo. W. Pacaud, *Social Idolatry*, 1920

Strange as it may seem, there is often a sensation of pleasure in the very sharpness of a pain.
J.J. Procter,
The Philosopher in the Clearing, 1897

PAINTER

The only significant difference between the painter and the poet is one of means.
John W. Bilsland, *Vision of Clarity*, 1960

They are strange animals, and, as such, merit suspicion.
William Arthur Deacon, *Local Colour*

PARENTS

However hellish parents may be, the duty is as real as the duty that exists in marriage.
Robertson Davies, *Leaven of Malice*, 1954

The child pays, not only for the sins of the parents, but also for their mistakes and for their lack of knowledge.
Nina Moore Jamieson, *The Hickory Stick*, 1921

PASSION

If you keep waiting for the grand passion it will never come and then you'll know that what you had was all that there was to have.
Janet Bonellie,
Why Are The People Staring?, 1968

I find, . . . that absence and amusement are the best remedies for a beginning passion.
Frances Brooke,
The History of Emily Montague, 1769

Time only proves the truth of worth and love,
The one may be a cheat, the other change,
And fears, and jealousies, and mortal hate
Succeed the sunshine of the warmest passion.
Robert Rogers, *Ponteach*, 1766

Passion ripens a woman as the sunshine ripens a peach.
Robert Service, *The Ballad of the Brand*, 1907

PAST

If only you could wind up your yesterdays, make them, even tinnily, repeat themselves.
Leslie Gordon Barnard, *The Dancing Bear*, 1945

I do not begrudge
The past for being past; I only
Forbid the future any further choice,
Having, at last, come home.
Ronald Bates, *Orpheus and Odyseus*, 1952

O Time, whose song Lethean has eased our pain, —
Call us not back to agony again!
Irene Chapman Benson, *A Plea for Peace*, 1938

That was our world —
But oh — it was long ago.
Freda Newton Bunner, *In The Far-Off Times*, 1954

Ah! happy days, with these innocent
crimes and fleeting remorses, how
bravely we faced them, and how gaily we
lived them, and how yearningly we look
back at them now!
Ralph Connor, *Black Rock*, 1900

And weeping for the days gone by, my
heart
grew cold as stone.
James Dollard, *The Fairy Harpers*

We can live nobler when the past we
know;
Look farther forward, as we see behind.
Donald A. Fraser, *To Memory*, 1931

Canadians have forgotten the tempests in
their own past, and few have known any at
all in a direct way.
John Graham, *From the Lion's Mouth*, 1957

I know nothing now of things I cried for
yesterday
or other pain that scooped me hollow.
Now I am breathing air and looking east.
Ester Gridjonson, *Nostalgia*, 1949

Faraway comes close
and long ago is now.
Marion Kathleen Henry, *Pinewood Evening*,
1956

To be part of the land seemed almost possible when the gun grew in the hand and
the finger bent on the trigger.
D.G. Jones, *Sequence of Night*, 1969

I think about my past and try to change
Into a singing metaphor a silent heart.
Eli Mandel, *Children of the Sun*, 1960

Oh, dreams to be no more!
All — all in life would I forsake, To dream
them o'er and o'er
To know that innocence again,
That felt not nor imparted pain.
J.R. Newell, *A Youthful Reminiscence*, 1881

I have learned little from the years that fly;
But I have wrung the colour from the
years.
Frances Pollock, *Sonnet III*, 1937

The past is for the old, not the young.
Edwin R. Procunier, *The Second Duchess*,
1962

Don't brood on what's past but never
forget it either.
Thomas H. Raddall, *A Harp in the Willows*

Worlds do change and people cannot con-
tinue to live in the past, however gracious.
Joseph Lister Rutledge,
This Stubborn Breed, 1956

I have no history
but the length of my bones.
Robin Skelton, *Report on Arrival*, 1963

the world is getting
dark but I carry
icons I remember
the summer
I will never forget
the light.
Miriam Waddington, *Icons*, 1969

So much for the past: there is really none,
or none that has much bearing on the
present.
Christopher Wanklyn,
Going Tangerine, 1959

PATIENCE

Patience sings a small song
not a fine song like joy or grief.
Anne Margaret Angus,
All These My Children, 1967

If patience be of God
Then I am none of His.
Freda Newton Bunner, *Anno Domini*, 1966

There's nothing like a few hard knocks to
learn a man patience.
D.M. Currie, *And Be My Love*

One must have patience, endurance;
these brought resignation and with
resignation might come wisdom.
W.B. Holliday,
F.P. Grove: An Impression, 1960

Patience is an old man's virtue, but I could
be so patient, so serene, if only I saw in
the future a glimmer of hope for that
which is beyond my reach today.
Nina Moore Jamieson, *The Hickory Stick*,
1921

What can't be cured, must be endured: let
us have patience.
Thomas McCulloch, *The Stepsure Letters*,
1821

Patience is a tired mare but she jogs on.
L.M. Montgomery, *Rilla of Ingleside*, 1921

Patience is nothing but Self's heartless
text
That age expounds to torture us withal.
Samuel James Watson, *Ravlan*, 1876

PATRIOT

The true patriot is one who is neither a
sycophant to the government nor a tyrant
to the people, but one who will manfully
oppose either when they are wrong.
T.C. Haliburton, *Sam Slick*, 1853

Most men, as you know,
Are not repelled by base considerations
Food and warmth and women are their
need;
It is the job of patriots to provide them;
Within the structure of society.
Lister Sinclair, *Return to Colonus*, 1955

PATRIOTISM

The same brand of patriotism is never
likely to exist all over Canada. Each race
so violently disapproves of the tribal gods
of the other I can't see how any single
Canadian politician can ever imitate
Hitler.
Hugh MacLennan, *Two Solitudes*, 1945

There are a great many things that are
sweet and fair-seeming besides dying for
one's country.
Nobody does that now-a-days.
J.J. Procter,
The Philosopher in the Clearing, 1897

A nation's patriotism is generally in
proportion to its literature.
J.R. Ramsay, *Some Canadian Books*, 1873

PATRONIZING

Now
They patronize me — damn their in-
solence!
Marjorie McKenzie, *Satan Complains*, 1936

PAYMENT

All
must be taken into account
sooner or later
later or sooner; eyeglasses
only magnify the mysteries.
Gwendolyn MacEwen, *Poem for G.W.*, 1963

So eat, drink and be merry, have a good
time if you will,
But God help you when the time comes,
and you
Foot the bill.
Robert Service, *The Reckoning*, 1907

PEACE

He has learned to possess his soul. He is
without haste.
Bliss Carman, *The Kinship of Nature*, 1904

As for me, I'm time-weary,
I await my release.
Give to others the struggle,
Grant me but the peace.
Nicholas Flood Davin, *Poem*, 1900

So again I will search, for there must be a
way
To attain peace of mind, to emerge from
this grey
And passionless sea to life's surface.
Linda Drew, *The Search*, 1961

Peace, in crowds, shows not her gentle
face
But stands revealed in quietude and
space.
Margaret Fulton Frame,
The Cathedral, 1947

We peacemakers are all agreed that there
must be no question of religion raised.
Stephen Leacock, *Further Foolishness*, 1916

There is very little peace to be had for you,
or for me, or for any animate thing in this
world, for perfect peace here means
stagnation and stagnation means death.
J.J. Procter,
The Philosopher in the Clearing, 1897

The symbol of the dove is not enough,
The god has departed from it, and it rattles
ominously.
Elfreida Read, *To the Peace-Makers*, 1956

Peace has its charms for those who love
their ease,
But active souls like mine delight in blood.
Robert Rogers, *Ponteach*, 1766

When our children's children shall talk of
War as a madness that may not be;
When we thank our God for our grief to-
day, and blazon from sea to sea

In the name of the Dead the banner of
Peace . . . that will be Victory.
Robert Service,
The Song of the Pacifist, 1916

Should we ask for days without strife
When this is the secret of life.
Phyllis Catherine Wright, *Life,* 1952

PEOPLE

We will never with people people this
country
no matter how much white seed our hot
poets spurt.
R. Gibbs, *Crossward Country,* 1969

Don't you think that it is possible to know
people too well for their comfort and
yours?
Raymond Knister, *White Narcissus,* 1929

There are two sorts of people in whom
other people are likely to place their confidence: those who are frank since they
are believed honest, and those who are
secretive because they are thought experienced.
Irving Layton, *Vacation in La Voiselle,* 1946

The young have always been young, and
the old always old . . . men and women
don't change.
Stephen Leacock,
Are Witty Women Attractive to Men

It is the wishes and likings of the mass
which largely dictate what the rest of us
shall see and hear.
Stephen Leacock,
Humor, Its Theory and Technique, 1935

We're a people without anything to pass
on to the next generation.
Edward McCourt, *Home Is the Stranger,*
1949

The only people one can feel truly at ease
with are those who are disinterested.
C.J. Newman, *An Arab Up North,* 1968

"Ithers" are to us, not
necessarily what they really are,
but what we conceive them to be.
J.J. Procter,
The Philosopher in the Clearing, 1897

PERFECTION

There is a passion for perfection which
you will rarely see fully developed; but you
may note this fact, that in successful lives
it is never wholly lacking.
Bliss Carman, *The Friendship of Art,* 1904

The blameless life is often hidden under a
mask of woebegone unloveliness.
Bliss Carman, *The Kinship of Nature,* 1904

If a man wants to be of the greatest possible value to his fellow-creatures let him
begin the long, solitary task of perfecting
himself.
Robertson Davies, *A Jig for the Gypsy,* 1954

A perfect thing is a gift of the gods — a
sort of compensation for what is coming
afterwards.
L.M. Montgomery, *Rilla of Ingleside,* 1921

PERSEVERANCE

I do not know a greater charm than, after
years of toil and privation, to see what
perseverance and industry have accomplished.
Samuel Strickland,
Twenty-Seven Years in Canada West, 1853

PIONEERS

During the first few years it is really the
woman that makes the living on a pioneer
farm. She keeps chickens, cows and pigs.
The man makes the land.
Frederick P. Grove, *Settlers of the Marsh,*
1925

A visit is an event in the bush!
Frederick P. Grove, *Snow,* 1932

A Canadian settler hates a tree, regards it
as his natural enemy, as something to be
destroyed, eradicated, annihilated by all
and any means.
Anna Brownell Jameson, *Winter Studies,*
1838

Let your imagination wander along the
lines of the rivers marked on the maps
and try to think — just a little, try to think
— what manner of human being lies
behind this peculiar nation.
Hugh MacLennan,
The People Behind This Peculiar Nation

There's no peace in the woods where the
settler has come,
He must kill and destroy for his life and a
home,

And make war on the ranks of the firs.
Frederic Philips, *The Passing of the Fir*, 1909

Pioneer women are good at business, even if they seem to handle it in a funny way sometimes.
R.D. Symons, *Many Trails*

Taking possession of a new land psychologically is a far slower process than merely occupying it physically.
R.E. Watters, *Original Relations*, 1959

Pioneers did not produce original works of art, because they were creating original human environments; they did not imagine utopias because they were shaping them.
George Woodcock, *An Absence of Utopias*, 1969

PITY

The madman under the quilt has not one friend
except Pity — no others call.
R.G. Everson, *Department Thirteen*, 1963

Above pity, we're above despair.
Raymond Knister, *White Narcissus*, 1929

Grieve not for me, I have chosen the harder way;
Nor would I retrace one step and elsewhere go.
Wilson MacDonald,
The Song of a Plutocrat, 1926

A woman loves to pity the captive, whatever his fault, if he be presentable and of some notice or talent.
Gilbert Parker,
The Seats of the Mighty, 1896

PLANS

My idealistic schemes and plans of life, like those of other people, are apt to be upset by the small motives — of pique, ill-temper, nervous distaste — with which my everyday decisions are often swayed.
M. Allerdale Grainger,
Woodsmen of the West, 1908

All his grand schemes were as open as sunlight — and as empty.
Stephen Leacock, *My Remarkable Uncle*

Every poet has the foul papers of a 'long poem' in his desk; every professor a 'project'.
Millar MacLure, *Two First Novels*, 1958

PLEASURE

Gentle and just pleasure
It is, being human, to have won from space
This chill habitable interior.
Margaret Avison, *New Year's Poem*, 1956

Dis is my day for sinful pleasure.
Frank Parker Day, *Rockbound*

Pleasure . . . is the last faint crimson flush which a setting sun has left to die alone in a cold gray sky.
George V. Hobart, *Experience*, 1914

I have the Canadian's remorseless conscience, unalloyed by the experience of raw pleasure.
Hugh Hood, *It's A Small World*, 1967

As a rule the cheap fun that excites the rustic to laughter is execrable to the man of education.
Stephen Leacock,
My Discovery of England, 1922

Time cannot filch from me mine ancient pleasure:
They grow but greener as the years slip by.
Wilson MacDonald, *Immortal*, 1938

How ardently we anticipate pleasure, which often ends in positive pain!
Susanna Moodie, *Roughing It in the Bush*, 1852

POEMS

A poem is a tear drop, told in superlative, so you are able to see the rainbow in it!
Tibor Baranyai, *What is a Poem?*

A poem is the passionate cry of the man himself, and should reflect all the searching and striving of his own soul, and its ultimate fulfilment.
Clara Bernhardt, *The Poet's Function*, 1939

To write a poem
one must experience
and then forget,
waiting for blood

to become spirit
and return.
Marguerite Edmonds, *(no title)*, 1966

On these nights
my poems turn away from me
like cold women.
Craig Sterry, *Looking at My Hands*, 1969

POETS

Men's souls are sick, and to whom shall
they go, if the poets fail them?
Clara Bernhardt, *The Poet's Function*, 1939

The poet is stone —
Cold, isolate.
Doreen Gordon Davis, *Of Ivory Towers*, 1953

The poet, living in a cloud of violent dream,
congested with energy,
illuminates only as lightning does, fitfully,
with less light than thunder.
Louis Dudek, *Danger*, 1952

Talented women poets seem on the whole
to be less embarrassed by their limitations.
Chester Duncan, *Poetry Chronicle*, 1957

The poet must be driven, not a driver.
Joseph Fisher, *The Finishing Touches*, 1937

Perhaps the poet speaks his heart
In what he leaves unsung.
Margaret Fulton Frame, *To a Poet*, 1947

The poet . . . is not heard, but overheard.
Northrop Frye,
The Function of Criticism, 1954

Only poets ask questions that no one can
answer.
Harry Green, *The Death of Pierrot*, 1926

Why do you call the poet lonely,
Because he dreams in lonely places?
He is not desolate, but only
Sees, where ye cannot, hidden faces.
Archibald Lampman, *Poems*

With only a few exceptions — the modern
poet has been an empty windbag and
chatterer.
Irving Layton,
the Foreword to:
"Balls For A One-Armed Juggler", 1963

Committee chairmen speak no language at
all, but poets speak the language of all
mankind.
Eli Mandel, *The Language of Humanity*, 1963

One of the distinguishing marks of a major
poet is that his work continues, changes,
develops, and increases in strength and
vitality as he grows older.
A.J.M. Smith, *A Poet*, 1958

A poet cannot change the world
Nor add to human worth,
He can but plant a tiny seed
Beneath the crust of earth.
Don W. Thomson, *Fulfilment*, 1956

It's the style for poets to be inspired liars,
insane prophets and tormented human
beings.
Miriam Waddington,
All Nature Into Motion, 1969

POETS—Canadian

Poets are a fastidious race, and in
Canadian poetry we have to give some
place, at least at the beginning, to the anti-
Canadian, the poet who has taken one
horrified look at the country and fled.
Northrop Frye,
"Preface to an Uncollected Anthology" 1956

Our poets must give themselves to a kind
of unsensible madness;
they must hear music not meaning as they
write.
Eldon Grier, *Stanza XIV*, 1963

The surprising thing is that our poets have
accomplished so much good work with so
little encouragement.
Lorne Pierce, *The Interpreter's House*, 1937

A Canadian poet is a man who gets
snowed on.
Elizabeth Rodriguez, *a Report*, 1970

Our poets are inclined to think that they attain inevitability by letting their thoughts
and impressions pour out in a congested
mass, by opening their mouths.
Lord Tweedsmuir, *Return to Masterpieces*,
1937

The Canadian poet has all the models in
the language . . . at his disposal, but lacks
the deadening awareness that he is
competing with them.
Milton Wilson,
Other Canadians and After, 1958

POETRY

The poetry of to-day is looking for its material in another region where the forms of life are more robust and actual and the atmosphere more electrical than they are in the old legendary world of Arcadia.
James Cappon,
"Roberts and the Influence of His Time"

Some poetry is addressed to the mind and some is not. The best poetry, of course, addresses the mind and emotions as well.
Bliss Carman, *The Kinship of Nature,* 1904

Humanity is the most precious thing about us and the essence of humanity is in poetry.
Alan Creighton, *Conquest by Poetry,* 1942

Poetry is not the product of any one faculty of the mind: it is the offspring of the whole mind.
Edward Hartley Dewart,
the Introduction to:
"Selections from Canadian Poets", 1864

Poetry is an experience in novelty, like eating strange foods, before one becomes committed to preference and admiration.
Louis Dudek,
The Writing of the Decade, 1969

Feeble poetry is an offence against society, but great poetry is the most important intellectual asset a country can possess.
Pelham Edgar, *a speech,* 1937

If I may take the golden cup,
And drain the mead of song,
I, too, shall know the ecstasies
That to the gods belong.
Eric F. Gaskell, *The Poet and His Muse,* 1936

But even though we speak, and think, in prose
We ought to try to feel and live in verse,
Else life is not a blessing but a curse.
Daryl Hine,
Letter from British Columbia, 1970

Rhyme does not make a poem,
For true poetry is abstract.
Elizabeth Hiscott, *When a Poet Speaks,* 1967

Poetry is a voice art. A poem does not exist on the page any more than a song exists on a piece of sheet music.
Lionel Kearns, *Stacked-Verse,* 1962

And me happiest when I compose poems.
Irving Layton, *The Birth of Tragedy,* 1954

If all life is to be the stuff of poetry, and it should be, poetry will be banal occasionally.
Alden Nowlan, *a review,* 1960

The poetry that haunts the marrow bone is elusive and rare.
Henry Noyes, *"William Butler Yeats",* 1939

Poetry is the impassioned soul of man speaking through the impassioned utterances of a man or a woman.
Bluebell Stewart Phillips, *Editorial,* 1961

We need not go to the books for poetry, it is nature everywhere.
Catherine Parr Traill,
The Canadian Settler's Guide, 1855

Every lover of poetry should be also a critic if he is to have full enjoyment of it.
Lord Tweedsmuir, *Return to Masterpieces*

In all poetry, everything
Is either in the infinitude or in the limitation.
Wilfred Watson,
A Manifesto for Beast Poetry, 1960

POETRY—Canadian

A good deal of the best verse in American magazines is written in Canada.
W.D. Lighthall,
Introduction to:
"Songs of the Great Dominion", 1889

Perhaps Canada is too gigantic a geographic entity to have a readily recognizable poetic identity, many-faceted as that would need to be.
Padraig O'Broin, *Editorial,* 1965

Canada was not discovered until our poets found it, nor was this land explored until our poets made it known.
Lorne Pierce, *The Interpreter's House,* 1937

The world of Canadian poetry is like some lonely farmhouse at the centre of a remarkably large and bleak farm.
James Reaney, *The Third Eye,* 1960

POLITENESS

There are too many books in the world who trade on the politeness of others in order to

air their own ineptitude.
Robertson Davies,
The Double Life of Robertson Davies, 1954

Stalemate. Politeness is the only way out.
What would we do without these well-
thumbed phrases to extricate us?
Margaret Laurence, *The Stone Angel*, 1964

POLITICIANS

The ambitions and actions of politicians, if
one does not stand too near to them, are
powerfully romantic.
Robertson Davies,
Preface to: "A Jig for the Gypsy", 1954

We have ministers talking like children
about political economy — a science they
never studied, and if they had, they
couldn't have mastered it.
Nicholas Flood Davin, *The Fair Grit*, 1876

Party leaders are admired for their keen
knowledge of the winds of opinion, and
their capacity for 'compromise'.
Louis Dudek, *Editorial*, 1958

Why is it...that when people have no
capacity for private usefulness they should
be so anxious to serve the public.
Sara Jeannette Duncan, *The Imperialist*, 1904

I have no great faith in him as a politician:
he is too honest a man!
William Dunlop, *Recollections*, 1847

I know what a statesman is. He is a dead
politician. We need more statesmen.
Robert C. Edwards, *Calgary Eye Opener*

But weary it is the Commons house
Where men talk loude loud and longe.
William Henry Fuller,
Ye Ballad of Lyttel John A., 1873

We be all humbugs, but the greatest of all
is the politician.
Francis W. Grey,
The Curé of St. Philippe, 1899

A democrat can't condescend.
He's down already. But when a
conservative stoops, he conquers.
Stephen Leacock, *My Remarkable Uncle*

There are two classes of politicians: those
who sit still, and make all the money; and

those who go about the country, and make
all the speeches.
J.J. Procter,
The Philosopher in the Clearing, 1897

POLITICS

The success of Canada has been that we
turned war into politics. The war of the
French and English, of the Americans and
Canadians, of the Indians and whites,
have all been coverted into issues, elec-
tions, debates and solutions.
James Bacque, *Notes for a Native Land*, 1970

We have our own dread of the world com-
ing to an end, though the nearest thing we
have yet produced to compare with a Last
Judgement is a series of Summit
Meetings.
Robertson Davies, *A Millenary Parallel*

In Opposition all is virtue; in power all the
reverse.
Nicholas Flood Davin, *The Fair Grit*, 1876

Canadian political parties have no policies
at all; they cultivate the art of elec-
tioneering.
Louis Dudek, *Editorial*, 1958

What need has a man of brains when he
goes into politics? Brainy men make the
trouble.
Nellie L. McClung,
Sowing Seeds in Danny, 1911

Our party struggles have never been raised
to the higher intellectual plane in which
they become of universal interest.
Frank H. Underhill,
In Search of Canadian Liberalism, 1961

POLLUTION

The circle is complete:
Fate is resolved;
The god created
And the man destroyed.
Martin Bartlett, *Elegy*, 1956

Grey Factory Smoke against a murky sky!
In days more prosperous I've grimly
muttered
Dark maledictions seldom thought or
uttered
When you've besmirched white linens out
to dry.
Gladys Knox Donahue, *Retraction*, 1938

129

Lord, Lord, pollution everywhere
But I breathe still.
E. Mandel, *An Idiot Joy*, 1969

Under the dark industrial sky we wonder
why we have to die.
James Wreford, *Kirkland Lake*

THE POOR

I'm sick and tired of those stupid platitudes
about the poor, . . . A Christian is entitled to
self-respect, to warmth and good clothing
in any kind of decent society.
Morley Callaghan, *Such Is My Beloved*, 1934

I found out the poor have no brains. They
believe whatever they're told so long as it's
easy to remember. But the main thing is,
they're all lazy.
Hugh MacLennan, *Two Solitudes*, 1945

Poor people can't afford to be disorderly —
not if they want to hold any kind of
reputation.
Edwin R. Procunier, *The Beginning of
Summer*, 1962

Regret is not great for the loss of the lowly;
The poor are expected to give up their
breath.
J.R. Ramsay, *Old Stephen, A Dirge*, 1873

POPULARITY

That's popularity, . . . soon won, soon lost.
T.C. Haliburton, *Sam Slick*, 1853

POSSESSIONS

Possessions are good and delightful and
necessary. But they are only good and
delightful and necessary in so far as they
minister to happiness.
Bliss Carman, *The Friendship of Art*, 1904

It is the peculiarly American philosophy of
life that to have is more important than to
be or to do; in fact, that to be is dependant
on to have.
Frederick P. Grove, *In Search of Myself*

If the standard man can be defined by his
possessions, then rob his house and you
steal his identity.
Mordecai Richler, *Son of a Smaller Hero*,
1955

POVERTY

Nothing can be more true, . . . than that
poverty is ever the inseparable companion
of indolence.
Frances Brooke,
The History of Emily Montague, 1769

You can't be a Christian when you're
hungry and have no place to sleep, for then
you're hardly responsible for what you do.
Morley Callaghan, *Such Is My Beloved*, 1934

Children do not mind poverty. It is not until
they grow and cultivate their wilful individuality, that unhappiness and discontent overtake them . . . They enjoy being barefoot and having nothing, until
some mistaken grown-up makes them
ashamed of it.
Bliss Carman, *The Kinship of Nature*, 1904

We're all poor in some way too, each of us
reaching for different riches.
Terry Crawford,
Statement in Storm Warning, 1971

Have you ever known an instance of a man
who tasted the bitterness of poverty in his
youth who ever felt that he had enough
money in his maturity?
Robertson Davies, *On Stephen Leacock*, 1957

Let us be bare,
let us be poor,
such poverty makes honest souls,
and solitude is capital for love.
D.G. Jones,
Soliloquy to Absent Friends, 1959

You can never have international peace as
long as you have national poverty.
Stephen Leacock, *To Every Child*, 1969

Better by far
be a penniless bum that a penniless
homeowner.
David McFadden, *Just Off the Junction*, 1971

That is one consolation when you are poor
— there are so many more things you can
imagine about.
L.M. Montgomery, *Anne of Green Gables*,
1908

A poor man's road to independence is
always up-hill work. Duty fences the path
on either side, and success waves her flag
from the summit; but every step must be

130

trod, often in ragged garments and with bare feet, if we would reach the top.
Susanna Moodie, *Geoffrey Moncton,* 1855

Happiness and poverty do not travel well together.
Geo. W. Pacaud, *Social Idolatry,* 1920

When poverty is seen poisoning the springs of human love, the compassionate artist has no need of a political platform to move the indifferent.
F.W. Watt, *Morley Callaghan as Thinker,* 1959

Your poorness is a thing of the spirit.
Adele Wiseman, *The Sacrifice,* 1956

POWER

Oh, for a tongue of flaming fire
To smite the souls of Men of Power,
And kindle there a living flame
To purify them in this hour!
Jonathan Hughes Arnett, *Save Our Land,* 1938

If taxation without representation is tyranny, still more is power without responsibility.
Nicholas Flood Davin, *The Fair Grit,* 1876

Power has a natural tendency to corpulency.
T.C. Haliburton, *Sam Slick,* 1836

Power and control are in all cases paid for by loss of freedom and flexibility.
Marshall McLuhan,
Culture without Literacy, 1953

Famous poets know
how power runs
It ticks in youthful gonads
like a bomb.
Peter Thomas, *Hearing the Famous Poet,* 1970

PRAIRIES

As sterile as November's womb
Immutable the snow-bound prairies lie
In bleak, unbroken line of earth and sky
Interred within the winter's frosty tomb.
Margaret Fulton Frame,
November Night, The Prairies, 1947

The world of prairie, the world of plain,
The world of promise, and hope, and gain,
The world of gold, and the world of grain,
And the world of the willing hand.
E. Pauline Johnson, *Prairie Greyhounds*

Between Regina and Moose Jaw the great plains stretch uninterrupted to the horizon. This is the authentic wheat country, the original breadbasket of the world.
Edward McCourt,
Overland from Signal Hill to Victoria

PRAISE

Angels live on praise,
Take it, it is all I can afford.
Daryl Hine, *A Vision,* 1960

It is both traditional and original. This is high praise indeed, but not unjust praise.
A.J.M. Smith, *A Reconsideration,* 1958

PRAYERS

When strong men pray
bowing the stubborn knee,
celestial choirs must chant for joy.
Carol Cassidy, *Prayer in Battle Dress,* 1941

Saying one's prayers isn't exactly the same thing as praying.
L.M. Montgomery, *Anne of Green Gables,* 1908

Prayer and a rigorous attention to one's religious duties will contribute far more towards one's personal salvation than the bickering that goes on about church bazaars.
Brian Moore, *Judith Hearne,* 1955

Our prayers are but a cloud of desert-dust
Blown up by winds to silent pyramids!
Robert Norwood, *The Witch of Endor,* 1916

O God, most earnestly we pray,
Make every day Remembrance Day!
Margaret Wright Ritchie, *Blind Veteran,* 1938

PREACHING

Whenever you hear a man going up and down the world reviling the times continually — he is a preacher. If he isn't a preacher by profession, he is a preacher by nature, which is worse.
Bliss Carman, *The Friendship of Art,* 1904

The fault nowadays is not with the preaching so much as with the hearing.
Ralph Connor, *The Prospector,* 1904

PREJUDICE

Narrow-mindedness is like anaemia — it is due to a lack of something.
Nina Moore Jamieson, *The Hickory Stick,* 1921

Even the pure waters of truth, when filtered through the sieve of public opinion, are apt to become tinctured by the rust of prejudice.
J.R. Ramsay, *Lo!*, 1873

THE PRESENT

These days are halcyon, they
grope quietly with winter
in our eyes.
Douglas Barber, *The Lake Ice Razed*, 1970

I shall lack nor tent nor food,
Nor companion in the way,
For the kindly solitude
Will provide for me to-day.
Bliss Carman, *At the Yellow of the Leaf*

Ah! how one forgets
All the high moments of love. For the living
Present is all.
Norman Gregor Guthrie, *Sweetheart Rose*, 1928

One day at a time — that's all a person has to deal with. I'll not look ahead.
Margaret Laurence, *The Stone Angel*, 1964

If not here, where?
Jack Ludwig,
Celebration on East Houston Street, 1963

If I have a failing, it is of too keen an enjoyment of the present, rather than an indulgence in unavailing regrets for the past.
William McLennan and J.N. McIlwraith,
"The Span O'Life", 1899

There is no real escape from the present. Here and now is where Everyman lives.
Hugo McPherson, *The Garden and the Cage*, 1959

The present is inescapable; it is now; the past and the future are delusions.
Hugh McPherson,
The Garden and the Cage, 1959

'Now is forever'
These are the sounds that murder.
Anne Wilkinson, *Italian Primitive*, 1969

PRIDE

I am not proud. Who can be proud
Of a fact.
Ronald Bates, *Orpheus and Odyseus*, 1952

Without pride in ourselves, in our work, and in each other, life becomes sordid and vulgar and slovenly; the work of our hands unlovely; and we ourselves hopeless and debased.
Bliss Carman, *The Kinship of Nature*, 1904

There is no sophist like pride.
Sara Jeannette Duncan, *The Imperialist*, 1904

Was ever pride portent of anything
Save sure destruction by a greater pride?
Verna Loveday Harden, *All Valiant Dust*, 1939

Pride walks in majesty but she's been known to stub her toe.
George V. Hobart, *Experience*, 1914

Pride has so often been my demon, the tempting conviction that one is able to see the straight path and to point it out to others.
Margaret Laurence, *The Rain Child*, 1962

They could not know how greatly proud hearts grieve.
Lois Loring, *Entre Nous*, 1939

If I can't love you I mean to be proud of you at least.
L.M. Montgomery, *Rilla of Ingleside*, 1921

PRIEST

They're human beings, young men without much guile or experience, full-blooded and healthy, right out of the seminary into a world where many silly women dote on them.
Morley Callaghan, *Such Is My Beloved*, 1934

The highest ambition of a Canadian parish priest is to build a Church.
Francis W. Grey,
The Curé of St. Philippe, 1899

This is just like any other parish in Quebec. The priest keeps a tight hold.
Hugh MacLennan, *Two Solitudes*, 1945

The cloth he wore had raised him above ordinary mortals.
Hugh MacLennan, *Two Solitudes*, 1945

PRINCE EDWARD ISLAND

In Prince Edward Island you are supposed to nod to all and sundry you meet on the road whether you know them or not.
L. M. Montgomery,
Anne of Green Gables, 1908

PRIVACY

Privacy is a privilege not granted to the aged or the young.
Margaret Laurence, *The Stone Angel*, 1964

Weel, . . . every man's business is his own.
Willard Mack, *Tiger Rose*, 1917

PROFESSIONALISM

We live in a world of increasing professionalism in which the PhD man is respected as being qualified, whereas the amateur who responds acutely to literature is a suspicious, carping misfit.
Paul West, *Canadian Attitudes*, 1963

PROFESSORS

I am no professor; I hold no card in the wise man's union.
Robertson Davies, *On Stephen Leacock*, 1957

A university professor is now a busy, hustling person, approximating as closely to a businessman as he can do it.
Stephen Leacock,
My Discovery of England, 1922

PROMISES

I never made a promise but I wished to break it. This one shall balance all I've broken, for I'll never unwish it.
Gilbert Parker,
The Seats of the Mighty, 1896

A promise made is a debt unpaid.
R.W. Service,
The Cremation of Sam McGee, 1907

PROSPERITY

Prosperity does various things for people. It makes most of them to the best of their ability drop intellectual pursuits and run to exciting, more material things.
Suzanne Marny, *The Unhappy House*, 1909

We are all of us fed with a species of providential bacon, in which the fat of prosperity is intermingled with the lean of adversity, and sorrow, and disappointment; and we cannot take our lean uncomplainingly: it spoils our enjoyment of the fat.
J.J. Procter,
The Philosopher in the Clearing, 1897

PUBLICATIONS

Thanks be to God for the heritage
Of a printed word on a plain white page.
Rosa Mary Clausen-Mohr, *Print*, 1953

There is no publication as agonizing or charged with elation as the first.
Mordecai Richler, *The Uncertain World*, 1969

No good publication just happens. Excellence is the result of skill, devotion and plain worry on the part of an editor.
Donald Stainsby,
The Press and Literature, 1961

PURITANS

Occidental prudery is a necessary condition of occidental progress.
Christopher Wanklyn, *Going Tangerine*, 1959

QUEBEC CITY

Strong and tall and vast
She lies, touched with the sunset's golden grace,
A wondrous softness on her gray old face.
Jean Blewett, *Quebec*

Your idea of Quebec, . . . is perfectly just; it is like a third or fourth rate country town in England; much hospitality, little society.
Frances Brooke,
The History of Emily Montague, 1769

My city, my old terraces,
With the few cobble roads that remain,
The men that work and sweat at your ferry,
Why have you remained so inarticulate
Why so impassive? The clash of traffic
Defiles you; you have forgotten your past.
Brenda Fleet, *Quebec*, 1971

Nature has lavished all her greatest elements to form this astonishing panorama.
Susanna Moodie, *Roughing It in the Bush*, 1852

Quebec is an oasis in the great Canadian Wilderness.
J.J. Procter,
The Philosopher in the Clearing, 1897

QUEBEC (province)

The history of Quebec since the conquest has been largely the story of an in-folded soul.
Marilyn I. Davis, *Pilgrim Unto Life*, 1960

Quebec where sexless nuns take care of orphans — turining out schizophrenics.
Louis Dudek,
The Problems of Education, 1960

The Quebec village looked medieval, because it was medieval. The church dominated the village visually because it did in fact.
Alan Gowans,
Architecture in New France, 1960

This soil is in the hands of God and the French.
Don Gutteridge, *Champlain,* 1967

When in Rome — so in Quebec.
Armitage Hargreaves,
Two-Way Tolerance, 1965

Every inch of it is measured, and brooded over by notaries, and blessed by priests.
Hugh MacLennan, *Two Solitudes,* 1945

Storied Quebec! Soil-wedded Jean Baptiste!
Living from land to lawyer, plough to priest;
Schooled in a science dogma simplifies
The state divides, the family multiplies.
William Robbins, *Canadiad,* 1947

QUIET

What greater pleasure
Than to sit, talking, thinking, drinking coffee
Gazing out at snow in turmoil.
Mary Humphrey Baldridge,
The Solitary Tree, 1967

Nobody it seems admires the soft word.
Louella Booth, *The Soft Word,* 1963

Here in this house of wind and willow boughs
Quietness is my constant only guest.
Audrey Alexandra Brown,
The Unbidden Guest, 1948

The stillness is the echo of an explosion!
Eldon Grier, *On the Subject of Waves,* 1963

How much like boredom is this quiet world.
D.G. Jones, *Standing in the April Noon,* 1959

How blest, remote from business strife,
Is he who leads a quiet life.
M.H. Nickerson, *Country Life,* 1963

QUOTATIONS

A wise saw is more valuable than a whole book, and a plain truth is better than an argument.
T.C. Haliburton,
Nature and Human Nature, 1855

Maxims are deductions already drawn.
T.C. Haliburton,
Nature and Human Nature, 1855

Nothing can stand against a really resolute quoter.
Goldwin Smith, *Empire Club Speeches,* 1911

RACE

You must get close to the great men of a race to appreciate it in all its fineness.
Nathaniel A. Benson, *The Paths of Glory,* 1927

RAILROAD

If your're looking for your true royalty in North America,...you look at the railroad. There is aristocracy.
W.O. Mitchell,
The Princess and the Wild Ones

RAIN

This is the rain that weeps Spring into summer.
Hyman Edelstein, *The Hidden Gleams,* 1916

The rain is only the river
grown bored, risking everything
on one big splash.
Raymond Souster,
The Rain Is Only the River, 1963

READING

Reading is the source of education and style.
Lord Beaverbrook,
The Three Keys to Success

Are you sure you're not getting your notions from authors of books. Are you sure your reading doesn't tend to destroy your faith? What have you been reading?
Morley Callaghan, *Such Is My Beloved,* 1934

Reading confers status.
Robertson Davies, *A Voice from the Attic,* 1961

Good reading is the only test of good writing.
Robertson Davies, *A Voice from the Attic*, 1961

Reading is a simple, cheap but intellectual way of escaping from unhappiness.
Silas N. Gooch, *A Season in Limbo*, 1962

I read. . . for enjoyment. If it's a labour, it's a labour of love.
L.A. MacKay,
Bliss Carman: A Dialogue, 1933

The reader reads for stimulation, pleasure, and even for information, and by that form of osmosis which true readers share with writers, he acquires perhaps discrimination.
Ethel Wilson, *A Cat Among the Falcons*, 1959

People read today for instruction, to keep up with their neighbours, and to be informed.
Ernest H. Winter,
Introduction to:
"Our Century in Prose", 1966

REALISM

What is known as realism is only a means to an end, the end being a personal projection of the world.
Philip Child,
Introduction to:
"White Narcissus" (R. Knister), 1962

Realism which is unsupported by imaginative force and vision can be drearily dull and utterly worthless as art.
Desmond Pacey,
Introduction to:
"Book of Canadian Stories", 1950

REALITY

I've tasted my blood too much to abide what I was born to.
Milton Acorn, *I've Tasted My Blood*, 1958

Fact and fancy cannot be long divorced; the one cannot live without the other; they are the body and soul of the universe.
Bliss Carman, *The Kinship of Nature*, 1904

We are like children living in fear of the fabulous giant, if we do not remember that fact is solidified fancy.
Bliss Carman, *The Kinship of Nature*, 1904

You can only believe safely in that which you know and have ceased to expect miracles of.
Cicely Louise Evans, *Antic Disposition*, 1935

shall I keep my feet
upon the ground
when the earth itself
is become an ooze
of shit puke quicksand.
Gerald Fulton, *An Answer from Job*, 1963

Who are we? What is the reality in us? That which we feel ourselves to be? Or that which others conceive us to be?
Frederick P. Grove, *The Master of the Mill*, 1944

I touch but the things which are near;
The heavens are too high for my reach:
Kate Seymour Maclean, *Questionings*, 1881

I have always been tethered to reality, always compelled by an unfortunate kind of probity in my nature to prefer a barefaced disappointment to the luxury of a future I have no just claims upon.
Sinclair Ross, *Cornet at Night*, 1968

Things are never what they seem:
Let a star be just a star,
And a woman — just a dream.
Robert Service, *Dreams are Best*, 1912

Let us keep melodrama out of this scene, Eye open to daylight, foot on the firm earth.
A.J.M. Smith, *Son-And-Heir*, 1943

Fantasy is commonplace,
actuality the dream.
Don W. Thomson, *Cybernetics*, 1961

REASONING

If one loves, one dares not reason; if one reasons, it is difficult to love.
Arnold Haultain, *Hints to Lovers*

You may depend upon it, a four-legged creature, unlike a two-legged one, has a reason for everything he does.
Marshall Saunders, *Beautiful Joe*

Free men ain't bound by reason.
George Woodcock,
Encounter with an Archangel, 1963

REBELLION

Rebellions against the codes of society begin at the top, not at the bottom. Stir the bottom and you get nothing but mud.
Robertson Davies,
At the Gates of the Righteous

If you'd done a little rebelling yourself you'd be a happier woman today!
Hugh MacLennan, *Two Solitudes,* 1945

REFORM

Reformers are no timid souls,
Their brains are lined with brass;
They set their minds on distant goals
That rarely come to pass.
Charles Clay, *Reformers,* 1938

RELAXATION

It has all been very sweet, but it will also be sweet to loaf awhile.
Robert Service,
Ballads of a Bohemian, 1921

RELIGION

Religion and politics are invitations to didacticism.
Claude Bissell
the Introduction to:
"The Imperialist" (S.J. Duncan), 1961

The essence of religion is the emotion, not the thought — the sure and certain conviction, not the logical conclusion.
Bliss Carman, *The Kinship of Nature,* 1904

A heavy chain forged by priests to keep mankind upon its knees.
Robertson Davies,
At the Gates of the Righteous

The greatest danger to religion does not arise from opinions that are absolutely false; but from partial and exaggerated views which possess truth enough to make them plausible and popular; and yet are misleading half-truths, or speculations that are substituted for facts.
E.H. Dewart, *Essays for the Times,* 1898

Pure religion is like pure gold; — it cannot be alloyed without being depreciated.
William Dunlop, *Statistical Sketches,* 1832

About the only people who don't quarrel over religion are the people who haven't any.
Robert C. Edwards, *Calgary Eye Opener,* 1910

If a religion is a going concern, in the sense of helping a man to face life and death honestly, it has already proved its substantial worth.
Maurice Hutton, *The Englishman*

Each religion tolerated by the state should be by the state maintained.
Anna Brownell Jameson, *Winter Studies,* 1838

I, . . . no longer know what salvation is. I am not sure that it lies in the future. And I know now that it is not to be found in the past.
Margaret Laurence,
The Drummer of All the World, 1956

Religion is not fun, . . . It is serving God.
Margaret Laurence,
The Drummer of All the World, 1956

I certainly know that many attitudes manage to mask themselves under the name of religion.
Hugh MacLennan, *Two Solitudes,* 1945

Religion teaches man to bear his sorrows with becoming fortitude, but tears contribute largely both to soften and to heal the wounds from whence they flow.
Susanna Moodie, *Roughing It in the Bush,* 1852

Human nature is so selfish, left to its own guidance, that it needs the purifying influence of religion to life the soul from grovelling in the dust.
Susanna Moodie, *Geoffrey Moncton,* 1855

Religion, a comfort for the next world, not this.
Brian Moore, *Judith Hearne,* 1955

Religion was insurance. It meant you got security afterwards. It meant you could always turn over a new leaf. Just as long as you got an act of perfect contrition said before your last end, you'd be all set.
Brian Moore, *Judith Hearne,* 1955

Religion is a comfort, even in conversation.
Brian Moore, *Judith Hearne,* 1955

Catholicism emphasizes man's spiritual condition and his responsibility for that condition, whatever it may be.
F.W. Watt,
Morley Callaghan as Thinker, 1959

REMEMBRANCE

So richly time-wrought are the later years
Remembrance may be overly encumbered
With dids and weres, . . .
Myrtle Reynolds Adams, *Child Eyes,* 1955

I am but a little child: when night falls upon the labor of my day I remember the morning!
Norman Duncan, *Every Man for Himself,* 1908

Remembrance is a foolish act, a double-headed snake
striking in both directions.
John Newlove, *The Double-Headed Snake,* 1969

The sharp remembrance of a hideous evil
Being as poignant as the evil's self,
And, lasting longer, often worse to bear.
Samuel James Watson, *Ravlan,* 1876

Remembrance of things past is more frequent in those with a brighter past than future.
R.E. Watters, *Original Relations,* 1959

REMORSE

All the mistakes and desires are here, old nameless shame for my lies.
John Newlove, *By the Church Wall*

REPUTATION

Mud-throwing may hurt a person's reputation, it cannot hurt his or her character; only inward impurity will affect that.
Minnie Smith, *Is It Just?,* 1911

RESEMBLANCE

Is there a misfortune so fraught with annoyance as a strong physical resemblance between two very different human creatures.
Robertson Davies,
The Double Life of Robertson Davies, 1954

RESIGNATION

I shall keep silence, since your world and mine
Immutably are alien, each to each.
Clara Bernhardt, *Resignation III,* 1940

True resignation meant accepting one's destiny.
Frederick P. Grove, *Fruits of the Earth,* 1933

RESPECTABILITY

There is no virtue in respectability, for virtue is an active principle, and the essence of respectability is dull, stupid, selfish, timid inaction.
Bliss Carman, *The Kinship of Nature,* 1904

In Canada we may know little about literature, but we are great experts on questions of respectability.
Robertson Davies, *On Stephen Leacock,* 1957

Like disparagement, respect is also catching.
Vincent Massey, *in a speech,* 1965

RESPONSIBILITY

The first was to make my own law.
The second was to break it. To distinguish the limits
Apparently, the third is to pay for it.
Ken Belford, *Omega,* 1971

Great gifts carry with them great burdens.
Robertson Davies, *On Stephen Leacock,* 1957

REST

It is late,
And must rest preface war's hot work tomorrow,
Else would I talk till morn.
Charles Mair, *Tecumseh*

Let the mind rest awhile, lower the eyes,
Relieve the spirit of its Faustian clamor.
E.J. Pratt, *The Good Earth,* 1958

RESULTS

When gales of circumstance
Shake orchards of the soil
Then, only then, they yield
Their fruit complete and whole.
Margaret Fulton Frame, *Parable,* 1947

In goodly faith we plant the seed,
Tomorrow morn we reap the weed.
Paul Hiebert, *Sarah Binks,* 1947

RETRIBUTION

Thy prayers are profanation. Heaven is dumb.
Go, taste of retribution.
Thomas Bush, *Santiago,* 1866

REVENGE

The spice of revenge is to make men feel your power.
M. Allerdale Grainger,
Woodsmen of the West, 1908

I am a dog that gnaws his bone,
I couch and gnaw it all alone —
The time will come which is not yet,
When I'll bite him by whom I'm bit.
William Kirby, *The Golden Dog*

Revenge is all the remedy that's left;
But what revenge is equal to the crime?
Robert Rogers, *Ponteach,* 1766

What good is revenge if you are not alive to taste it.
Norman Williams, *Night of Storm,* 1956

My work is now completed; — 'tis only tit for tat.
W.P. Wood, *The Woman of Wentworth,* 1871

REVOLT

The spirit of the age is a spirit of revolt, in religion first, in politics later on.
Francis W. Grey,
The Curé of St. Philippe, 1899

REVOLUTION

A people never rebel from a mere passion for attack — it is a people's impatience of suffering and that only which lights the fires of rebellion.
Nathaniel A. Benson, *The Patriot,* 1930

Was there salvation in revolution? Or did revolution — proletarian revolution — necessarily mean the destruction of what the past had built?
Frederick P. Grove, *The Master of the Mill,* 1944

Anything that is a revolution must keep moving or it doesn't revolute: by nature it contains within it the seeds of its own destruction.
Malcolm Lowry, *Under the Volcano,* 1961

RICHES

If you are rich you cannot be free. You have obligations you cannot shirk.
Bliss Carman, *The Kinship of Nature,* 1904

RIGHT

Righteousness is greatly to be desired, but a little wickedness is much more interesting, isn't it?
Nina Moore Jamieson, *The Hickory Stick,* 1921

It may be something that has to be done — but it will never be right.
Colin McDougall, *The Firing Squad*

Whatever is right can never be impossible; whatever is wrong can never be eternal.
H.A. Mitchell Keays,
He That Eateth Bread with Me

RIGHTS

He'd earned at least the right to childishness.
Charles Bruce, *The Sloop,* 1786

RIVERS

What that has travelled upon their far-spreading waters has not felt the compelling charm of the rivers of Canada?
Lawrence J. Burpee, *By Canadian Streams*

ROADS

Roads are friendly contrivances, helpful to lovers of mankind.
Archibald MacMechan,
Afoot in Ultima Thule

ROSES

He who buys red roses
Dreams of crimson lips.
Isabella Valancy Crawford, *Roses in Madrid*

THE ROYAL ALEX
(Theatre-Toronto)

The Royal Alexandra Theatre in Toronto, where touring companies come to die.
Robert Fulford,
The Yearning for Professionalism, 1959

ROYAL COMMISSIONS

Royal Commissions are instruments of national conscience or symptoms of national crisis.
Robert Weaver, *The Canada Council,* 1957

RUIN

When he fell he pulled all his glory with him to the ground.
Gwendolyn MacEwen,
The Day of the Twelve Princes, 1970

A thing does not need to be dishonorable to be ruinous.
William McLennan and J.N. McIlwraith,
"The Span O'Life", 1899

SACRIFICE

Sacrifice is the badge of motherhood, and the honour of it finer than any flower.
Raymond Knister, *White Narcissus,* 1929

SADNESS

Sadness is words spoken in careless anger
and greedy youth seeking life from the edge of Time.
George Frederick Cameron,
With All My Singing, 1887

If you can find any justification for putting an unhappy murderer to death, there surely ought to be some punishment for that unsocial creature who constantly shows a gloomy face to the world.
Bliss Carman, *The Kinship of Nature,* 1904

Sadness, whether from bereavement, or disappointment, or misfortune of any kind, may linger on through life.
James De Mille, *A Strange Manuscript,* 1888

I leave my fears
To fools to gather,
And my unshed tears
To the long cold winter!
Marion Ford, *My Last Will,* 1967

Shadows there are upon my wondering heart,
Weaving a pattern that I scarce would miss,
Painted by life upon unwilling ground.
Clara E. Hill, *Shadows on the Snow,* 1941

An end! No more! Never let melancholy
Again perch on our brows, and caw our folly!
A.M. Klein, *Hershel of Ostropol,* 1970

Nothing tends so much to increase our melancholy as merry music when the heart is sad.
Susanna Moodie, *Roughing It in the Bush,* 1852

What shall I do
Now my love is gone
Toss on an empty
Bed alone?
Padraig O'Broin, *Circle,* 1963

The world does not want a sad man.
Gilbert Parker,
The Seats of the Mighty, 1896

How can you grab hold of light with arms of dark!
James Reaney, *The Killdeer,* 1960

There is a sadness o'er my spirit stealing,
A flash of fire up-darting to my brain,
Sowing the seeds — and still the seeds concealing.
Charles Sangster, *Despondency*

Let virtue lie in joy and song,
The only sin is sadness.
Robert Service, *The Concert Singer,* 1921

Why repeat these strains of sadness,
Which but feed our fears?
Are there no clear notes of gladness
Straying down the years?
Bernard Freeman Trotter, *The Songs We Need*

Sad thoughts are but sad dreams that come by day,
When the sick body gives them invitation,
And the mind is too weak to say them nay.
Samuel James Watson, *Ravlan,* 1876

SAILOR

A sailor looks like a child when he smiles.
Ernest Buckler,
The Mountain and the Valley, 1952

Seamen are a lonely lot —
Stars are cold and blood is hot.
Marjorie Freeman Campbell,
The Sailor, 1956

Great naval commanders have always
had two qualities, audacity and iniative.
Thomas B. Costain,
The White and The Gold, 1954

For those who sweep the Seven Seas,
Lord of the Deep, we pray!
If theirs be the Sum of Sacrifice
Grant us the Right to Pay.
Elspeth Honeyman, *Out There*

SAINT JOHN (N.B.)

O city
With a Loyalist graveyard
In the centre
Of every brain.
John Drew, *Saint John,* 1967

SASKATCHEWAN

Saskatchewan is an idea of wheat.
James Dougherty,
Perils of an American, 1967

Down by the old Saskatchewan
It's lonely, and wild, and free,
And the old rough range by the river-side
Looks best in the world to me.
Rhoda Sivell, *The Old Saskatchewan,* 1911

SATIRE

Satire is a grappling hook thrown up the
high wall of the everyday world.
Jack Ludwig, *A Thermostats,* 1967

Satire is part of the healthy functioning of
a mature society that can look at itself
ironically.
George Woodcock,
A Spectre in Haunting Canada, 1963

SATISFACTION

Plenty to drink and plenty to eat
is how the country is run
Hungry and sober is merely confusion and
defeat
besides not being much fun.
George Johnston, *Home Free,* 1967

To the strong, the greater burden; to the
clever eye, the greater beauty; to the pure
soul, the greater happiness.
J.J. Procter,
The Philosopher in the Clearing, 1897

I am not carefree, yet I wish for nothing.
Alfred W. Purdy, *Visitors,* 1959

To love, to serve, this gave her joy and
there was the end of it.
Laura Goodman Salverson, *Queer Heart,*
1936

SCHOOL

School life is a miniature forecast of the
larger life of manhood and womanhood.
Its difficulties, tests of character, and
elements of success, are substantially the
same as those of mature years.
E.H. Dewart, *Essays for the Times,* 1898

The school is the one institution over
which the district has immediate and absolute control; and every ratepayer thinks
himself entitled to a share in the running
of it which is in inverse proportion to his
qualifications.
Frederick P. Grove, *Fruits of the Earth,* 1933

SCIENCE

Science gathers facts and puts them in
order. Then they become law.
Frederick P. Grove, *Fruits of the Earth,* 1933

Science is the new theology.
Hugh MacLennan, *Two Solitudes,* 1945

The scientist is the dilemma of the times.
The more he knows, the more he can
betray you.
Lister Sinclair, *Return to Colonus,* 1955

Science has taught us to kill before
philosophy has taught us to think.
Lister S. Sinclair, *No Scandal in Spain,* 1945

The voice of Science is the voice of God,
For the objects of Science are seen with
the eye of Faith.
Lister Sinclair, *Return to Colonus,* 1955

SEA

The sea was the first woman,
The eternal female.
She calls her men irresistibly
From every land.
Kathleen Brown, *The Sea,* 1936

Eternal in might and malignance is the sea! It groweth not old with the men who toil from its coasts.
Norman Duncan, *The Fruits of Toil,* 1903

The sea is tameless: as it was in the beginning, it is now, and shall ever be — mighty, savage, dread, infinitely treacherous and hateful.
Norman Duncan, *The Fruits of Toil,* 1903

The life of a man is a shadow, swiftly passing, and the days of his strength are less; but the sea shall endure in the might of youth to the wreck of the world.
Norman Duncan, *The Way of the Sea,* 1903

What's most like God
In the universe, if not this same strong sea,
Encircling, clasping, bearing up the world,
Blessing it with soft caresses, then, for faults,
Chiding in God-like surges of wrath and storm?
S. Frances Harrison, *Pine, Rose and Fleur de Lis*

Adventure was never chained to land.
Delight is born of keel and tide.
Margaret Lathrop Law,
Forbears of Cornwall, 1952

Oh Sea! thou art like my heart, full of infinite sadness and pity,
Of endless doubt and endeavor, of sorrowful question and strife,
Like some unlighted fortress within a beleagured city,
Holding within and hiding the mystery of life.
Kate Seymour Maclean,
The Voice of Many Waters, 1881

The sea, . . . is the mightiest thing we know. The sky is the most changeable and mysterious.
Hugh MacLennan, *Each Man's Son,* 1951

There is no silence upon the earth or under
the earth like the silence under the sea!
E.J. Pratt, *Silences,* 1937

SEARCH

Thus does ignorance, pricked by the soul's deep hunger,
Grope blindly after things intangible

And, groping, crush with crude, possessive hands
What cannot be owned.
Joan Birrell, *Butterfly Hunter,* 1948

Don't you know that what you search for
Lies far beyond the sands of time?
John F. Donnelly, *Beach Doll,* 1966

I watched and waited for a long time and finally, as kids will, I stopped looking.
Malcolm Lowry, *The Bravest Boat,* 1954

How pathetically
I reach
for the one person
I have met
that I seem to belong to.
Tom Marshall, *in: The Silences of Fire*

Wherever I go,
Wherever I wander
I never find
What I should like to find.
James Reaney, *The Red Heart,* 1963

SEASONS

Every phase of the seasons is so transient, so brief, one hardly expects to see the same sight twice.
Frederick P. Grove, *The Master of the Mill,* 1944

The changing of the seasons had only emphasized the impression of monotony, and he had been held by inertia, and uncertain hope of fulfilment, on the only soil he knew.
Raymond Knister, *White Narcissus,* 1929

SECRETS

Lest you should lightly prize me, I withold
Myself from you in countless little ways.
Clara Bernhardt,
Lest You Should Lightly Prize Me, 1939

Every man, no matter how debased, nor how carefully policed or brain washed, by a state, or on our side of the world, by a corporation or a school, has some kind of a small secret private world. It may frighten him to have it, but it is there.
Morley Callaghan, *Solzhenitsyn,* 1970

But the earth is as the future: it hath its hidden side.
Thomas D'Arcy McGee, *Jacques Cartier*

To maintain dignity, one must have at least one secret.
Margaret Laurence, *The Perfume Sea*, 1960

SECURITY

Security is a plate balanced
Upon a juggler's nose
While wilful children use his back
As target for their balls.
Mary Elizabeth Colman, *Hunger*, 1937

SELF

Only the sick are self-conscious; and the first step on the road to health is forgetfulness of self.
Bliss Carman, *The Kinship of Nature*, 1904

Self-pity is commonly held to be despicable; it can also be a great comfort if it does not become chronic.
Robertson Davies, *Tempest-Tost*, 1951

Self preservation, which, next to self-interest — from which it doubtless springs — is the strongest of our instincts.
Francis W. Grey,
The Cure of St. Philippe, 1899

Open, O heart, and let me view
The secrets of thy den;
Myself unto myself now show
With introspective ken.
Charles Heavysege, *Self-Examination*

There are no objects outside of ourselves.
We learn our lessons wrinkle by wrinkle,
Humbly planting behind us now and then
The milestone of a missing tooth.
George Jonas, *To An Ex-Girlfriend*, 1969

Everything, it seems to me, has to be purchased by self-sacrifice. Our race has marked every step of its painful ascent with blood.
L.M. Montgomery, *Rilla of Ingleside*, 1921

Clothed in our own self-righteousness,
We look around us, and express
Our grief for other men.
J.R. Newell, *Self-Righteousness*, 1881

Ironic self-depreciation can be too easily taken by others as sober literal truth.
A.J.M. Smith, *A Self-Review*, 1963

Self is the centre of being, the source of our most vital impulses.
Warren Tallman, *Wolf in the Snow I*, 1960

SELFISHNESS

God knows, 'tis so . . .
My grief doth make me selfish.
Francis W. Grey, *Love's Pilgrimage*, 1931

He who would give nothing, what could he receive?
James E. Le Rossignol, *The Miser*, 1908

I do not hate my fellows, but I hate
The actuating selfishness of man.
J.R. Ramsay, *French Chaos*, 1873

SENSIBILITY

A man with any sensibility will find himself constantly curbed by his regard for the feelings of others.
William McLennan and J.N. McIlwraith, *"The Span O'Life"*, 1899

Just think what a dull world it would be if everyone was sensible.
L.M. Montgomery, *Anne of Green Gables*, 1908

SENSE

Evoking daily response,
the art of the fifth sense
vanishes like the dance.
Francis Maguire,
The Art of the Fifth Sense, 1967

Even age is no warrant for common sense when it meets with old gratifications.
William McLennan and J.N. McIlwraith, *"The Span O'Life"*, 1899

It must be a great deal better to be sensible; but still, I don't believe I'd really want to be a sensible person, because they are so unromantic.
L.M. Montgomery, *Anne of Green Gables*, 1908

What the devil's the good of sense when it comes to keeping a Frenchman from flying after petticoats?
Laura Goodman Salverson, *Queer Heart*, 1936

SENTIMENTALITY

Sentimentality merely does cheaply what high romance does greatly.
Douglas Bush, *A Vanished Race*, 1926

The sentimentalist belongs to the cat family. He is very imperfectly domesticated, but his habit of locality is phenomenally developed.
Bliss Carman, *The Friendship of Art*, 1904

Sentimentality is the philosophy of boobs.
Robertson Davies, *A Voice from the Attic*, 1960

I detest sentimental people. They are the greatest humbugs in the world.
Susanna Moodie, *Geoffrey Moncton*, 1855

SEPARATISM

Separatism, in the light of our history, is a backward - looking movement that turns away, once again, from the prospect and future that stands before French Canada.
Louis Dudek,
The Future of French Canada, 1964

SEX

Erotic books feed a part of that fantasy life without which man cannot exist.
Robertson Davies, *A Voice from the Attic*, 1960

Unconsummated relationships depress outsiders perhaps more than anybody else.
Alice Munro, *The Peace of Utrecht*, 1968

The biological demand seems to be the clearest explaination to the oddest people. But never for themselves.
Edwin R. Procunier, *Appassionata*, 1962

Pornography is another intellectual mode which serves as a substitute for feeling.
Miriam Waddington,
All Nature Into Motion, 1969

SHORT STORY

At its best, the short story is a flawless plant, carefully separated from the tangle of nature and pruned and displayed as for a flower show.
Hugo McPherson,
Morley Callaghan's April, 1959

SICKNESS

When you're sick, you're popular with nobody.
Brian Moore, *Judith Hearne*, 1955

Sickness is a crime
For habitual offenders the penalty is death.
Alden Nowlan, *X-Ray*, 1969

Pain and sickness may obscure for a time this exquisite pleasure of living, but it cannot efface it utterly.
J.J. Procter,
The Philosopher in the Clearing, 1897

SILENCE

You would like to keep me from saying anything: you would prefer it
if when I opened my mouth
nothing came out.
Margaret Atwood,
"Spell for the Director of Protocol", 1970

Silence about lofty aims is always best.
Mrs. Everard Cotes, *The Burnt Offering*

Silence, if deliberate, is artificial and irritating; but silence that is unconscious gives human companionship without human boredom.
Stephen Leacock, *A Lecture on Walking*

Silence was loudest near cemeteries.
Jack Ludwig, *A Woman of Her Age*, 1962

Silence, how I cry for silence! But the gods have hemmed me 'round
With the clamor of the builders and the street's unceasing sound.
Wilson MacDonald,
The Song of the Rebel, 1926

Silence has become a sign of taste.
Malcolm Miller, *To Be Muttered*, 1962

This was the monologue of Silence Grave and unequivocal.
E.J. Pratt, *Come Away, Death*, 1943

If you've got grace enough to hold your tongue other folks'll do all your lying for you.
Marshall Saunders, *Tilda Jane*

And there was silence till God spoke.
F.R. Scott, *Span*, 1969

Silence is only man's confession of his deafness. Life, Death, like Eternity, it is a word that means nothing.
Robert Service, *Ballads of a Bohemian*, 1921

A silent people is a dangerous sign
Both for the nation and whoever rules it.
Samuel James Watson, *Ravlan*, 1876

SIMPLICITY

Simplicity is the basis of all great art.
Arthur S. Bourinot, *After Four Years*, 1952

The only simplicity that is desirable is
simplicity of soul, a certain singleness of
aim and quiet detachment of vision, a
mood of enduring repose.
Bliss Carman, *The Friendship of Art*, 1904

It is my misfortune to be a plain man; and
my mistake to have told a plain story to
plain people in plain terms.
Thomas McCulloch, *The Stepsure Letters*,
1821

Man is large in his views; he loves size,
and he likes complexity rather than simplicity.
J.J. Procter,
The Philosopher in the Clearing, 1897

The simple life, I say, is the best. Now I
have learned.
Jane Van Every, *Isses Net Peculiar?*

SIN

What sins I have committed in the name
of my father's seed!
George Bowering, *Stab*, 1969

Only the sinner can become the saint
because only the sinner can understand
the need and the allness of love.
Hugh MacLennan, *Each Man's Son*, 1951

The infant hand that toys with flame
Is burnt, and knowledge is not given;
And so the judgements of high Heaven
Come down for sins we can not name.
J.R. Newell, *In Memoriam*, 1881

There is no good, nor is there any bad;
And sin—
Is but an arrow shot beyond the mark.
Robert Norwood, *The Witch of Endor*, 1916

We are taught that all making is sin;
To the pure, all things are pollution.
Lister Sinclair, *Return to Colonus*, 1955

The sins of the fathers are cast on the
sons.
Let them figure it out.
Wayne Stedingh, *Pigalle*, 1970

SINCERITY

Where shall I find a hired man
With a single passion for his job,

With thoughts of work,
And nothing else,
Within his knob.
Paul Hiebert, *Sarah Binks*, 1947

SKY

Grey, the sky and concrete
sets the mood.
George Ellenbogen,
At the Dorchester Bus Terminal, 1958

SLANDER

The wise man is deaf when Slander talks.
George V. Hobart, *Experience*, 1914

SLEEP

In the heat of sleep
we may dream . . .
someone elses terror.
Terry Crawford, *The Heat's On*, 1971

Like death is comes, the sleep upon your
brow.
Stanley M. Forkin, *Song to a Sleeper*, 1962

So sleep, and fill a temporary grave
With sleep's absurd deceit, continued
breath.
Stanley M. Forkin, *Song to a Sleeper*, 1962

Nobody loves the sandman, who comes to
us every night,
Scattering sand in our faces, shutting our
eyes up tight.
Edith Lelean Groves, *The Sandman*

I force sleep
down my throat
I take
and stuff it into my lungs.
Dorothy Livesay, *Insomnia*, 1969

Sleep, baby, the slumber-world waits for
you,
Opening its fairyland gates for you.
God guard the hours you are dreaming
away,
Bring you back safely again with the day.
Charlotte McCoy, *Slumber Song*, 1938

Turn Thou the key upon our thoughts, dear
Lord,'
And let us sleep;
Give us our portion of forgetfulness,
Silent and deep.
Virna Sheard, *At Midnight*

Oh, who will dare to wake the Sleeping Giant
Who slumbers on, all careless of our need?
Ada M. Strachan,
The Sleeping Giant of Thunder Bay, 1938

SMILE

Learn now
The imperturbable smile
That welcomes the guest.
Myrtle Reynolds Adams, *The Last Guest,* 1956

Why go through this world perpetually disgruntled, when men will concede so much to a smile?
Bliss Carman, *The Kinship of Nature,* 1904

When you smile, the sunlight glints metallic
Off the fillings which mar your teeth like metal staples on white paper.
Dave Solway, *Beautiful Woman,* 1960

The incalculable value of a smile — a smile from the heart, as a burden-lifter and care-scatterer is beyond computation.
Adeline Margaret Teskey,
Candlelight Days, 1913

SMOKING

The moment a man takes a pipe he becomes a philosopher; it's the poor man's friend; it calms the mind, smoothes the temper, and makes a man patient under trouble.
T.C. Haliburton, *Sam Slick,* 1838

Oh, it's good is grub when you're feeling hollow,
But the best of a meal's the smoke to follow.
Robert Service, *The Black Dudeen,* 1916

SNOBBERY

A little snobbery, like a little politeness, oils the wheels of daily life.
Robertson Davies, *Tempest-Tost,* 1951

There is a dash of pinchbeck nobility about snobbery. The true snob acknowledges the existence of something greater than himself, and it may, at some time in his life, lead him to commit a selfless act.
Robertson Davies, *Tempest-Tost,* 1951

Canada does not have a titled aristocracy or a very rigid class system, but it does have a snob problem where things cultural are concerned.
Wendy Mitchener,
Towards a Popular Theatre, 1959

SNOW

There's something that's haunting and tragic
In this slumber and acient repose,
And the phantom-like lights and the magic
Of the moon on Canadian snows.
Hyman Edelstein, *Contrast,* 1916

Snow is the greatest equalizer in Nature.
Frederick P. Grove, *Dawn and Diamonds*

Snow is hospitality — clean, impacted snow; restful and silent.
Gilbert Parker, *Pierre and His People*

SOCIALISM

So come my wellborn friends, my fellow drunkards,
We must all work toward the devaluation of volumes,
The reduction of all things to their proper place.
John Glassco, *To Save the World,* 1959

Let all men be equal in an economic sense and one incitement to live is gone.
Frederick P. Grove, *The Master of the Mill,* 1944

In a population of angels a socialistic commonwealth would work to perfection. But until we have the angels we must keep the commonwealth waiting.
Stephen Leacock,
The Unsolved Riddle of Social Justice, 1920

The Socialists are living in the future, not the real future, but some post-legislative utopia.
Millar Maclure, *English Notes,* 1959

SOCIETY

The slow-working yeast of weariness has belched its gases in the social dough.
Margaret Avison, *Factoring,* 1959

To have a real society, that shall have good form, you must have a real head of

society, and that head should find his or her inspiration not in the brackish waters and moral poverty of imitation, but at the springs and fountains of principle and nature.
Nicholas Flood Davin, *The Fair Grit,* 1876

Society can never offer more than an approximation to peace or justice or security, no matter how much we try for these good things.
Carlyle King,
Joyce Cary and the Creative Imagination, 1959

The greatest legacy given us by the class society is the institution of the domestic servant class.
Stephen Leacock, *Woman's Level*

The sheep call themselves idealists, and the wolves call themselves realists.
Hugh MacLennan, *Two Solitudes,* 1945

The world is made up of madmen and fools. It is better to belong to the first than to the latter class — to rule, than to be ruled.
Susanna Moodie, *Geoffrey Moncton,* 1855

Society, like a wolf, devours its own mutilated; and an unsuccessful person stands about equal chances with a rogue or a fool.
J.R. Ramsay, *Born in the Purple,* 1873

Society, . . . is like salt water, good to swim in but hard to swallow.
Arthur Stringer, *The Silver Poppy*

Just as excessive inbreeding is biologically weakening, so an abnormally isolated society will become culturally stagnant, repeating itself over the centuries with decreasing meaningfulness.
George Woodcock,
Views of Canadian Criticism, 1966

SOLDIER

A soldier has no business to consult his feelings!
Leslie Gordon Barnard, *The Traitor,* 1926

Great military leaders have confidence in themselves or they would not dare the improvisations and risks by which battles are won.
Thomas B. Costain,
The White and the Gold, 1954

The precarious life of a soldier gives him the habit of sacrificing every thing to the present moment and a certain callousness to the suffering and destruction which, besides that it ministers to the immediate want, is out of sight and forgotten the next instant.
Anna Brownell Jameson, *Winter Studies,* 1838

A modern soldier is an inhuman instrument. He drops bombs or fires a heavy gun, and half the time he doesn't see the consequences of his acts.
Henry Kreisel, *The Betrayal,* 1964

For fighting men have always stalwart sons to give away.
Fred E. Laight,
The Everlasting Trumpets, 1937

I know no better grave for a soldier than beneath the sod that has been moistened with his blood.
John Richardson, *Wacousta,* 1833

SOLITUDE

You cannot be lonely when you are doing a job that can only be done alone.
Janet Bonellie,
Why Are The People Staring?, 1967

One measure of a man is his capacity for enduring solitude.
Bliss Carman, *The Kinship of Nature,* 1904

One grows accustomed to solitariness, as to other hardships.
Mary Stewart Durie,
St. Columba's Spring, 1913

For he who once discerns the mountain-plain
Of solitude sees all horizons wane.
Robert Finch, *The Mountain-Plain,* 1948

We live in solitude. We cannot break Or mend our solitude. We are alone.
Robert Finch, *The Mountain-Plain,* 1948

All we have is our solitude, taken from the children we were.
Gail Fox, *Poem for Rilke,* 1970

One bliss of solitude is the bliss of hearing one's own voice.
Archibald MacMechan, *Afoot in Ultima Thule*

I have lived too long alone,
I have suffered too much alone, to look to

any human creature for such help or such comfort as you would bring.
William McLennan and J.N. McIlwraith, "The Span O'Life", 1899

Nought remains of all I cherished
In the days that now are gone;
Hope has withered, love has perished,
And I feel I am alone.
J.R. Newell, Song, 1881

A person is always alone — alone when he's born, and alone when he dies. He might think he's not, but he is.
Edwin R. Procunier,
The Strength of Love, 1962

What is in the houses?
Is other people's seclusion
Anything we can grow by?
Dorothy Roberts, The Houses, 1958

Alone! Alone! some time we each must be,
Before we reach that great eternity.
Rhoda Sivell, Alone, 1911

I am weary of these places — anything is better than this horrible solitude.
Catherine Parr Traill, Canadian Crusoes, 1850

SOLUTIONS

People tend to think that anything new will automatically help to make things all right, or at least a great deal better than they were before.
Vincent Massey, a speech, 1965

SON

There are times when you can only look at your son and say his name over and over in your mind.
Ernest Buckler, The Harness

Teach me, O Lord,
That when my years are done,
He, out of all the rest,
Remains my son.
Eve Hellyer,
Prayer for a Little Boy, 1934

SONG

The Canadian boat song is always some old ballad of Norman or Breton origin, pure in thought and chaste in expression, washed clean of all French looseness in its adaptation to the primitive manners of the colony.
William Kirby, The Golden Dog

Behind all poetry is the song.
Dorothy Livesay, Song and Dance, 1969

A song in the heart is worth two in the book.
Arthur Stringer, The Silver Poppy

SORROW

Who curseth Sorrow knows her not at all.
Isabella Valancy Crawford,
in Collected Poems

The Still Life, inanimate, continues its playlet
While I choke with sorrow, and yet cannot weep.
E. Hope Kerr, Still Life, 1939

The rich man can all things command,
But all his gifts are in his hand,
And seldom can he understand
The lonely heart of sorrow.
Wilson MacDonald,
A Song of Two Houses, 1926

I cloaked my mind with velvet
To keep all sorrow out.
No music burned to brighten
The dark that stood about.
Isabel McFadden, The Flame, 1938

Alas! there is no region
On this side of the tomb
Where mortals know no sorrow
Where spirits know no gloom.
J.E. Pollock, Felicity, 1883

Fashioned of sorrow, my mood's a silent thing
Covered by clouds and shrouds that cling
In remorse to sinew and bone.
Else Ransom, November's Child, 1966

It is hard to know why people enjoy being so sad, yet one enjoys it, the sorrow being vicarious and unimportant.
Ethel Wilson,
On a Portuguese Balcony, 1956

I sometimes think that whereas some people are born to joy, I was born to sorrow.
Ethel Wilson, A Drink With Adolphus, 1961

147

SOUL

The soul is not happy in exactitude, but loves the overbrimming measure.
Bliss Carman, *The Friendship of Art*, 1904

It is not the province of the soul to labour. Its proper office is to exist, to be and enjoy, to sorrow if it must, to rejoice when it can, to direct, order, and govern.
Bliss Carman, *The Kinship of Nature*, 1904

Money may be lost, but the treasures of the soul could never be taken away.
James E. Le Rossignol, *The Miser*, 1908

Soul-ache doesn't worry folks near as much as stomach-ache.
L.M. Montgomery, *Anne of Green Gables*, 1908

Once your soul is dirty, then what difference is the shade of black?
Brian Moore, *The Luck of Ginger Coffey*

Man's soul needs all the avenues of sense For its high purpose.
Robert Norwood, *Bill Boram*, 1921

SPECIALIZATION

To the artist, the scientist, the man of action, the danger lies in specialization.
Bliss Carman, *The Friendship of Art*, 1904

Westerners hold experience and expertness in small esteem; they prefer the young girl who will dance and gad about.
Frederick P. Grove, *Fruits of the Earth*, 1933

SPEECH

Men of laconic speech say much by tone and gesture, and often by silence.
Ralph Connor, *The Prospector*, 1904

There is no speech like heart-speech.
Ralph Connor, *The Prospector*, 1904

Between heart and heart speech is the paltriest of channels.
Arnold Haultain, *Hints to Lovers*

Time is not the same for the speaker as for the audience. To the speaker it is too, too brief for what he has to say. For the audience it is grim foretaste of eternity.
Marshall McLuhan,
Culture Without Literacy, 1953

Speech — the interchange of ideas.
S. Morgan-Powell, *Memories That Live*

Look wise, say nothing, and grunt. Speech was given to conceal thought.
William Osler, *Oslerisms*, 1905

A fluent tongue is more than match for brains
When you go wooing.
Samuel James Watson, *Ravlan*, 1876

SPOKESMAN

I speak for my generation, for eyes that never have beheld the Lord.
William Robbins, *Glow, Worm!*, 1947

Do I speak for my generation?
Can any man speak?
William Robbins, *Who's Who*, 1947

SPRING

I know of nothing that can so elicit,
Such great relief as spring; I know no boon,
That's quite so welcome as the annual visit,
Of spring between the equinox and June.
Sarah Binks, *Spring*

I can feel joy at her coming, but 'tis a tranquil joy,
For I have known Winter long.
I have lost much of the exuberance and fervour of youth.
Charles Frederick Boyle,
The Quiet Spring, 1938

It is only in the north that we fully love the spring. After these iron months of unremitting struggle with the giant cold, the spirit is glad when relief comes at length; and the season of returning vitality has a festal charm all its own.
Bliss Carman, *The Kinship of Nature*, 1904

Spring magic always comes on wings of song
Plucked from the heart-strings of an April day.
Amy Bissett England, *Spring Magic*, 1938

Let Spring speak now.
Grim Winter prattled long
And gave no hope 'til now
When 'he is tired,
And can stand no more.
Barbara Gage, *Let Spring Be Now*, 1952

Spring is young and fair,
With laughing eyes and blossoms in her hair
So Winter hates her.
Norah Mary Holland,
The Awakening of the Lily, 1924

It comes as a slow thing out of the sun,
This telling of Spring.
Don James, *Equanimity*, 1963

So wake! O wake! Open wide the doors!
Come join the Jubilee!
All winter long the sleepy snow
But sighs their melody.
Grace Nutting Moore,
"Ornithographic Songs Grand Opera in May",
1934

Through stacks of years I've seen,
With waxing love and awe,
Spring's spanking blades of green
Thrust through the years of straw.
Alan C. Reidpath, *Spring*, 1958

O spring wind, sweet with love
And tender with desire,
Pour into veins of mine
Your pure impassioned fire.
Charles G.D. Roberts, *The Good Earth*

Oh, how sweet is life, how tender!
Spring is here, rejoice, rejoice!
Dorothy Murray Slitter, *April*, 1938

I saw Spring coming in the hills
Not as a maiden shy with footfalls soft
As fleeting showers, but radiant, flushed
With all the imperial beauty of the earth.
A.M. Stephen, *Spring*

When the long, grey mornings of spring renew their invitation they cannot be denied. Snow lingers in secluded corners and frost is still in the ground, but spring is awaiting a welcome.
S.T. Wood,
Rambles of a Canadian Naturalist

STARS

Stars are the signs of dreaming earth; in them
Is light like pearls upon a garment's hem.
Sheila Barbour, *Symbols*, 1939

What are stars?
Beacon lights,
hung by God in far, blue places
for us fools who through the nights
pass with pale, bewildered faces.
Gloria Lauriston, *Queries*, 1936

ST. LAWRENCE (river)

Immortal river, from whose shores forlorn,
The sea-spent eyes of Cartier swept the heights —
Glimpsing beyond the bourne of primal nights
A vision of a nation yet unborn.
Irene Chapman Benson,
To the St. Lawrence River, 1938

Waterway supreme
Glorious and proud
Channel unsurpassed,
Mighty as a sea;
River king uncrowned,
Lord of ships and waves,
Emperor of shores
Where all men are free!
Margaret Fulton Frame,
Hymn to the St. Lawrence, 1947

STORY

Few people realise how extremely difficult it is to tell a story so as to reproduce the real fun of it — to 'get it over' as the actors say.
Stephen Leacock, *Further Foolishness*, 1916

You ask me what he's done? I'll tell his story,
Although the tale corrupts my wholesome tongue.
John Newton McIlwraith, *Ptarmigan*, 1895

Reading stories is bad enough but writing them is worse.
L.M. Montgomery, *Anne of Green Gables*, 1908

STRANGE

To be a stranger is enough, to be a stranger
in two worlds: that is the ultimate loneliness.
Alden Nowlan,
At the Edge of the Woods, 1970

They don't like strangers,
So be careful how you smile.
Alden Nowlan,
Stoney Ridge Dance Hall, 1969

The dazzle of the strange reminds us of
the facts of the familiar.
Kent Thompson, *Editorial*, 1968

STRENGTH

Lionism is a dream that has no use for
dreamers.
Irving Layton,
Some Observations and Aphorisms, 1968

Weakness is always vengeful, prompt,
cruel;
But Strength, like to a lion in a dream,
Will not, unless roused through wan-
tonness,
Strike for the sake of striking.
Samuel James Watson, *Ravlan*, 1876

STUBBORNNESS

Once folks has set their sights they can't
stand to be nudged out of the line of fire.
E.G. Perrault, *The Silver King*

STUDENT

Whoever ceases to be a student has never
been a student.
George Iles, *Canadian Stories*, 1918

The real thing for the student is the life
and environment that surrounds him. All
that he really learns he learns, in a sense,
by the active operation of his own intellect
and not as the passive recipient of lec-
tures.
Stephen Leacock,
My Discovery of England, 1922

The true citizen is a citizen of the world,
the allegiance of whose soul, at any rate,
is too precious to be restricted to a single
country.
William Osler, *The Student Life*, 1905

The student often resembles the poet —
he is born, not made.
William Osler, *The Student Life*, 1905

Except it be a lover, no one is more
interesting as an object of study than a
student.
William Osler, *The Student Life*, 1905

STUPIDITY

All down the ages, the stupid men have
been swatting the clever men on the jaw.
It's their only retort.
Fred Jacob, *The Clever One*, 1925

People seemed so constructed as they
were unable to use ideas as instruments
to discover truth, but waved them instead
like flags.
Hugh MacLennan, *Two Solitudes*, 1945

Conviction is the executioner of the
stupid.
Gilbert Parker, *The Seats of the Mighty*, 1896

One has to talk a great deal of nonsense if
one wishes to get the attention of the
public directed to a little sense.
J.J. Procter,
The Philosopher in the Clearing, 1897

Sometimes, I think you're an ass, my pet,
and sometimes I wonder if that grey stuff
inside your head
is brain or cigarette ash.
Dave Solway, *Dedication*, 1960

SUCCESS

My enemies were certain I was starving,
It must have given them a fearful shock
Through the binoculars to see me carving
A roast of beef up on the barren rock.
Roy Daniells, *Psalm 23*, 1963

There is no search when nothing is left to
seek,
Nothing to find when what was found is
lost,
Nothing to lose when what is lost was all.
Robert Finch, *Over*

A man cannot be expected to rise above
his training, — except of course, in the
very rare instances, and at a cost which
would deter most of us — any more than
water can rise higher than its source.
Francis W. Grey,
The Curé of St. Philippe, 1899

The best thing a man can say of himself is
that he has grown with the growth of his
dreams.
Frederick P. Grove, *Fruits of the Earth*, 1933

When all a man's gifts have been bent on
the realization of material and realizable
ends, the time is bound to come, unless

he fails, when he will turn his spiritual powers against himself and scoff at his own achievements.
Frederick P. Grove, *Fruits of the Earth*, 1933

Once you have learned what to unlearn, Success will come, so work and wait.
Ronald Hambleton, *The Immigrant*, 1947

Why use your triumph if you could not tell The fools how blind they are, how deep the well?
Verna Loveday Harden,
Lines to a Prophet, 1952

It takes more than a few minutes to get to Easy Street. The railroad service is very poor.
George V. Hobart, *Experience*, 1914

Art, quality, genius, talent, have nothing whatever to do with it. Success is salesmanship.
Alexander Knox, *Old Master*, 1939

Out of failure, the cruel crucible of censure,
Bruised, bleeding, beaten at last to form,
Fashioned of heart's harsh rending;
Success is born.
Murla I. McKinnon Latta, *Achievement*, 1938

Out of infirmity, I have built strength.
Out of untruth, truth.
From hypocrisy, I weaved directness.
Irving Layton, *There Were No Signs*, 1963

Success is like some horrible disaster
Worse than your house burning, the sounds of ruination.
Malcolm Lowry,
"After Publication of Under the Volcano", 1961

Few people know how to be pleased at the successes of their friends.
Hugh MacLennan, *Barometer Rising*, 1941

He who hugs closest the enemy's wall has often a better chance than he who lies at a distance.
William McLennan and J.N. McIlwraith,
"The Span O' Life", 1899

To conquer is to gain courage and unusual powers of endurance.
Gilbert Parker,
The March of the White Guard, 1902

We work like slaves, we eat too much, we put on evening dress;
We've everything a man can want, I think.
. . . but happiness.
Robert Service, *The Joy of Being Poor*, 1921

SUFFERING

We may be merciful and just,
Yet pride of character remain,
Hence they who would be humble must
Endure from pain to pain.
Grant Balfour, *From Pain to Pain*, 1910

Suffering has been the lot of all living things, from the giant of the primeval swamps down to the smallest zoophyte.
James De Mille, *A Strange Manuscript*, 1888

We all must suffer
For those the higher things life has to offer.
A.M. Klein, *The Diary of Abraham Segal*

To suffer is to be alive.
Malcolm Lowry,
Letter to David Markson, 1954

Oh what a female Jesus.
Always suffering for others.
James Reaney, *The Killdeer*, 1960

Men and women suffer equally.
The tragedy is not that they suffer, but that they suffer alone.
Margaret Laurence,
the Introduction to:
"The Lamp at Noon" (S. Ross), 1968

SUMMER

Sweet is the earth when the summer is young
And the barley fields are green and gold!
Jean Blewett, *The Barley Fields*

O Canada, your summer comes at length,
A troubadour in purple, drunk with wine!
Laura A. Ridley, *Late Spring in Canada*, 1938

SUNSET

Just when the sun behind the purple hills
Dips, leaving yellow - luminous tracts behind,
Like fame or memory of good deeds; the heart

Is touched, and pleasing sadness steals into
The soul.
Nicholas Flood Davin,
Eos (A Prairie Dream), 1884

My soul always vanishes at dusk. I am always sad at dust, when the day passes away and the night is coming.
Norman Williams, *A Battle of Wits,* 1956

SURVIVAL

People who don't believe in survival, haven't yet begun to live.
Mackenzie King, *attributed*

The mere fact of survival makes gods out of martyrs and transforms defeat into victory.
Miriam Waddington,
All Nature Into Motion, 1969

SUSPICION

Knowing I live in a dark age before history,
I watch my wallet.
Milton Acorn, *I've Tasted My Blood,* 1969

Confidence reposed in a third party is always hazardous, and generally betrayed.
Susanna Moodie, *Geoffrey Moncton,* 1855

SYMPATHY

If you didn't sympathize you couldn't know anyone perfectly.
Raymond Knister, *White Narcissus,* 1929

A certain dole of sympathy, a casual mite of personal relief is the mere drop that any one of us alone can cast into the vast ocean of human misery. Beyond that we must harden ourselves lest we too perish.
Stephen Leacock,
The Unsolved Riddle of Social Justice, 1920

Man's happiness depends in a great measure on the sympathy of others.
Susanna Moodie, *Geoffrey Moncton,* 1855

TALENT

My talent is my union card.
Robertson Davies, *A Masque of Mr. Punch,* 1962

TALK

It is not sufficient to say something well; the thing said must be worth saying.
Clara Bernhardt, *The Poet's Function,* 1939

I do not believe in wasting good talk on people who are plainly unable to appreciate it.
Robertson Davies,
The Table Talk of Samuel Marchbanks, 1949

I have been talking for a long time now but nobody listens to me, listens to me.
Joan Finnigan, *At The Party,* 1964

Garrulity is an affliction of the soul.
Margaret Laurence, *The Tomorrow-Tamer,* 1961

She talks only to fill silence.
Gwen Pharis Ringwood,
The Courting of Marie Jenvrin

TASTE

Incredible, . . . the authority of simple good taste.
Clark Blaise,
A Class of New Canadians, 1970

Variety is the spice of life, and no person can afford to confine his taste in one narrow groove.
Franklin Graham, *Histrionic Montreal,* 1902

Well, there's no explaining tastes, and ugliness is pretty nowadays.
Margaret Laurence, *The Stone Angel,* 1964

Discrimination has never been an essential part of a Canadian anthologist's equipment. Enthusiasm, industry, sympathy, yes; but taste, no.
A.J.M. Smith,
A Book of Canadian Poetry, 1939

TEACHERS

He had the educator's peculiar genius for imparting knowledge without himself assimilating it.
Paul Hiebert, *Sarah Binks,* 1947

There are two nightmares that haunt school - teachers; one is in the form of the class that gets beyond control, and one is in the guise of the Inspector who tells them to go ahead as if he were not there.
Nina Moore Jamieson, *The Hickory Stick,* 1921

152

A very important rule with the normal teacher is to laugh convincingly at his jokes, no matter how feeble they may be.
Duncan McLaren,
How to Win Marks and Influence Masters, 1956

Nowadays the most progressive teachers try to find out what their pupils like best, with the idea that those are the things they are most fitted for.
Leslie Reid, *Trespassers*

He could have been a success at anything he wanted. Instead he's devoted his life to teaching.
Mordecai Richler,
The Apprenticeship of Duddy Kravitz, 1959

The ideal teacher of literature should be able to interpret a poem by means of his or her voice in the same way that a skilled musician interprets a musical composition.
A.M. Stephen,
the Introduction to:
"The Voice of Canada", 1926

A dull teacher, with no enthusiasm in his own subject, commits the unpardonable sin.
R.C. Wallace, *A Liberal Education*, 1932

TEACHING

Teaching children is a fine profession for those who enjoy the company of children, and who are happiest among those whose minds are less well - stored than their own.
Robertson Davies, *On Stephen Leacock*, 1957

School teaching is properly a profession for old men.
Stephen Leacock, *Woman's Level*

TEARS

There are tears of passion and tears of sorrow but the sounds of an old man crying in the night, has in it, the whole meaning of life and of the death that yawns ahead . . dark . . lonely and unknown.
Harry J. Boyle, *The Inheritance*

What are tears?
Only these
passionate or futile fees
paid for sacred memories.
Gloria Lauriston, *Queries*, 1936

Tears are the best balm that can be applied to the anguish of the heart.
Susanna Moodie,
Roughing It in the Bush, 1852

Ah! there are tears that must be shed
In depths of solitude.
J.R. Newell, *A Lament*, 1881

TEMPTATION

Temptation is the same as inspiration; it is the tiger's pounce of the imagination.
Caryle King,
Joyce Cary and the Creative Imagination, 1959

THEATRE

And here tonight within this spacious hall
Built by kind labour volunteered by all,
We meet again — and by your beaming eyes
You're pleas'd once more to see the curtain rise.
James Anderson, *Prologue*, 1869

Theatre is not realistic in a vulgar, wide-awake fashion: it is realistic as dreams are realistic; it deals in hidden dreads, and it satisfies hidden, primal wishes.
Robertson Davies, *A Voice from the Attic*, 1960

The Canadian theatre will move a step or two towards some sort of individuality when it finds a way to abandon mock professionalism.
Robert Fulford,
The Yearning for Professionalism, 1959

To have great plays you must also have great audiences. Art has never flourished in a vacuum and it never will.
Hugh MacLennan,
The Art of City-Living, 1954

Today theatre is taken seriously: you don't joke about something that makes money.
Wendy Michener,
Towards a Popular Theatre, 1959

Theatre is people.
Theatre belongs not to a special class or cultural elite, but to us all.
Alvin J. Shaw,
in the Introduction to:
"Theatre Canada 71", 1971

An active theatre is often a reflection of a country's spirit and vitality.
Pierre Elliott Trudeau,
in the Introduction to:
"Theatre Canada 71", 1971

The living theatre is a growing, changing theatre. Always it moves forward; always it seeks new sources of strength.
Herman A. Voaden,
in the Introduction to:
"Six Canadian Plays", 1930

Most Americans do not like to go to the theatre unless they are visiting in New York.
Gerald Weales, *American Drama*, 1959

The creation of a fine play for the theatre, awaits its first Canadian master.
Herbert Whittaker,
the Preface to: "Worlds Apart", 1956

The best way to make a good play ridiculous is to summarize its plot.
Milton Wilson, *On Reviewing Reaney*, 1963

THEORY

Every one who adopts a new theory or fad, on any social or religious subject, feels bound to disparage and condemn all existing beliefs or practices which stand in the way of the acceptance of his theory.
E.H. Dewart, *Essays for the Times*, 1898

One should never spoil a good theory by explaining it.
Peter McArthur, *To Be Taken with Salt*, 1903

THINKING

So you stay the underdogs.
Because you think . . . it is better to 'ave the big fist than to 'ave the big brain.
Hugh MacLennan, *Each Man's Son*, 1951

I think a lot all day.
I haven't anything else to do.
Thinking is fun.
Edward Meade, *Remember Me*, 1946

You think too darn much. That's what's the matter with you.
J.E. Middleton, *Lake Dore*, 1930

Concentration is the price the modern student pays for success.
William Osler, *The Student Life*, 1905

That's the only way. You mustn't think. You just got to go on.
Michael Spivak, *Secret of the Trade*, 1963

The best philosophers are only jesters, Who upon ignorance build up their fame.
Samuel James Watson, *Ravlan*, 1876

THOUGHT

If wisdom lies inside the door of studious thought, madness is also sleeping there; and the mortal who knocks does so at his peril.
Bliss Carman, *The Kinship of Nature*, 1904

My thought has wings, and springs
From the Source, —
God thought!
Vina Bruce Chilton, *Thought*, 1962

Thought, by Truth's compulsion bred,
Once born, is never, never dead.
Margaret Lathrop Law, *The Word*, 1952

It's strange that thoughts often sound silly when you try to put them into words.
Edwin R. Procunier, *The Second Duchess*, 1962

In the black absence between thoughts, waves rush my inlets. Coastlines dissolve. I wait in harbour for a crowning sea.
Mark Young, *Eye of the Gull*, 1970

TIME

Time is moving faster
And, maybe, space is curling in.
Margaret Avison, *Mordent For a Melody*, 1960

O Time whose song Lethean has eased our pain,
Call us not back to agony again!
Irene Chapman Benson, *Call Us Not Back*, 1937

Time is a nagging friend, and the mind blurs,
Wearied with this and then, today and the past.
Charles Bruce, *The Native*, 1948

Time exacts what is has given you.
Louis Cormier, *Sequence,* 1970

Almost before it has had time to fill
The year tears up summer's engagement book
And winter's pages open white to take
Notes that will fade as quickly as leaves fell.
Robert Finch, *The Daily Heart,* 1961

Come sit at our table
And feast in the presence of the sun
And gather the spinning fruit at your feet
Though know we will
That all these houses shall fall
Under the steady gaze of Time.
Joel Fox, *Beneath the Running Sun,* 1968

I have looked on time, and been afraid.
Mary Hall, *Time Is the Fire,* 1948

This life
We live but cannot fathom;
We hold it hungrily, and cry
For Time, the thief, to pass us by.
Verna Loveday Harden,
This Life We Live, 1937

But time's fire burns away all unities
Grass grows on gods and queens and courtesans.
David Helwig,
After Watching "The Nature of Things", 1967

So slow the unprofitable moments roll,
That lock up all the functions of my soul,
That keep me from myself.
Anna Brownell Jameson, *Winter Studies,* 1838

Time is my ancient enemy;
Implacably he and I
Wage many a tireless battle
Beneath the timeless sky.
Jane Johnson, *My Ancient Enemy,* 1960

Time is the ultimate thief
Of beauty, power and glory.
Margaret Lathrop Law, *Indestructible,* 1953

Time is the small change of eternity.
Irving Layton,
Some Observations and Aphorisms, 1968

The way to improve time is by some useful activity that leads directly or approximately to the making of money.
E.W. Nichols, *On Lying Awake,* 1929

The answer lies locked up and Time alone will bring his master key.
Lister S. Sinclair, *Oedipus the King,* 1946

And everybody has weekends off and goes to bed
with their lovers or their wives.
Raymond Souster, *Phoney War*

Time, the great humourist, I toast,
He pays all scores and cleans each slate.
Lewis Wharton,
Time, the Great Humourist, 1936

TOLERANCE

Tolerance snickers behind doors closed on integrity.
Theresa E. Thomson, *What of the Night?,* 1966

TORONTO

If Toronto stinks, as some of our fellow-Canadians aver, then a slight aroma ought certainly to be discernible from me.
Gregory Clark, *Two Anecdotes*

Toronto is like a fourth or fifth-rate provincial town, with the pretensions of a capital city. We have here a petty colonial oligarchy, a self - constituted aristocracy, based upon nothing real nor upon anything imaginary.
Anna B. Jameson, *Winter Studies,* 1838

Toronto is in general tone "the most American" of Canadian cities.
Robert McCormack, *Letter from Toronto,* 1963

Toronto, O city of callipygous whores.
Alfred Purdy, *Towns,* 1960

Toronto! Queen! Trunk of our family tree!
Thou last great prophet of propriety!
William Robbins, *Canadiad,* 1947

Toronto is the largest small town in the British Empire.
Lister Sinclair, *We All Hate Toronto,* 1946

In Toronto the good, it's quite understood
That sin is a thing to beware-i-O!
But if you are bad, you've got to look sad,
For nothing is fun in Ontario.
Lister S. Sinclair, *We All Hate Toronto,* 1946

TRADITION

Tradition is the father of persecutions, the uncle of falsehoods, the brother of ignorance, and the grandsire of a thousand hideous sins against sweetness and light.
Bliss Carman, *The Friendship of Art*, 1904

Tradition makes men bigots and slaves and tyrants and superstitious yokels.
Bliss Carman, *The Friendship of Art*, 1904

The world is full of people whose notion of a satisfactory future is, in fact, a return to an idealized past.
Robertson Davies, *A Millenary Parallel*

It is the lack of a vital tradition that explains how, in Canada, a die-hard conservatism acts as the counterpart of a desire to ape the latest fashion.
John Sutherland,
editorial in 'First Statement', 1944

TRAGEDY

You know the tragedy is not — not all in the future.
Raymond Knister, *White Narcissus*, 1929

Tragedy celebrates man in a hostile world that overwhelms him, mocks his ideals, denies his hopes.
J. Percy Smith, *G.B.S. on the Theatre*, 1960

TRAINS

The sound of a train whistle at night — is the key experience of North Americans.
Kildaire Dobbs, *Running to Paradise*, 1962

TRAVELING

I am done with journeys.
They weary me beyond all thought,
As women weary me.
Ronald Bates, *Orpheus and Odyseus*, 1952

There is no logic in journeys.
They are all allegories.
Nancy L. Bauer,
A Christmas Pilgrimage, 1969

What makes the foot strain to be off and away?
What lures the heart from the known, the rear, the beloved?
Marjorie Freeman Campbell, *Green Light*, 1955

I cannot stay, I cannot stay!
I must take my canoe and fight the waves,
For the Wanderer spirit is seeking me.
Hermia Harris Fraser, *Song to the Wanderer*, 1939

It appears that many people when they travel really see nothing at all except the reflection of their own ideas.
Stephen Leacock,
Brotherly Love Among the Nations, 1926

The morning freshness is on him,
Just wakened from his balmy dreams;
The wayfarers all soiled and dim,
Think longingly of mountain streams.
Agnes Maule Machar, *Untrodden Ways*

Travel books are generally less concerned with 'how the natives live' than with 'how the natives took to me' — even those travel books that call themselves anthropology.
Christopher Wanklyn, *Going Tangerine*, 1959

TREASON

Eve was a woman . . . yes, of course,
But Judas was a man!
Masie Nelson Devitt, *In Defence of Eve*, 1936

Treason, . . . is caution come too late;
Is caution, turned to desperation, when
It sees the chance of gaining what it lost
By its own cowardice, gone by for ever.
Samuel James Watson, *Ravlan*, 1876

TREES

Perhaps we were not faithful to our trees;
We laid no water-shadows at their feet
In pledge of our delight . . .
And all the lovely place
Has vanished now into a city street —
Only these lines remain!
Katherine Hale, *Lost Garden*

A white birch is a beautiful Pagan maiden who has never lost the Eden secret of being naked and unashamed.
L.M. Montgomery, *Rilla of Ingleside*, 1921

There are pleasures you cannot buy,
Treasures you cannot sell,
And not the smallest of these
Is the gift and glory of trees.
Robert Service, *Trees Against the Sky*, 1940

TROUBLE

Trouble is a thing one can allow other people to have, if one doesn't throw oneself in its path.
Robertson Davies, *Tempest-Tost*, 1951

There is always one little trouble to keep us from being too happy.
James E. Le Rossignol,
The Poor of this World, 1908

Trouble! I guess you think you have troubles; but what are they to mine?
Susanna Moodie,
Roughing It in the Bush, 1852

Trouble . . . makes a man forget every one's affairs but his own.
Susanna Moodie, *Geoffrey Moncton*, 1855

TRUTH

The deepest truths
are in their opposites.
Gustav Davidson, *In Their Opposites*, 1966

If a thing is supposed to be true, it can be immeasurably more lurid and crude than if it is labeled as fiction.
Robertson Davies, *A Voice from the Attic*, 1960

What it hurts to be told is always untrue or unjust.
A.M.D. Fairbairn, *The Tragedy of Tanoo*, 1935

Truth is not necessarily so much a matter of often disgusting detail as it is a matter of atmosphere.
Frederick P. Grove, *A Search for America*, 1927

The truth is a fine thing if you use it wisely and in moderation — but did you ever stop to consider that too much truth can be just as dangerous as too many lies?
Vera Johnson, *The Huckelmeyer Story*, 1953

It takes almost as much practice to be able to recognise the truth as to state it.
Alexander Knox, *Old Master*, 1939

My Blasphemy's a synonym for truth.
Gwendolyn MacEwen, *Child of Light*, 1962

Sin ever doubts and is not sure;
But truth forever shall endure
When future worlds their years begin.
J.R. Newell, *In Memoriam*, 1881

No human being is constituted to know the truth, the whole truth, and nothing but the truth; and even the best of men must be content with fragments, with partial glimpses, never the full fruition.
William Osler, *The Student Life*, 1905

What is truth but a game, eh?
It isn't what's true that matters but who Is the more powerful.
James Reaney, *The Killdeer*, 1960

One cannot tell the truth and go unscathed!
Fred Swayze, *The Great Canadian Novel*, 1952

I walk
Groping the dark in search of truth,
Wondering have I lost the way.
Pauline E. Wagar, *Broad Is the Way*, 1942

THE TWENTIETH CENTURY

The twentieth century belongs to Canada.
Joseph T. Clark
editorial in: Saturday Night around 1890

Our age has robbed millions of the simplicity of ignorance, and has so far failed to lift them to the simplicity of wisdom.
Robertson Davies, *A Voice from the Attic*, 1960

One of the really notable achievements of the twentieth century has been to make the young old before their time.
Robertson Davies, *Tempest-Tost*, 1951

Where now are the frontiers we defend?
Where are the edges of our villages?
F.R. Scott, *TV Weather Man*, 1969

UNCERTAINTY

Nothing is absolute any longer, . . . There is a choice of beliefs and a choice of truths to go with them. If you choose not to choose then there is no truth at all. There are only points of view.
Mordecai Richler, *Son of a Smaller Hero*, 1955

UNDERSTANDING

At last I have had my vision
all this has happened to me.
Patrick Anderson,
Ballad of the Young Man, 1970

I know my lawful heritage,
Although I stand on alien ground;
I know what kingship is, although
I go uncrowned.
Helena Coleman, *Prairie Winds*

A man, to see far, must climb to some
height.
Ralph Connor, *Black Rock*, 1900

The eye sees only what the mind is
prepared to comprehend.
Robertson Davies, *Tempest-Tost*, 1951

And all the understanding on the earth
Can never light a fire on a cold hearth.
Robert Finch, *The Formula*, 1946

No one does ever understand any one
else. People are too busy living their own
lives to be troubled with investigating the
motives and feelings of others.
Nina Moore Jamieson, *The Hickory Stick*,
1921

There is no better way to know people
than by living in the house with them.
Nina Moore Jamieson, *The Hickory Stick*,
1921

People don't like to be understood.
Raymond Knister, *White Narcissus*, 1929

If you did know a person perfectly you
would be compelled to sympathize with
him.
Raymond Knister, *White Narcissus*, 1929

This clarity is mercy for our sight:
Deformed, we seek the therapy of light.
Dorothy Livesay, *On Seeing*, 1955

I have you fast and will not let you go:
Your nature and your name I know.
Jay MacPherson, *Reader*, 1956

Few words —
We needed so very few,
For even without the phrases
We looked at each other and knew.
Bonnie McConnell, *Shades*, 1967

We all have moments of self-realization.
Brian Moore, *an Interview*, 1962

I have weighed every word so long
That I cannot speak;
Have searched each thought so deep
That my mind is bare.
Dale Scott, *Renunciation*, 1956

Knowledge of self is destruction.
B.A. Veldhuis, *Narcissus*, 1967

UNHAPPINESS

The great majority of people are not happy, and unhappy people are always com-
plaining people.
E.H. Dewart, *Essays for the Times*, 1898

The unhappy are the most cruel of people.
Raymond Knister, *White Narcissus*, 1929

UNITED EMPIRE LOYALISTS

Loyalist blood — those are proud words
still in Canada, nowhere more than in
Nova Scotia.
Thomas H. Raddall, *A Harp in the Willows*

UNITY

Men of the East and West
Of kindred blood are we;
We heed one's country sure behest,
We seek one liberty.
Mary Kinley Ingraham, *East and West*, 1934

The lack of any real sense of community
can make life more difficult than it needs
to be.
Robert McCormack,
Letter From Toronto, 1961

UNIVERSITY

The most important thing you learn at
college
is how to live your life selectively.
Kenneth Leslie, *Cobweb College*, 1938

A university cannot live without students:
when the under-graduates are away it
arranges its memories and promises, and
then settles into stone.
Millar Maclure, *English Notes*, 1959

O it's not hard to see why these poets
give us little poetry
nourished, sustained by the dried up drugs
of the university.
Raymond Souster, *La Belle Dame*, 1954

UNKNOWN

Even to science, there is a margin of
unknown which makes the known seem
to wear the guise of the miraculous.
Bliss Carman, *The Kinship of Nature*, 1904

I'm living with you yet I don't know you.
You seem to go only so far and then . . . .
There is a part of you that I can't reach or
understand.
Mordecai Richler, *Son of a Smaller Hero*,
1955

Vancouver is a city that should have
grown straight up, like Manhattan,
instead of despoiling great mountainsides
and blotching fair valleys.
Edward McCourt,
Overland from Signal Hill to Victoria

U.S.A.

We often say that we fear no invasion
from the south, but the armies of the
south have already crossed the border,
American enterprise, American capital, is
taking rapid possession of our mines and
our water power, or oil areas and our
timber limits.
Sara Jeannette Duncan, *The Imperialist*,
1904

VALUE

We always undervalue what we have
never been without.
Robertson Davies, *Tempest-Tost*, 1951

She treasured her virginity with all the
tenacity of a poor girl who knows it is her
only asset and never forgets that it can be
lost only once.
Hugh MacLennan, *Two Solitudes*, 1945

Men talk of the intrinsic value of things;
the intrinsic value of anything is that
which each individual assigns to it for
himself.
J.J. Procter,
The Philosopher in the Clearing, 1897

According to the world today, he really is
a prince.
He has money.
Norman Williams, *The King Decides*, 1956

VANCOUVER

A clean-cut city
Demolishing the last embarrassing skid
row.
George Holmes,
An Aerial View of Vancouver, B.C., 1958

Vancouver is culturally as dead as the
dodo, and by no stretch of the imagination
could it supply you with what Europe
would at this stage.
Malcolm Lowry,
Letter to David Markson, 1954

VANITY

All is vanity, vanity, the Siamese twin of
the flesh which only dies with the flesh.
Suzanne Marny, *The Unhappy House*, 1909

VICTIM

Sport have we been for them, lugubrious
sport,
Jesters who had a continent for court . . .
Performing sorry antics for the scum
That giggled at the gags of martyrdom.
A.M. Klein, *Hershel of Ostropol*, 1970

You hold the Fate of my Fool's deserving,
For I am prey to Life's carrion law.
Ruth E. Scharfe, *The Vulture*, 1952

VICTORIA (B.C.)

This is a town of memories, of gardens, of
cultivated voices. One thinks of the past,
one feels the past, but it is not the
recognizably Canadian past of farmers
and fishermen.
Michael Macklem, *A Book a Mile*, 1970

When a British colonel anywhere in the
world is wounded or feels death at hand,
unerring instinct leads him eventually to
the windswept waste of whitening flannel
that is Victoria, and there, after snorting
defiance through the local press, he
passes on.
Eric Nicol, *Sense and Nonsense*

VIRTUE

I never met a virtuous person who didn't
make me think of castration.
Irving Layton,
Some Observations and Aphorisms, 1968

Virtue would be an easy thing
If we were never tempted.
Alexander McLachlan,
Poverty's Compensations, 1856

My nobility
Is that of virtue not of birth, if I
Have any!
Lister S. Sinclair, *Oedipus the King*, 1946

VOICES

The voice gives the keynote of the soul.
Ralph Connor, *The Major*, 1917

Oh, when I hear
The music absolute
Of your beloved voice, I stand entranced and mute.
John Daniel Logan, *Flute of God*

A voice like hers sounded sorry all the time.
Hugh MacLennan, *Each Man's Son*, 1951

WAITING

Waiting, always waiting.
Everyone here is waiting.
Silas N. Gooch, *A Season in Limbo*, 1962

It's very hard to stand and wait
When those we go to
meet — are late.
Anahid Hagopian, *Waiting*, 1960

Waiting is a woman's lot
Whether liking it or not.
Mary Matheson, *Spinster's Reverie*, 1960

WALTZ

The waltz is surely the music of young love, which is why the old folks are so fond of it.
D.M. Currie, *And Be My Love*

WAR

War is a glorious thing at times, but the causes of it never are!
Nathaniel A. Benson, *The Paths of Glory*, 1927

War is so small, so sad, so inexcusable.
Gregory Clark, *La Mer*

Out of war's cataclysm
Come deeds of heroism.
Spontaneous . . . sublime!
Caroline D'Aguilar Henderson,
War Breeds Heroes, 1943

The straining hounds of war, unleashed again,
Have crushed the world between their dripping jaws.
Verna Loveday Harden, *All Valiant Dust*, 1939

There's a wail of bugles blowing,
There's a trouble on the wind;
Marching feet are coming, going,
But who heeds the tear-drops flowing
Of the women left behind?
Norah Mary Holland, *Cradle Song*, 1924

If war be unchristian and barbarous, then war as a science is more absurd, unnatural, unchristian, than war as a passion.
Anna Brownell Jameson, *Winter Studies*, 1838

They say perchance that war will come again;
Men talk of gas and bombs and awful pain.
I see, while they discuss their different creeds,
Death, passing briskly in her new cut tweeds.
Murla I. McKinnon Latta, *Aftermath*, 1938

The whole world would need a sort of acclimatization drug when this war was over, but they wouldn't get it. They would have to live in the ruins for quite a while.
Hugh MacLennan, *Barometer Rising*, 1944

No man ever went to war who did not, at some time, reckon on his chances of casualty and escape.
Edward Meade, *Remember Me*, 1946

For a man at sea in wartime there was monotony and discomfort, but there was a prospect of adventure always. For the woman left ashore there was only monotony — and fear.
Thomas H. Raddall, *A Muster to Arms*, 1954

Of, War's the thing!
It gives us common, working chaps our chance,
A taste of glory, chivalry, romance.
Robert Service, *Wounded*, 1916

Shall the passing of the seasons always record the grim procession of military preparations?
Lister S. Sinclair, *Day of Victory*, 1945

Strip war of its song and story,
And underneath you'll find
A hydra-headed monster
That preys upon mankind.
Caroline Eleanor Wilkinson,
War's Unholy Might, 1938

WEAKNESS

I am like an uprooted tree, dying at the core, yet with a strange unreasonable power at times of mocking at my own most miserable weakness.
Anna Brownell Jameson, *Winter Studies*, 1838

WEALTH

A rich man is also an unusual man, and a great financier is as rare a creature as a great painter.
Robertson Davies,
Introduction to:
"Moonbeams from the Larger Lunacy", 1964

Come sweet riches, come to me
From earth's brown treasury!
Louis Blake Duff, *Calling,* 1937

Wealth that is not acquired by industry, is seldom retained by prudence.
Susanna Moodie, *Geoffrey Moncton,* 1855

Gold turns all crabs to plums,
And makes all bastards legal.
J.R. Ramsay, *French Chaos,* 1873

Well groomed, we stand on broadloomed floors
Inhaling deeply the smell of money,
Well-adjusted children of the new era
Blankly awaiting the next pogrom.
David Lewis Stein, *Poem,* 1956

WEEPING

Mine eyes, O Lord,
Grow dim with too much weeping,
My throat is weary
With yet unshed tears.
Eve Hellyer,
Prayer For a Little Boy, 1934

Shallow is grief that weeping can subdue.
Wilson MacDonald, *The Loon,* 1926

We have no time to mourn. Leave that to women. They are wont to weep.
Daisy McCleod Wright,
Those Other Battle Fields, 1938

THE WEST

There is one in nearly every town and village in Western Canada, and anybody raised on the prairies has affection for the Chinese café and the gentleman from China who runs it.
Ed Arrol, *The Chinese Café*

The trouble with you . . . is that you're from the West where everything was born yesterday.
Allan Bevan
Introduction to:
"At the Tide's Turn" (T.H. Raddall), 1959

No men are so truly gentle as are the Westerners in the presence of a good woman.
Ralph Connor, *Black Rock,* 1900

In the West all dimensions are spatial. There is no past. Everything happens now.
Michael Macklem, *A Book a Mile,* 1970

WICKEDNESS

It has always been my opinion that the souls of bad men turn into crows and, as such, subsist on carrion.
Janey Canuck, *In a Monastery Garden*

The prince of darkness is twin-brother to the god of light.
Gustav Davidson, *Sing, Paradox,* 1966

There is a spirit of Malignance which makes people say offensive things to lovers about those they love.
Robertson Davies, *Tempest-Tost,* 1951

Wrong-doing need not be personal to produce evil.
William McLennan and J.N. McIlwraith,
"The Span O' Life", 1899

If God made me in His likeness, sure He let the devil inside.
Robert Service, *The Parson's Son,* 1907

WIFE

A woman with an ambitious husband can find plenty of burdens to bear, if she wants them.
Robertson Davies, *A Jig for the Gypsy,* 1954

Wives with too much education can cause a lot of trouble, . . . They're never satisfied.
W.D. Valgardson, *Bloodflowers,* 1970

WILDERNESS

Who goes out into the wilderness goes not in vain, if he see naught but a reed shaken by the wind.
W.H. Blake, *Brown Waters*

The wilderness is a foster-mother that teaches hard, strange paradoxes. The first is the sin of being weak; and the second is that death is the least of life's harms.
A.C. Laut, *Heralds of Empire*

WILL

When you're making a will, you likely think all will be harmony and concord afterwards.
Hugh Hood, *Getting at Williamstown*

The less I leave, the less the children will have to fight over.
Mordecai Richler,
This Year at the Arabian Nights Hotel

WIND

Come, O Wind, from the dreaming west,
Sweeping over the water's breast,
Bring my unquiet spirit rest.
Norah Holland, *West Wind*, 1924

Cold blows the wind
Through cities of night,
Through towns and hamlets,
Leaving nothing untouched
Not even the hearts of men.
Thelma Nadler, *The Wind*, 1951

Wind is featureless as my belief
In what you are and what you guard so jealously. . .?
Kay Smith, *Remember the Wind*, 1943

The south wind saps the strength of men,
The north wind makes men grow.
William Whitney, *Palm and Pine*, 1941

WINNIPEG

You have pioneer blood to make you strong.
You have dreamer's fancy to make you great.
Paul Grescoe, *Winnipeg*, 1956

WINTER

In winter everything is frozen — Even the heart.
Clara Bernhardt, *When Winter Comes*, 1951

Genius will never mount high where the faculties of the mind are benumbed half the year.
Frances Brooke,
The History of Emily Montague, 1769

Though the cold of a Canadian winter is great, it is neither distressing nor disagreeable.
William Dunlop, *Statistical Sketches*, 1832

It would seem that this wintry season, which appears to me so dismal, is for the Canadians the season of festivity.
Anna Murphy Jameson, *Sketches in Canada*

Our best days are now a winter sky
White with coruscations of the clouds.
D.G. Jones,
Soliloquy to Absent Friends, 1959

The northern winters of Europe are seasons of terror and gloom; our winters are seasons of glittering splendor and incomparable richness of colour.
Archibald Lampman, *Two Canadian Poets*, 1891

In the solitude of the dark winter nights the stillness was that of eternity.
Stephen Leacock, *My Remarkable Uncle*

The winters are long and full of hardship and the weak cannot always survive them.
Alice Munro, *The Peace of Utrecht*, 1960

The Canadian winter is a cold and excessive mistress.
Howard O'Hagan, *Grey Owl*, 1958

Now Winter lords it o'er the land.
Bow the neck! Bow the neck!
King is he of mighty wand
Bow the neck!
Frederic Philips, *Winter*, 1909

Soon, all too soon
winter will storm in
fall heavily on us.
Raymond Souster, *Pact*, 1968

We must content ourselves with wintry landscapes, snowflakes and frost-flowers, and the crystal casing that covers the slender branches of the birches and beeches.
Catherine Parr Traill,
Studies of Plant Life in Canada

WISDOM

And I — I have no wisdom but the child's,
That knows its own simplicity.
Audrey Alexandra Brown, *Lammastide*, 1936

The wise man is he who sets himself to
cultivate both faculties — the heart that
always loves, the mind that is never
deceived.
Bliss Carman, *The Friendship of Art*, 1904

To be clean and temperate and busy, . . . to
simplify the mechanism of living and
enrich the motive, and to avoid
fanaticism, this is the part of wisdom.
Bliss Carman, *The Kinship of Nature*, 1904

The idea that a wise man must be solemn
is bred and preserved among people who
have no idea what wisdom is, and can
only respect whatever makes them feel
inferior.
Robertson Davies, *A Voice from the Attic*,
1960

Being oneself, . . . is really the essence of
all wisdom!
Roland Goodchild, *The Grand Duchess*

WOMAN

'Tis woman rules the whole world still,
Though faults the critics say she has;
She smiles her smile and works her will—
'Tis just a little way she has.
Jean Blewett, *Her Little Way*

A raw country makes the old male fear of
the female loom larger in the male's
mind.
Robert Bly,
For Alden Nowlan, With Admiration, 1970

Man doesn't destroy the heart that loves
him. Woman does. Only the female of the
species can choke affection until the
source that she depends on is strangled.
Janet Bonellie,
Why Are The People Staring?, 1968

A woman is either a face or a voice.
Mary Wallace Brooks, *Voices*, 1926

How the hell something could be wrong
with the woman if she ain't breeding?
Austin Clarke,
The Woman with the BBC Voice, 1963

Youth and charm in a woman makes any
deviation from ordinary conduct doubly
reprehensible.
Robertson Davies, *Leaven of Malice*, 1954

No woman wants to be loved; she only
wants to love.
James De Mille, *A Strange Manuscript*, 1888

Nothing! That's like your sex. It's always
'nothing' when they want to vex.
F.A. Dixon,
Fifine, The Fisher-Maid, 1877

When she sat down, . . she seemed to un-
tie and fling herself as you might a parcel.
Sara Jeannette Duncan, *The Imperialist*,
1904

And this was an artful woman: artful
enough not to speak.
Frederick P. Grove,
Settlers of the Marsh, 1925

A woman wants to be taken, not adored.
Frederick P. Grove,
Settlers of the Marsh, 1925

You are a woman, therefore you,
Have had your lonely tears,
Black waters flowing noiseless to
The gulf of hopeless years,
After the radiance was lost.
Norman Gregor Guthrie, *Resurrection*, 1928

I have always found that the road to a
woman's heart lies through her child.
T.C. Haliburton, *Sam Slick*, 1836

The invincibly taciturn woman is so rare
as to have escaped objurgation. Yet she
too is a terror to men.
Arnold Haultain, *Hints to Lovers*

The woman who enriches her husband
with her admiration and her ready response gets her reward on earth, from her
husband.
Marion Hilliard,
A Woman Doctor Looks at Love and Life,
1956

'Tis woman that inspires
The soul of man to grand unselfish deeds,
As worshippers lay down their lives for
shrines.
John Hunter-Duvar, *The Enamorado*, 1879

Go to your room and pray.
That is all women are good for.
Fred Jacob, *The Basket*, 1925

At certain moments, even an ugly woman, if she has lived for some time with the wind and the sun, can be sexually attractive.
Irving Layton,
Vacation in La Voiselle, 1946

You are a woman and for you a thing does not exist until it has been given a name.
Irving Layton,
Vacation in La Voiselle, 1946

This is the inglorious age of the mass - woman. Her tastes are dominant everywhere — in theatres, stores, art, fiction, houses, furniture — and these tastes are dainty and trivial.
Irving Layton,
in the Foreword to:
"A Red Carpet for the Sun"

In point of intellect, the average woman cannot reason and think. But she can argue.
Stephen Leacock,
the Preface to:
"Winnowed Wisdom", 1926

the woman I am
is not what you see
move over love
make room for me
Dorothy Livesay, *The Unquiet Bed*, 1965

You can get a man to change his mind if you're in the right, but all the angels in heaven can't make a woman change her mind if she's in the wrong, — which is always the case.
L.A. MacKay, *The Freedom of Jean Guichet*

She jerks a string;
attached to those pink fingertips
I'm a marionette
at her slightest whim!
Seymour Mayne, *Puppetry*, 1964

Of all the wearisome things in the world, I can imagine nothing worse than being a woman.
William McLennan and J.N. McIlwraith,
"The Span O' Life", 1899

A cat will hunt a mouse,
Why not a woman man?
Robert Norwood, *Bill Boram*, 1921

A woman's wit is in a woman's love.
Robert Norwood, *The Witch of Endor*, 1916

A woman's handwriting will do more than a man's word any time.
Gilbert Parker,
The March of the White Guard, 1902

What bliss that private life attains,
How happy is that earthly lot,
How blest to man that sacred spot
Where woman's genial influence reigns!
J.E. Pollock, *Woman's Influence*, 1883

When a woman closes up her lips tight, you may depend upon it she is going to bite.
J.J. Procter,
The Philosopher in the Clearing, 1897

Ye bes a fool over a woman — an' that be the weakest kind o' fool! What would a lady like her be wantin' wid ye for a husband?
Theodore Goodridge Roberts,
The Harbormaster, 1911

O, woman-heart be strong,
Too full for words — too humble for a prayer —
Too faithful to be fearful — offer here
Your sacrifice of patience.
L. Annie Rothwell-Christie, *The Woman's Part*

Do you really think a man can have of a woman what she will not give?
Laura Goodman Salverson, *Queer Heart*, 1936

Woman has a great influence over man on account of her womanly qualities; when she enters on a public career, she loses those qualities, and has less influence than if she had remained in her own sphere of life.
Minni Smith, *Is It Just?*, 1911

The heart of a woman is seldom cold to those who cherish their offspring.
Catherine Parr Traill, *Canadian Crusoes*, 1850

What man wants a Nice Girl when he may have a lovely pagan?
Frances Fenwick Williams, *Which?*, 1926

WOMEN

Women always want more than they get.
Ted Allan, *Lies My Father Told Me*

There is not perhaps on earth a race of females, who talk so much, or feel so lit-

tle, of love as the French; the very reverse is in general true of the English.
Frances Brooke,
The History of Emily Montague, 1769

There are chiefly two kinds of women in the world: those who listen to agreeable things and those who say them.
Mary Wallace Brooks, *Voices*, 1926

Next to womankind there is nothin' so deceitful as horse - flesh that I ever seed yet. Both on 'em are apt to be spoiled in the breakin': both on 'em puzzle the best judges sometimes to tell their age when well vamped up, and it takes some time afore you find out all their tricks.
V.L.O. Chittick, *The Gen-u-ine Yankee*

Women, in a variety of ways, played a primary role in shaping French - Canadian society even before the Conquest.
Ramsay Cook, *Word from New France*, 1968

There is nothing men like so much as generalizing about women; all women are alike, except the one they love.
Robertson Davies, *Tempest-Tost*, 1951

Circe was a beautiful woman
and she did to all her men
what all your beautiful women
have done to you
used you
out of sheer revenge.
Joan Finnigan, *For A Poet*, 1968

What can I be but sad
knowing that you have learned nothing about beautiful women?
Joan Finnigan, *For A Poet*, 1968

After you have been loved by a Russian, all other women seem tame.
Diana Goldsborough,
Ville superbe, que fais-tu là?, 1957

Is't not ever so?
And doth not every woman of them all
Know better than ourselves what we should do,
Or leave undone?
Francis W. Grey, *Love's Pilgrimage*, 1931

If politicians are humbugs by profession, women — or, at all events, some women — are humbugs by nature.
Francis W. Grey,
The Curé of St. Philippe, 1899

Any man, . . . that understands horses has a pretty considerable fair knowledge of women, for they are jist alike in temper, and require the very identical same treatment.
T.C. Haliburton, *Sam Slick*, 1836

Women . . . were made for labour; one of them can carry, or haul, as much as two men can do.
Samuel Hearne, *A Journey*, 1795

Chaste women are best,
but married women are wisest
in the ways of love and safest
to make play with.
John Hulcoop, *A Fable for James*, 1968

Women are truly God's best handiwork,
And better every way than are we men.
John Hunter-Duvar, *De Roberval*, 1888

I have not often in my life met with contented and cheerful - minded women, but I never met with so many repining and discontented women as in Canada.
Anna Brownell Jameson, *Winter Studies*, 1838

For what will not your sex do and dare for the sake of us men creatures, savages that we are?
Anna Brownell Jameson, *Winter Studies*, 1838

Modern women I see cast in the role of furies striving to castrate the male; their efforts aided by all the malignant forces of a technological civilization that has rendered the male's creative role of revelation superfluous.
Irving Layton,
the Foreword to
"A Red Carpet in the Sun"

We women ought to be as elaborate as possible, so as to frighten away all those who are not rich enough to marry.
W.D. Lighthall, *The False Chevalier*, 1898

It is the taste . . . of all women, to co-quette. It is their privilege, and I for one would not deny it to them.
Blanche Lucile Macdonell,
Diane of Ville Marie, 1898

We women see our own images mirrored several times daily, and the face and the form of our youth lurks perpetually in our minds.
Suzanne Marny, *Distant Youth*, 1909

It is horrible what animals women can be when once they begin!
William McLennan and J.N. McIlwraith, *"The Span O' Life"*, 1899

There's only two kinds of women, the good ones and the bitches. We marry the good ones and whore with the bitches.
Edward Meade, *Remember Me*, 1946

In her quiet dwelling,
In singing, sighing flow,
Came love and parting, birth and death,
And all that women know.
John Hanlon Mitchell, *Farm Wife*

Tis a bad thing to make too much of woman-kind.
Susanna Moodie, *Geoffrey Moncton*, 1855

Most women don't even live lives of quiet desperation. (Quiet desperation is far too dramatic.)
Brian Moore, *I Am Mary Dunne*

Women are into everything nowadays. I tell you it keeps us men hustling to keep up with them.
T.M. Morrow, *The Blue Pitcher*, 1926

How much easier life would be if only women were ugly?
John Newlove, *The Fat Man*, 1969

Thank God that good women are born with greater souls for trial than men; that given once an anchor for their hearts they hold until the cables break.
Gilbert Parker,
The Seats of the Mighty, 1896

Man's lot is hard
And woman's harsher, being more sensitive.
J.R. Ramsay, *French Chaos*, 1873

The divil bes in the women, lad, — the women from up-along.
T.G. Roberts, *The Harbormaster*, 1911

Women exert too much influence on us men.
Mazo de la Roche, *The Building of Jalna*, 1927

Get all the lasting things out o' men you can. Small, costly, things like joolery that is easy to carry 'round, and can always be pawned, if necessary.
Mazo de la Roche, *Delight*, 1926

Women talk too much even to make good checker players. It takes concentration.
Sinclair Ross, *One's A Heifer*, 1944

There's nothing to life,
And women are not to be trusted.
Arthur Stringer,
The King Who Loved Old Clothes, 1940

Poor simpleton, hast thou not learnt by now
That none can hate like women?
Samuel James Watson, *Ravlan*, 1876

This, then, is women's part — do hide the heart wounds'
smart at what they reap —
While winds and waves alone chant funeral hymns along
the firing line.
Daisy McCleod Wright,
Those Other Battle Fields, 1938

WORDS

To know what we see or feel involves stating it.
Margaret Avison, *Poetry Chronicle*, 1956

Thought, sentiment, desire, these are our rulers, and they have their only embodiment in expression. It is by the help of the wandering word that they hold sway and move in power.
Bliss Carman, *The Kinship of Nature*, 1904

Words age
in the mouths of men
my own age.
John Robert Colombo, *My Generation*, 1966

Words must be clear bells,
or sound gravelly along like horns.
They should detonate, explode
like lightning under the sea.
Eldon Grier, *Stanza XIV*, 1963

Words are bold troubadours that sing through space.
Pauline Harvard, *Words*, 1937

Words are but symbols of a poet's thoughts.
Elizabeth Hiscott, *When a Poet Speaks*, 1967

I am drunk with the wine of words,
Of the mead of sound.
Kathleen Lang, *Aspiration*, 1961

Words are the real trouble-makers.
Hugh MacLennan, *Each Man's Son*, 1951

He is one of your dealers in fine words, who conceal their want of sense under a garbage of fustian which they call the flowers of Parnassus.
Thomas McCulloch, *The Stepsure Letters*, 1821

Choice words are good, but saves no lives at all.
Norman Newton,
Lullaby for a Young Poet, 1966

Words no sooner said become clichés.
A.W. Purdy, *an interview*, 1969

Images increase as words diminish.
J.R. Ramsay, *One Quiet Day*, 1873

I found it in my thoughts today —
That little word I meant to say,
So long ago.
Frank F. Robertson, *So Long Ago*, 1934

Loving words will fade from memory,
And gentle words will seem less dear;
Warm, sweet lips that spoke the message,
Will seem unreal when they're not near.
Rhoda Sivell, *Good-Bye*, 1911

Take the words, nor seek to find
What, if anything, lies behind.
Damn the meaning! Take the sound!
It's words that make the world go round.
John Smalacombe,
From The Ill-Tempered Lover, 1937

Words may varnish facts, they cannot alter them.
Harry James Smith,
Mrs. Bumpstead-Leigh, 1917

Words . . . words . . . they are so precious to women!
Arthur Stringer, *The Oyster*, 1939

What matter the words when all is clear?
Jane Van Every, *Isses Net Peculiar*

Words are comforting to hold against one's heart when one is alone.
Eva-Lis Wuorio, *Call Off Your Cats*, 1955

WORK

Work is a great thing to make you forget who you are entirely.
Nathaniel A. Benson, *The Patriot*, 1930

When you get the feel of it there's nothing to compare with the satisfaction of hard work.
Harry J. Boyle, *Jezebel Jessie*

How soon things would cease to be ugly and become beautiful, if only every stroke of work in the world had some expression in it!
Bliss Carman, *The Kinship of Nature*, 1904

It is necessary, in order to secure good work, that we should throw ourselves into it whole-heartedly.
Bliss Carman, *The Kinship of Nature*, 1904

Work is not a burden, but a pleasurable activity, a natural function of the healthy and happy.
Bliss Carman, *The Friendship of Art*, 1904

To each hand is given
Its capacity of work
For one day.
Cecile Cloutier, *Morning* 1960

A man's home is where his heart is, and his heart is where his work lies.
Ralph Connor, *The Prospector*, 1904

One value of work is not that crowds stare at it.
Ralph Connor, *Black Rock*, 1900

I s'pose mos' ev'ry boddy t'ink hees job's about de hardes'
From de boss man on de Gouvernement to poor man on de town
From de curé to de lawyer, an' de farmer to de school boy
An' all de noder feller was mak' de worl' go roun'.
William H. Drummond,
The Canadian Country Doctor, 1897

There's no business in it, and I haven't time for pleasure.
Sara Jeannette Duncan, *The Imperialist*, 1904

Why should I work to support a bum like me?
L.W. Ellis, *"E.J."*, 1964

Exacting nothing, one receives no less
Than one exacts, possibly an excess.
Robert Finch, *Ask For No Promise*, 1946

Imagine me vainly trying to survive
My environment when I'm most alive
Buried deepest in the work I love.
Len Gasparini, *The Marginal Man,* 1969

Sweat is their speech.
Each day is the same.
Len Gasparini, *Grapes,* 1968

When a man's working he wants to work.
Work and booze don't mix.
M. Allerdale Grainger,
Woodsmen of the West, 1908

Is not the best, most satisfying work, work
that is intermittent, that gives one rest
after toil, time for recuperation?
M. Allerdale Grainger,
Woodsmen of the West, 1908

Work, and plenty of it saves every man.
S. Frances Harrison, *The Forest of Bourg-Marie*

If you concentrate your full energies on
the things that are at hand, you will,
through the mercy of Heaven, be able to
attain to your heart's desire among the
things that are not at hand.
Albert Hickman, *An Unofficial Love Story*

This is a job, it's money, that's all. To tell
you the truth, I consider the time here
wasted. It's a job: I don't let it interfere
with my life.
Theodore Kitaif, *The Arch-Criminal,* 1969

Work is only toil when it is the
performance of duties for which nature
did not fit us, and a congenial occupation
is only serious play.
Archibald Lampman, *Happiness,* 1896

The world is out of work for the simple
reason that the world has killed the goose
that laid the golden eggs of industry.
Stephen Leacock,
My Discovery of England, 1922

All things we would gain must be won by
pursuit:
Loose now for the capture the hounds of
your soul!
Wilson MacDonald, *Why Not I?,* 1926

Whenever a man courts unnecessary
work — and believe me you've been doing
it — it's not natural.
Hugh MacLennan, *Each Man's Son,* 1951

No matter how good his work might be, . .
. it would never be good enough to satisfy
him.
Hugh MacLennan, *Each Man's Son,* 1951

The slave works because he is compelled
to; the artist because he loves to; the fool
does unnecessary work because he is a
fool. Each one of us is part slave, part
artist, and part fool. The wise man is he
who strives to be all three in due
proportion, and succeeds in being not too
much of any one.
Andrew Macphail, *Essays in Politics*

I am the sort of woman who must have
work to do. If I don't, my mind will grow
dim and misty.
Joyce Marshall, *The Old Woman,* 1952

In the warfare of life, labour and
perseverance fight a hard battle; and,
unless the odds against them be very
great indeed, they never fail to be
rewarded with victory.
Thomas McCulloch, *The Stepsure Letters,*
1821

If you haven't no pride in your work you
haven't no pride in yourself.
John Metcalf, *Our Mr. Benson,* 1969

Strange how it comes to be
True of all precious things, that man must
earn
Afore he spends!
Robert Norwood, *Bill Boram,* 1921

The joy is only in the task —
What would you do with days removed
from work?
Robert Norwood, *The Man of Kerioth,* 1919

Lift up your heads heed not the words of
scorning,
From those whose earnest life is not
begun;
Blessed are they who on the judgment
morning
Hear from the Master, "Servant, 'tis well
done."
Nora Pembroke, *Servants,* 1880

He who despises and wastes the hours of
dawn is less fitted to endure the heat of
the mid-day; he who has not toiled in the
mid-day cannot appreciate the rest of the
sunset; and for him whom the sunset of

life has no real repose, night, the long night that comes to all, has no sheltering veil; is nothing but blackness and a void.
J.J. Procter,
The Philosopher in the Clearing, 1897

The trouble with me . . . is I'm too light for heavy work and a bit too heavy for light work, so I'm out o' luck all round.
Thomas H. Raddall, *A Harp in the Willows*

The great trouble with our way of society is that we do too much unnecessary work. Two-thirds of time are frittered away pandering to vitiated tastes and the unusual requirements of luxurious living.
J.R. Ramsay, *One Quiet Day,* 1873

Awake to work, and do not shirk
What duty bids to do;
The strength of life is in the strife,
Tho' dreadful storms ensue.
J.R. Ramsay, *Awake,* 1873

Work, work, always work.
Nought to show, an aching back.
The help of God is what I lack.
Beverley Rosen, *Twisted Roots,* 1956

He made the best of the fate which compelled him to depend for his living on something he disliked.
Duncan Campbell Scott, *Paul Farlotte,* 1896

In all labour
there is profit.
Samuel Strickland,
Twenty-Seven Years in Canada West, 1853

Good work creates an audience.
Kent Thompson, *Editorial,* 1968

It depends upon ourselves to better our own condition.
Catherine Parr Traill,
The Canadian Settler's Guide, 1855

In this country honest industry always commands respect: by it we can in time raise ourselves, and no one can keep us down.
Catherine Parr Traill,
The Canadian Settler's Guide, 1855

WORKER

I call every honest workman brother, but you are neither honest nor a workman.
Robertson Davies, *A Jig for the Gypsy,* 1954

Harvest hands are like hobos, their friendships are casual as the mating of a pair of flies.
Hugh Garner, *Hunky,* 1963

Come all ye weary sons of toil
And listen to my song,
We've eat oppressions bitter bread,
And eat it far too long.
Alexander McLachlan, *The Workman's Song*

I never had a holiday long as I can remember. Who the hell ever heard of a hired man takin' a holiday!
W.O. Mitchell, *The Golden Jubilee Citizen*

The holiest alliance by love ever planned
Is the warm hearted grasp of a workingman's hand.
J.R. Ramsay, *A Warm Hearted Grasp,* 1873

You are this man
Who labours so
To build a world all his alone.
Dorothy Murray Slitter, *Creator,* 1967

The man who is industrious, thinks for himself and acts accordingly, increases the value of his neighbor's property by increasing that of his own.
Minni Smith, *Is It Just?,* 1911

WORLD

Now having walked in shadows I emerge,
To find the world a glory long concealed.
Clara Bernhardt, *Awakening,* 1937

The mind feeds upon the events and aspirations of its time as a plant feeds upon the soil and air in its own valley.
Bliss Carman, *The Friendship of Art,* 1904

The world is made forever
In likeness of a dream.
Bliss Carman, *Earth Voices*

The world is a beautiful piece of jade;
Each small part gives it a subtle shade
Of quiet beauty.
Elizabeth Challis, *The World,* 1939

I seek this world to its end. This world
Owns me and all I have — and yet
This world is mine.
Edward Hunt, *Untilled,* 1966

Fellow flesh affords a rampart,
And you've got along for comfort
All the world there ever shall be, was, and
is.
Jay Macpherson, *The Boatman*, 1957

The world is wiser than its wisest men,
And shall outlive the wisdom of its gods,
Made after man's own liking.
Charles Mair, *Tecumseh*, 1886

And all the world is one wide waste of
lone, uncharted sea.
Where never beacon lifts its flame above
a friendly quay.
F. Robina Monkman, *A Song of the Admirals*,
1937

Is the agony in which the world is
shuddering the birth-pang of some
wondrous new era?
L.M. Montgomery, *Rilla of Ingleside*, 1921

The world, . . . was a good school for
teaching people the art of falsehood.
Susanna Moodie, *Geoffrey Moncton*, 1855

The day of dull-eyed teachers is at end —
The world needs men.
Robert Norwood, *The Man of Kerioth*, 1919

Harden thy heart to look on cruelties,
To look on truth, to look on life, and see
That the world is what it must ever be—
An evolution of alternate tyrannies.
Francis Pollock, *Sonnet I*, 1937

O wonder!
How many goodly creatures are there
here!
How beauteous mankind is! O brave new
world,
That has such people in't!
James Reaney

O love this world
If you can.
Wilfred Watson,
Graveyard on a Cliff of White Sand, 1955

This is a blessed place. A little world
Laid on the green foundations of the
earth.
P.P. Watson, *Old Man at His Door*, 1937

WORRY

May He forgive all people whose lives
overflow with plenty of everything, and
who fret their souls for petty ills.
Ralph Connor, *Beyond the Marshes*, 1900

Worrying helps you some — it seems as if
you were doing something when you're
worrying.
L.M. Montgomery, *Anne of Green Gables*,
1908

Without our cares our joys would be less
lively.
Catherine Parr Traill, *Canadian Crusoes*,
1850

WORTH

Fools but talk of blood and birth —
Ev'ry man must prove his worth.
Alexander McLachlan, *Acres of Your Own*,
1874

To own a Prince,
One must be a Prince.
Jacob Zilber, *The Prince*, 1960

WRITERS

To the state and the politicians the writer
is simply not important.
Morley Callaghan, *Solzhenitsyn*, 1970

There are two kinds of writers: the one
who tries to see the world out of his own
eyes, and the other one, the commercial
writer, who tries to see the world out of
the eyes of others.
Nathan Cohen,
Heroes of the Richler View, 1958

Once scholarship has its grappling -
hooks on a writer's work there is no room
for doubt.
Robertson Davies, *Leaven of Malice*, 1954

The vice of the literary mind is excessive
subtlety, just as that of the theatrical mind
is trivial profusion.
Robertson Davies, *A Voice from the Attic*,
1960

The errors which are maintained by a
writer are often more injurious in their influence on others than to himself.
E.H. Dewart, *Essays for the Times*, 1898

There cannot be, for a writer or for any
other man, complete isolation.
Roderick Haig-Brown,
The Writer in Isolation, 1959

A writer is, by definition almost, a man
sensitive to influences; he may reject

them or accept them, search for them or flee from them, but he cannot be neutral or unfeeling about all of them.
Roderick Haig-Brown,
The Writer in Isolation, 1959

Working with people of lesser competence and experience can be not only discouraging but actually harmful for the writer.
Peter Haworth,
Playwrights in Vancouver, 1961

The man wrote good.
Who cares what he was?
Margaret Laurence, *Roses and Yew,* 1970

Many writers have the courage to show us the hairshirt they are wearing, but only the greatest will display the raw and itchy skin it conceals.
Irving Layton,
Some Observations and Aphorisms, 1968

No writer in his senses writes solely to make money. If money is what he wants most, he needs his head examined if he becomes a writer.
Hugh MacLennan, *The Story of a Novel,* 1960

Both the incredulity and belief of the world are so capricious, that no man who writes for the public is sure of getting justice.
Thomas McCulloch, *The Stepsure Letters,* 1821

Any serious writer is a moralist, and only incidentally an entertainer.
Mordecai Richler, *The Uncertain World,* 1969

Every serious writer has one theme, many variations to play on it.
Mordecai Richler, *The Uncertain World,* 1969

Nobody is more embittered than a neglected writer.
Mordecai Richler, *The Uncertain World,* 1969

Art which is both fine and immediately or ever popular is too rare a thing for any writer to expect, least of all in Canada.
F.W. Watt, *Western Myth,* 1959

A writer's mind seems to be situated partly in the solar plexus and partly in the head.
Ethel Wilson,
A Cat Among the Falcons, 1959

The technical expert is essential to the advancement of our scientific world, but it is the essayist who integrates this knowledge for us and presents it in understandable terms.
E.H. Winter,
Introduction to:
"Our Century in Prose", 1960

Like the conductor who, without his orchestra, can only wield his baton in silence . . . an editor is nothing without his writers.
George Woodcock,
Getting Away With Survival, 1969

French writers seem at present to be abandoning a traditional position of revolt, and to be accepting a mood of disinvolvement which extends far beyond merely intellectual circles.
George Woodcock,
The Disengaged: A Letter from France, 1958

All writers are derivative; all good writers plagiarize; theft is a literary virtue.
George Woodcock,
The Absorption of Echoes, 1970

WRITERS — Canadian

Canadian writers are hungry writers!
Hugh MacLennan, *The Story of a Novel,* 1960

Most Canadian writers belong to a single social group identifiable with a university-based Establishment.
Robert L. McDougall,
The Dodo and the Cruising Auk, 1963

For the great bulk of Canadian writers the environments of childhood and of "the struggle for a living" are uniform in kind; professional, relatively well-to-do, 'genteel', above all, academic.
Robert L. McDougall,
The Dodo and the Cruising Auk, 1963

It is characteristic of Canadian writers to forget that to write in the English

language is to compete with the best writers in Britain and the United States.
Donald Stephens, *A Maritime Myth,* 1961

We're not the stuff of which great books are made:
No national pride to amount to a hill of beans;
No local cause for which men will fight and die.
Fred Swayze,
The Great Canadian Novel, 1952

Welcome to all young writers, but prepare yourselves for the cold climate here.
Robert Weaver,
Editorial in Tamarack Review, 1970

Those who speak English, whether in Canada or abroad, are still too much inclined to take for granted that Canadians — and Canadian writers — live either in the Maritimes or west of Montreal.
George Woodcock, *Cautious Inevitability,* 1962

If we try to envisage an "average Canadian writer" we can see him living near a campus, teaching at least part time at university level, mingling too much for his work's good with academics, doing as much writing as he can for the CBC, and always hoping for a Canada Council Fellowship.
George Woodcock, *Away From Lost Worlds,* 1964

WRITING

(That line hath "quality" of loftiest grade.)
And I have eased my soul of its sweet pain.
William Wilfred Campbell, *At Even,* 1893

There is nothing that cannot be written.
Frank Davey, *The Reading*

It is this hunger for words
That makes writing pain!
Irene G. Dayton, *Poem,* 1953

Write whatever you write not as prose, but as rhythmic poetry.
Louis Dudek, *Functional Poetry,* 1959

Plodding prose expository, endless, rhymeless prose has won over poetry.
Louis Dudek, *Functional Poetry,* 1959

Great thoughts by Art are shrined in Magic Words;
The Writer's fluent Pen has set them down,
To send them winging through the Land like Birds.
In eager hope of winning Fair Renown.
Donald A. Fraser, *Printing*

Publication means nothing.
What matters is solely that the work be done, the book be written, the beauty created.
Frederick P. Grove,
a letter to W.B. Holliday, 1960

Sure there are better lines, but that one sticks.
Anahid Hagopian, *Postscript,* 1960

Writing is the most natural of the arts because it stems directly from man's daily habit of using words to express his thoughts and emotions.
Roderick Haig-Brown,
The Writer in Isolation, 1959

In the end, all writing is isolation.
Roderick Haig-Brown,
The Writer in Isolation, 1959

In letters I don't strike a match
I butt cigarettes
I mail only words.
Grant Johnson, *no title,* 1970

Writing is a fascinating, arduous and solitary profession. The technical skills necessary to produce even a commonplace novel are quite as complicated as those necessary for a brain operation.
Hugh MacLennan, *The Story of a Novel,* 1960

Wise men speak — fools write their thoughts.
Susanna Moodie, *Geoffrey Moncton,* 1855

The fact is that I am more enamoured of the act of writing than of the act of meaning.
John Newlove, *in: Moving in Alone*

Being a married man, I am denied the privilege of lengthy conversation, and so have to talk in writing.
J.J. Procter,
The Philosopher in the Clearing, 1897

What, prostitute my soul across some un-published page for every artful eye to gaze upon?
Irene Richards, *Does It Pay?*, 1954

Last night, in fact, I burned the midnight oil;
I picked up words like pebbles from a beach,
Selected, polished, matched them rich with plain,
And strung them like fine jewels upon a chain.
Anna Letitia Wales, *Breakfast Trio*, 1949

The absence of an enriching university education does not prevent the practice of the art of writing.
Ethel Wilson, *A Cat Among the Falcons*, 1959

The business of writing is one of the four or five most private things in the world.
Ethel Wilson, *A Cat Among the Falcons*, 1959

Canadian novelists and poets, writing on politics, become as dull as the experts.
George Woodcock, *The Muse of Politics*, 1961

YANKEE

Now Yankee betokened a separate race. All the story of the Revolution was summed up in the changed meaning of a word.
Thomas H. Raddall, *At The Tide's Turn*

YOUTH

Is there a sorrow on us, who are young, And have no grief.
Audrey Alexandra Brown, *Lammastide*, 1936

He 'was not born for age'. Ah no, For everlasting youth is his! And part of the lyric of the earth With spring and leaf and blade he is.
Bliss Carman, *A Seamark*

The young are often accused of ex-aggerating their troubles; they do so, very often, in the hope of making some impression upon the inertia and the im-movability of the selfish old.
Robertson Davies, *Tempest-Tost*, 1951

It is a pity that we ourselves can never see the promise that others see in us when we are young.
Lovat Dickson, *The House of Words*, 1963

There is . . . a complacence among adolescent peoples which is vaguely irritating to their elders; but the greybeards need not to be over-captious; it is only a question of time, pathetically short-lived in the history of the race.
Sara Jeannette Duncan, *The Imperialist*, 1904

In the whirlyworld of youth soon the music slackens and the motors stop they have to get off and make room for the next ones.
Peggy K. Fletcher, *Let Them Have Their Fling*, 1968

When I was young The fields were there To sing a song, To answer care.
Marion Ford, *On Growing Old*, 1968

The affairs of the young are the envies of the middle-aged.
Hugh Garner, *Hunky*, 1963

Play, children, play the time for song is short and age and sorrow come like frost to wither up the heart.
Phyllis Gotlieb, *Ordinary Moving*, 1970

God help the young and teach them to be humble.
John Gray, *When Elephants Roost in Trees*, 1957

It's the privilege of Youth to enjoy first and suffer after.
George V. Hobart, *Experience*, 1914

Youth is the store-house of all poetry. He looks upon the world as a garden of roses and dreams never of winter nor decay.
George V. Hobart, *Experience*, 1914

Don't grow old too suddenly, . . . Your youth will go of its own accord — don't hurry it.
Nina Moore Jamieson, *The Hickory Stick*, 1921

Youth realizes love, but sees marriage as only a vague something in the distance.
Nina Moore Jamieson, *The Hickory Stick*, 1921

173

Do not contend
That youth holds all worthwhile of our
life-scene:
Remember, hearts can break at
seventeen.
Margaret Hurdon Keifer, *Seventeen*, 1963

The youth o' this day are jist fair daft!
Marion Keith, *Duncan Polite*, 1913

When people are young they think they're
the only ones who can understand
anything.
Margaret Laurence, *The Stone Angel*, 1964

Suddenly I recall
with an agony of loss
how glorious it felt
to be young.
N. West Linder, *To Be Young*, 1968

The youngest thing in a youthful world
Is a young soul in an old heart.
Wilson MacDonald, *The Last Portage*, 1926

One can be young but once. When old age
overtakes me I shall devote myself to good
works.
Blanche Lucile Macdonnell,
Diane of Ville Marie, 1898

I wish I could grow backwards!
I wish I could grow young again.
Gwendolyn MacEwen
The Day of the Twelve Princes, 1970

Alas for youth and beauty!
What a short, tantalizing lease of them we
poor humans have!
Suzanne Marny, *Distant Youth*, 1909

In extreme youth in our most humiliating
sorrow we think we are alone. When we
are older we find that others have
suffered too.
Suzanne Marny, *The Unhappy House*, 1909

When early work is already more than
promising, how then does one predict
growth?
Joyce Marshall,
A Young Writer on Her Way, 1958

The youthful mind pants for enjoyment;
and what it desires, it is prone to consider
as the grand object of life.
Thomas McCulloch, *The Stepsure Letters*,
1821

It does not do to laugh at the pangs of
youth. They are very terrible because
youth has not yet learned that "this too,
will pass away."
L.M. Montgomery, *Rilla of Ingleside*, 1921

Boys and girls in their teens, are beings
without much reflection. Their knowledge
of character, with regard to themselves
and others, is too limited and imperfect to
enable them to make a judicious choice.
Susanna Moodie, *Geoffrey Moncton*, 1855

What fantasies we build around the frail
figures of our child-selves, so that they
emerge beyond recognition incorrigible
and gay.
Alice Munro, *The Peace of Utrecht*, 1968

Wanted to trade:
A tranquil mind
For a foolish day
Of a youthful kind.
Gladys Nolan, *For Trade*, 1962

To tell you the truth
I am no longer envious of youth
For they won't know older age
If nuclear bombs come on stage.
Stan Obodiac, *Lived Is Better*, 1961

How freely came belief when we were
young!
Unruffled by an argument, the tongue
Had left the mind a garden where the
seeds
Sprouted and grew and blossomed
without weeds.
E.J. Pratt, *Magic in Everything*

We are not young forever, but our years
Seem for the while eternally suspended
Upon the bough that bears our budded
dreams.
Margaret Rempel, *Green Is Forever*, 1967

In youth we ask for bonfires,
Fed by the fuel of ecstasy, passion,
To light our way.
Hilda Ridley, *Little Fires*, 1951

Somewhere I failed him, somewhere I let
him depart —
Youth, who could only sleep for the
morn's fresh start.
Theodore Goodridge Roberts,
The Lost Shipmate

We are called the· young generation because we may never grow old.
Jill Robinson, *(no title)*, 1967

Young manhood sees no farther
Than the radiant face of love.
Dale Scott, *Vantage*, 1955

Youth is the season of enterprise.
Samuel Strickland,
Twenty-Seven Years in Canada West, 1853

Young minds have a natural poetry in themselves, unfettered by rule or rhyme.
Catherine Parr Trail, *Canadian Crusoes*, 1850

The half-illicit spell of young awareness, all careless alchemy and rebellions retreat, too easily becomes a flood of information. How it felt is nearly impossible to establish.
Paul West, *I, Said the Sparrow*, 1963

Not ours to have again
those laughing days of shrugging youth.
Clifton Whiten, *In the Gay Days*, 1966

Unless one is young and very, very beautiful, one's self-esteem is thereby diminished.
Ethel Wilson,
On a Portugese Balcony, 1956

INDEX of AUTHORS